PRINCIPLES AND PERSONS

An Ethical Interpretation of Existentialism

PRINCIPLES AND PERSONS

An Ethical Interpretation of Existentialism

Frederick A. Olafson

The Johns Hopkins Press, Baltimore, Maryland

To the Memory of My Father and Mother

ACKNOWLEDGMENTS

I wish to thank the Humanities Council of Princeton University for appointing me to their Hodder Fellowship for the year 1960–61 and thus enabling me to undertake the studies on which this book is based. The intellectual debts I have incurred in the writing of this book are unfortunately too numerous to acknowledge here; but I must express my gratitude to my wife for her invaluable editorial assistance over a period of years, and to Mrs. Dorothy Spotts for her excellent typing of the manuscript.

I should also like to thank Editions Gallimard and Alfred A. Knopf, Inc. for their courtesy in permitting me to translate the passages from Jean-Paul Sartre's *Critique de la raison dialectique* which appear on pp. 228–29.

CONTENTS

INTRODUCTION

Among contemporary philosophical movements, none has addressed itself more directly to ethical issues than has existentialism. As popularly understood, it is, in fact, not so much an ethical theory as itself an ethical attitude; and in this form it has attracted and repelled large numbers of people who have no knowledge of the philosophical position on which this attitude is allegedly based. As a result, "existentialism" has come to designate almost any sort of unconventional or arbitrary style of living or thinking; and the very idea that an understanding of existentialism might require the making of careful distinctions and sustained argument would undoubtedly strike many of its partisans and its critics as incongruous.

This state of affairs is unfortunate because, as I hope to show, the real interest of existentialism lies not in any special affinity it may have with the contemporary *Zeitgeist* nor in the self-conscious attitudinizing it has inspired, but in what it has to say about the nature of value and choice and moral freedom. It is as an ethical theory, i.e., as a reasoned interpretation of the fundamental concepts of morality, that existentialism deserves serious consideration; and it is as an ethical theory and not as a set of prescriptions for our moral practice that it will be presented and appraised in this book. Whether or not that theory has implications, direct or indirect, for the conduct of life is, of course, one of the principal questions that a study like this will have to consider. But it is important to see that this is itself a question of ethical theory, and that it must be answered at the level of ethical theory before any existentialist ethic in the usual sense can be promulgated.[1]

In this connection, it must be noted in passing that most current philosophical accounts of existentialism do little to correct mistaken popular assumptions, particularly with respect to the alleged irrationalism of the existentialist ethic. One recent study, for example, explicitly endorses the prevalent view of existentialism as the philosophy of irrationalism and defends it as such, apparently on the ground that man has in fact been shown to be strongly influenced by irrational motives and drives.[2] It is not difficult, to be sure, to collect passages from the writings of the existentialists which sound very much like a repudiation of reason and a glorification of action for action's sake. In most cases, however, it turns out on closer inspection that the point being made is a point about the nature and circumstances of human action and not a piece of special pleading in favor of some drastically curtailed conception of our responsibilities as moral agents. In short, if existentialist ethical theory is to be described as "irrationalistic" at all, it must be understood that the rationality in question is one that it regards as merely specious and delusive; and it must be pointed out that within their positive account of human action the existentialists make room for what we ordinarily call *reasons* for acting. Certainly existentialism involves a reinterpretation of the "place of reason in ethics," but it is unfair and inaccurate to represent it as exalting instinct and impulse at the expense of deliberation and foresight in the conduct of life. There is much that is highly controversial in the existentialist po-

[1] For an interesting study of the moral and social aspect of existentialism that leaves aside questions of ethical theory, see Norman Greene, *Jean-Paul Sartre: The Existentialist Ethic* (Ann Arbor, Mich.: University of Michigan Press, 1960).

[2] William Barrett, *Irrational Man* (New York: Anchor Books, Doubleday and Co., Inc., 1958). In this book, existentialism is declared to be "the counter-Enlightenment come at last to philosophical expression," and its message is said to be "to bring the whole man—the concrete individual in the whole context of his everyday life, and his total mystery and questionableness—into philosophy." (p. 274–75) For a better balanced account that is also more detailed in its treatment of points of philosophical interest, see James Collins, *The Existentialists: A Critical Study* (Chicago: H. Regnery Co., 1952).

sition, correctly understood, but I shall try to show that what is at issue is not whether the existentialists are giving bad moral advice but whether their general interpretation of the relation of individual choice to moral rules is a correct one.

To treat existentialism as an ethical theory may occasion surprise for many reasons, not least among them the fact that the chief existentialist writers have in some cases explicitly disclaimed any interest in such an interpretation of their thought and in others have failed to present anything readily recognizable as an analysis of leading ethical concepts. It is certainly true that neither Heidegger nor Sartre has given more than a sketch of an ethical theory in the current Anglo-American sense of that term; but I hope to show that the difficulty of recognizing even that sketch for what it is is due to the special philosophical context in which it is developed and more specifically to the unfamiliar philosophical idiom in which it is presented. None of the philosophers whose views will be considered in this book conceives of philosophy as a whole or of philosophical ethics in particular as an activity of conceptual analysis. They are all in their different ways ontologists, and their views of the nature of value are accordingly stated in terms of "structures" that are held to be particular to certain modes of being. The central contention of this book is that it is both possible and worthwhile to disengage the elements of an ethical theory from the forbidding ontological terminology which the existentialists use and to restate them in terms that are intelligible to those philosophers who do not share this special "ontological" orientation.

In spite of the hazards that such an attempt to translate out of one philosophical idiom into another inevitably faces, there is reason to think that the resulting restatement of existentialist ethical theory may have real advantages over the original by virtue of lending itself less readily to a number of misinterpretations that distort much current discussion of existentialism. It can also contribute materially to the correcting of the widespread but erroneous belief that the interests and views of European philosophers of the phenomenological persuasion are absolutely different from those of philosophers in this country and in Great Britain. While such differences obviously exist, it is one of the guiding assumptions of this study that there has been nevertheless a substantial parallelism in the development of ethical theory on the Continent and in the English-speaking countries during the twentieth century.[3] More specifically, I think it can be shown that much contemporary moral philosophy in this country and England of the kind that is usually called "prescriptivistic" or "noncognitivistic" has close affinities with the ethical theory of existentialism, and that both are descended from a common tradition of ethical theory of which the principal stages are briefly outlined in Part I.[4]

The common strain that unites the ethical theories assignable to this tradition is their progressive elaboration of the idea of moral autonomy and their substitution of this idea for the older conception of moral truth as the fundamental concept of morals. I have accordingly presented the ethical theory of existentialism as essentially an attempt to give a definitive account of what autonomous moral personality is; and I have neglected many other aspects of the existentialists' contribution to ethical theory. I have also been led, by this choice of a focus for this study, to use as my primary representatives of the "ethical theory of existentialism" only those writers who conceive moral autonomy as the final and ineluctable condition of man and not as a kind of interim state that may possibly be surmounted by an eventual intuition of ultimate being or by a mystical communion with God. As I understand them, this view is the one held by those religious or Christian existentialists who, like Marcel and Jaspers, are critical of traditional metaphysical conceptions of natural teleology, but do not despair entirely of the possibility of an external source

[3] A very helpful review of the development of twentieth century ethical theory in both continental Europe and the English-speaking world is provided by William Frankena in his contribution, "Ethics," to R. Klibansky (ed.), *Philosophy in the Mid-Century: A Survey* (Florence: Nuova Italia, 1958–59), Vol. 3, pp. 42–77.

[4] I have in mind especially the work of R. M. Hare whose principal works, *The Language of Morals* (Oxford: Clarendon Press, 1952) and *Freedom and Reason* (Oxford: Clarendon Press, 1963) show many obvious points of affinity with the views of such existentialists as Sartre. It would not do, however, to press these affinities too hard, as Hare's essay, " 'Rien n'a d'importance,' " in *La philosophie analytique* (Cahiers de Royaumont, Philosophie, No. 4 [Paris: Editions de Minuit, 1962], pp. 305–19) clearly shows.

of moral direction.[5] By contrast, Heidegger and Sartre, at least in a certain period of their philosophical development, do seem to me to have committed themselves to the idea of moral autonomy in a truly radical way, and to have produced a view of value that breaks much more sharply with established traditions in ethical theory than does that of the religious existentialists.[6] Needless to say, all of the general statements I make about the "ethical theory of existentialism" must be understood as applying only to this more restricted group of writers—Heidegger and Sartre, together with Maurice Merleau-Ponty and a number of French writers who seem to be principally influenced by them.[7] Even in the case

[5] For a study of these philosophers and of the relationship of their views to one another, see Paul Ricoeur, *Gabriel Marcel et Karl Jaspers* (Paris: Editions du Temps présent, 1948). Both Jaspers and Marcel have written extensively on what they regard as the spiritual and moral crisis of our time, and these works have done much to identify existentialism as a philosophy which addresses itself to the variously defined malaise of modern Western civilization. See Jaspers' *Die geistige Situation der Zeit* (Berlin: W. de Gruyter and Co., 1931) and Marcel's *Les hommes contre l'humain* (Paris: La Colombe, 1951). A critical review of Sartre's *L'Être et le néant* can be found in Marcel's *Homo Viator* (Paris: Aubier, Editions Montaigne, 1945), pp. 233–256.

[6] Even in the case of Heidegger and Sartre, some question arises as to whether they have maintained this position in their more recent work. It seems clear to me, as it has to many critics, that Heidegger's writings from the late thirties onward reflect a quite different spirit and a quite different conception of the relationship of man to being than was characteristic of his earlier works; and I have accordingly based my interpretation of his thought mainly on the latter, especially *Sein und Zeit* (8th ed.; Halle: M. Niemeyer, 1957) and *Vom Wesen des Grundes* (4th ed.; Frankfurt-am-Main: V. Klostermann, 1955). Similarly, my treatment of Sartre rests primarily on *L'Être et le néant;* and while, as I try to show in Chapter VIII, the doctrines he is developing in his still incomplete *Critique de la raison dialectique* (Paris: Gallimard, 1960), are an extension rather than a repudiation of ideas he had developed earlier, I have relied heavily on only one section of that work.

[7] In this group, I would cite particularly Raymond Polin, whose *La création des valeurs* (Paris: Presses Universitaires de France, 1944) was one of the first statements in French of a non-cognitivistic theory of value; and Francis Jeanson, whose *Le problème morale et la pensée de Sartre* (2d ed.; Paris: Editions du Myrte, 1965) offers an interesting interpretation of Sartre's treatment of morality—an interpretation to which Sartre gave his express approval in the preface he contributed to the book. Simone de Beauvoir's *Pour une morale de l'ambiguité* (Paris: Gallimard, 1947) is useful for such light as it casts on Sartre's thought; and her larger work, *Le deuxième sexe* (Paris: Gallimard, 1949) contains much material that has an indirect bearing on questions of morality and moral theory. A highly original account of moral

of this restricted group, however, the account I give in Part I is intended primarily as a delineation of a type of ethical theory rather than as a faithful textual study of their *ipsissima verba*. My principal interest throughout has been to state clearly a very general position in ethical theory that is shared by a group of writers, and to do so without too great a concern for minor divergencies among them. In the footnotes to each chapter, however, I have given rather extensive references to the texts on which my interpretations are based; and I have also tried to illustrate in several especially important cases the principles of philosophical "translation" on which I have relied.

My original intention was to follow the historical review, in Part I, of the development of the ethical theory of existentialism with a full-scale restatement and defense of that theory in its mature form along the lines of interpretation I propose in Chapter V. I found this too ambitious a task, however, and I have chosen instead to deal in Part II with only three major questions that confront the ethical theory of existentialism. These questions concern: first, the adequacy of the grounds alleged by the existentialists for rejecting all objectivistic theories of value; second, the relationship between particular choices and universal moral principles; and finally, the place of moral obligation and moral community in an ethical theory based on the concept of autonomy. Criticism of the ethical aspect of existentialism frequently centers on these questions, and it must be admitted that the difficulties raised by critics have not often been met or even squarely faced by the leading existentialist writers. I believe that the objections to which I have alluded *can* be successfully answered and I have accordingly tried to show how the ethical theory of existentialism can be amplified and refined in such a way as to make it less vulnerable to criticism and misunderstanding on these three cru-

---

experience that runs parallel at many points to that of the existentialists was worked out by Jean Nabert in his *Éléments pour une éthique* (Paris: Presses Universitaires de France, 1943). By contrast with the above works, Georges Gusdorf's *Traité de l'existence morale* (Paris: A. Colin, 1949) is of only routine interest. A detailed bibliography of recent work in ethics by French writers is provided by Georges Bastide in his "Ethics and Political Philosophy," *French Bibliographical Digest* (February, 1961), No. 34, Series II.

cially important points. At the same time, while I feel that the kind of reconstructed existentialism I propose remains consistent with the deepest inspiration of the writers on whom I draw as my primary sources and is in fact adumbrated in their writings, I recognize that my emendations may strike some readers as dilutions of the authentic and heady brew of existentialism with an insipid analytical thinner. I would simply ask those who may be unable to recognize any true affinity between the existentialism of Heidegger and Sartre and the reformulation I propose, to consider the latter on its own merits alone without any concern for its degree of faithfulness to such originals, and with full appreciation of the seriousness of the criticisms it is designed to meet.

PART I

HISTORICAL

CHAPTER I

THE INTELLECTUALISTIC TRADITION

Existentialism is often regarded as a typical expression of a style of thought and sensibility that is characteristically contemporary. Certainly the widespread interest it has aroused and its numerous points of affinity with much that is peculiarly modern in the literature and other imaginative arts of the twentieth century speak in favor of such a view, which, in fact, is perfectly unexceptionable in the positive affirmation it makes. A one-sided emphasis on the contemporary character of existentialism could prove seriously misleading, however, if it encouraged the assumption that the philosophy of existentialism is capable of being stated or understood without a constant effort to relate it to the very philosophical tradition which it claims to supersede. As even the most famous and most cryptic formulation of that philosophy—"Existence is prior to essence"—shows, the terminology in which the existentialist couches his denials is, as often as not, drawn from the philosophies he is concerned to refute. Existentialism is, in fact, a reactive movement of thought which becomes fully comprehensible only when the philosophical positions against which it is reacting are identified and understood. Many of the commonest misunderstandings of existentialism as well as many "demonstrations" of its gross incompatibility with common sense have been due to an attempt to take its philosophy "neat," i.e., to interpret its theses without giving sufficient attention to the philosophical context in which these have been developed. Too often the result has been to mistake the sense of the existentialist's affirmations through having failed to grasp the point of his denials. This statement applies with special force to the relationship of existentialism to the main stream of Western moral philosophy; and in this chapter and the three that follow it, an effort will be made to describe, however briefly, the reactive or dialectical relationship in which existentialism stands to dominant trends in the history of ethical theory, and also to say something about earlier formulations of the alternative conception of value and choice of which existentialism claims to be the definitive statement.[1]

I

The belief that the concepts of truth and falsity are applicable to judgments of value has been a central theme of Western moral philosophy since its inception. While this view may have been first put forward by Socrates, it received an explicit philosophical interpretation at the hands of Plato; and it is not too much to say that the whole subsequent development of moral philosophy has been dominated by Plato's original statement of what may be called the intellectualistic thesis.[2] This is the view that value predicates have meaning by virtue of standing for objective qualities or relations that are independent of our feelings and volitions; that rational beings are able to apprehend these qualities; and that true (and false) statements can accordingly be made about them. In this first formulation, as later, intellectualism was intended as a refutation of skeptical views which made the moral quality of things relative to the attitudes and aspirations of individual human beings. Against the view that values are artificial

[1] In the brief historical review that follows, I pass over in silence a number of questions concerning the correct interpretation of the doctrines of the writers I discuss. These questions have their own considerable importance, but for my purposes, even setting considerations of space aside, they must be secondary. My concern here is primarily with the way such writers as Plato and Aristotle influenced the subsequent development of ethical theory; and in characterizing that influence I am not thereby denying the possibility that the traditional interpretation of their doctrines may be mistaken in certain important respects.

[2] For a contrasting view of the ethical thought of Socrates which assimilates him to Kierkegaard, and thus to at least one wing of the existentialist tradition, see John Gould, *The Development of Plato's Ethics* (Cambridge: Cambridge University Press, 1955). This view has been decisively refuted, I think, by G. Vlastos in "Socratic Knowledge and Platonic Pessimism," *Philosophical Review*, LXVI (1957), 226–238.

human conventions, intellectualism has always insisted that the goodness or badness of a thing and the rightness or wrongness of an action are functions of the nature of that thing or action rather than of our feelings about it. "Nature" in this context means simply the set of characteristics that an object possesses and by which it is classifiable as belonging to a certain kind or species of things. Since these characteristics define a class of things and are therefore not peculiar, at least in principle, to any single object, the natures they compose have traditionally been described as "universals."

Two features of Plato's account of moral knowledge were to play an important role in the subsequent evolution of intellectualism. First, his attribution of logical necessity to the relationship between universals suggested a similar conception of the relationship between the form of the good and other universals. Knowledge of the moral quality of things has thus often been conceived to be of a type with mathematical knowledge; and in both cases the test of truth is held to be essentially logical in character and to consist in a set of dialectical operations performed upon the definitions of the terms involved. At the same time, however, Plato often used the language of perception and of vision to characterize our apprehension of the good as well as of other universals. He did not, of course, mean that insight into moral relationships was literally seeing, but the metaphor of sight has a unique capacity to suggest the independence or "out-there-ness" of what is known, and it was therefore natural that Plato and the whole intellectualistic tradition which followed after him should make such extensive use of it. By combining these two features of moral knowledge, Plato worked out the conception of a necessity inherent in the object of moral knowledge itself that was perhaps his principal legacy to subsequent ethical theory. At the same time, by virtue of this very association of the idea of necessity with that of a vision directed upon self-subsistent entities, he created one of the most difficult problems that the intellectualistic tradition has had to resolve.

If Plato gave Western ethical theory its initial intellectualistic bent, it was Aristotle and the medieval Aristotelians who recast his teaching into the form of a detailed doctrine of human nature. Since it was this form of intellectualism that principally stimulated—by reaction—the developments in ethical theory that eventually led to existentialism, a summary review of the main relevant features of Aristotle's moral philosophy is in order.

A theory of natural teleology and a theory of natural kinds provide the basis of that doctrine. According to the latter, each individual thing is endowed with a nature or essence that it has in common with some other individuals and by virtue of which they are classifiable as belonging to a certain genus and species and so on down to the *infima species* in the lowest tiers of the classificatory pyramid.[3] This classification into kinds is natural in the sense that the distinction between defining traits and accidental or peripheral traits is conceived to be a real, and not a conventional, distinction. It is, in fact, a kind of prelinguistic datum that must be faithfully reproduced in language instead of being itself a pragmatically justified linguistic achievement. The metaphysical priority of the traits that constitute these "natures" generates a basic vocabulary for identifying individual things; and the way of cutting up the world that is thus imposed is emphatically not optional. To tinker with it would result not just in departures from a particular system of identifying reference but in a distortion of the natures of the things classified.

The doctrine of natural teleology can be described as a further stipulation attached to the theory of natural kinds. It asserts that the natures on which the "natural" system of classification is based are compounded in such a way as to define a function, or end, that is proper to the bearers of any given nature. According to this view, it will thus be impossible to identify a particular as having any specific nature without thereby committing oneself to a number of propositions with respect to the distinctive good of that thing; it is understood that right conduct for intelligent

[3] In the account I give here of Aristotle's doctrine of the ontological basis of systems of classification, I have been influenced by the views set forth in Stuart Hampshire, *Thought and Action* (London: Chatto and Windus, 1959), particularly in Chapter I. While Hampshire does not explicitly associate Aristotle with the conception of language and its reference to objects which he describes and criticizes there, there can be little doubt, I think, that Aristotle's philosophy offers a prime example of the kind of view that Hampshire has in mind.

beings consists in doing what realizes their distinctive *telos*. A conceptual system that would enable us to identify someone as a human being, while leaving open all questions as to what he ought properly to do, is thus in effect excluded. Once again, the reason is not to be sought in any linguistic conservatism on Aristotle's part but in his conviction that what is real, independently of all language, is a combination of actuality with a special potentiality for realizing certain distinctive ends, and that this fact must be reflected in any viable scheme of classification. In summary, then, one may say that Aristotle's normative ethic consists of a set of implications that is built into the very language he uses for the description of the subjects of that theory; and this language, in turn, is interpreted as reflecting metaphysical structures that are antecedent to language and immune to change.

If this theory is applied to human action, it is clear that principles of right action will be derivable from the *telos,* or proper end, of man; and this end will be implicit in the "nature" that is peculiar to human beings. These principles will have the status of moral or practical truths; and if we follow Aristotle, at least one of them (i.e., the principle that the end of man is the exercise of intellectual virtue), will be a necessary truth. Others that bear upon the means to this end, will be among those things "that could be otherwise." In any case, they will function as the major premises in practical syllogisms; taken together with factual premises describing a given situation as of the type to which the rule applies, they will generate a particular moral judgment that tells what action would be suitable in that situation. To this piece of moral knowledge the will is referred for guidance. Aristotle's way of putting this is to say that the conclusion in a practical syllogism is an action, but this seems to prejudge the question of whether a person may not act otherwise while knowing what he ought to do.[4] Intellectualism, as I am using the term, is a thesis

[4] Aristotle's theory of the practical syllogism has been the subject of much recent discussion, particularly as it bears upon the much-vexed problem of akrasia. Much of this discussion is summarized in James Walsh, *Aristotle's Conception of Moral Weakness* (New York: Columbia University Press, 1960); there is also a helpful analysis of the relationship of practical and theoretical reason which in general appears to support the view of that relationship which I am defending. (See especially pp. 131 ff.)

7

about the kind of knowledge that is involved in the apprehension of the truth of moral principles; and care should be taken to distinguish this thesis from the view that the will is somehow constrained to seek what the intellect represents to it as good. As we shall see, this distinction has not always been observed.

One very important effect of this doctrine of natural ends that are proper to each kind of being is the restrictions it imposes upon the concept of choice. According to Aristotle, choice is the outcome of deliberation, and deliberation is concerned with means to an end and not with the end itself.[5] Deliberation and choice thus operate within a framework of goals over which they exercise no control; and the proper goal for any being is determined by the *kind* of being it is, i.e., by its nature. The *telos* or proper end of human beings may, of course, be misapprehended by them, and when it is, choice will be directed to means that do not realize their peculiar good. But even in this case, it would presumably not be correct, in Aristotle's view, to speak of a *choice* of the mistaken end. Ends are apprehended (or misapprehended) by human reason, and precisely because our relation to them is cognitive, they are not objects of choice. If they were chosen, then there would either have to be some ulterior end to which they were means, and then this higher end would not be chosen; or the possibility would arise that in the absence of any end that has such a status, human beings might differ in their choice of the highest end. If such difference amounted to incompatibility, Aristotle's conception of man as a social being whose *true* good is necessarily compatible with that of other human beings would have to be called into question.

The view that man has a natural end and that the moral principles in which this end is defined have the status of necessary truths became a central tenet of the medieval theory of natural law by which the Greek tradition of ethical intellectualism was transmitted to the modern world.[6] In the classical formulation of

[5] Aristotle's analysis of choice and deliberation is given in chs. 2–4, Bk. 3, of the *Nicomachean Ethics*. For a discussion of some of the problems raised by his doctrine, see G. Anscombe, "Thought and Action in Aristotle," in R. Bambrough (ed.), *New Essays on Plato and Aristotle* (London: Routledge, Kegan, Paul, 1965), pp. 143–158; and also G. Anscombe, *Intention* (Oxford: B. H. Blackwell, 1957), pp. 57 ff.

[6] A compact review of the main stages in the development of natural law theory is to be found in Alessandro Passerin d'Entreves, *Natural Law: an*

natural law theory produced by St. Thomas, intellectualism has to accommodate itself to the Christian view that the ultimate basis of morality is the will of a personal God. Such a view has strongly anti-intellectualistic implications which, as we shall see, were to be fully developed in the later medieval and early modern periods. To meet this difficulty, St. Thomas tried to construct a theory of the divine personality in which intellect and will were related in such a way as to render compatible with one another the demands of a theistic ethic and the intellectualistic position which makes choice and will subordinate to intellect.[7] In constructing this theory of the relation of will and intellect in the divine personality, St. Thomas was also providing a model by which the relationship of these faculties within human personality might be understood.

The premise on which Thomas's theory of God's personality rests is that God has a nature, or essence. This divine essence differs from the essences of finite creatures in many ways, but most notably by virtue of the fact that God's essence and his existence are one, as man's are not. It also differs in that all of God's attributes are perfected or complete forms of attributes which finite beings possess only in partial and fragmentary form. In spite of these differences, there is a real sense in which St. Thomas may be said to apply Aristotle's theory of natural kinds to God, since his being is tied to a constellation of attributes. As a result, God can-

---

Introduction to Legal Philosophy (London: Hutchinson's University Library, 1951). An excellent treatment of much the same subject is Hans Welzel, *Naturrecht und materiale Gerechtigkeit* (Göttingen: Vandenhoeck and Ruprecht, 1955), although Welzel somewhat incongruously treats as one form of natural law theory the kind of ethical voluntarism which I interpret rather as a directly antithetical doctrine worked out by critics of natural law theory.

[7] St. Thomas's doctrine of the nature of God's intellect and will and of their relationship to one another is set forth in his *Summa Theologica* I, Qu. 14, 15, and 19 and in the *Summa Contra Gentes*, Bk. 1, chs. 44–96. In these discussions, St. Thomas often cites St. Augustine's "De ideis" [*De Diversis Questionibus* 83, No. 46, *Opera Omnia* (Paris: 1861–65), Vol. 6] which is unmistakably Platonic in inspiration. Although it is often claimed that St. Augustine developed a new conception of the will that ran counter to classical intellectualism, the passages most often cited in *De Trinitate* Bk. X, 11 (17–18) seem to indicate that this innovation should not be interpreted in such a way as to qualify the primacy of intellect as the touchstone of moral truth, which is clearly expounded in the "De ideis."

not be lacking in any of these attributes that constitute his essence; for if he were, he would not be what he is, and this is to say that the law of contradiction would have been violated. This is impossible even in the case of God, who must therefore act in a manner consistent with his own nature. St. Thomas certainly did not think that by this doctrine he was denying God a power that he might possibly have had, and he would doubtless have thought it senseless to assert that he was imposing real limits on what God could do, as some of his critics were to argue. On the other hand, if any of the things which, according to his theory, God cannot do, are not obviously unimaginable, the denial that God can do them will inevitably sound as though some real incapacity were being imputed to him. This is precisely what was to happen in the case of the moral limits assigned by St. Thomas to God's action.

St. Thomas assumes further that the object of God's knowledge is his own essence, and that God knows other things only mediately, i.e., as contained in his own essence. Now, one element in this essence is God's goodness which is thus, in the first instance, an object of knowledge—a *bonum intellectum*. Similarly, the good of each finite being that is included in the nature of God is included in the nature of that thing as it figures in the divine intellect. The crucial step in the argument is St. Thomas's assertion that the object of God's will cannot be something outside him, but must be his own essence. Otherwise, God would be in a state of privation, and this would be genuinely incompatible with his perfection. From this it follows that the will is addressed to the *bonum intellectum*, and that it is subject to the same law of contradiction that governs the intellect:

The will is only of some understood good. Wherefore that which is not an object of the intellect, cannot be an object of the will. Now things in themselves impossible are not an object of understanding, since they imply a contradiction. . . . Therefore things in themselves impossible cannot be an object of God's will.[8]

8 "Voluntas non est nisi alicuius boni intellecti. Illud igitur quod non cadit in intellectum, non potest cadere in voluntatem. Sed ea quae sunt secundum se impossibilia non cadunt in intellectum. . . . in divinam igitur voluntatem non possunt cadere quae secundum se sunt impossibilia." *Summa Contra*

God cannot, therefore, will evil; and since there cannot be any possibility of error in his apprehension of the good, he does in fact will only what is truly good and good by a standard that is independent of his will.

It is another very important thesis of the theory of natural law that the moral truths that God knows infallibly and perfectly in apprehending the goodness of his own nature are in some measure accessible to the human intellect and will. To the extent that they are, human beings are not exclusively dependent upon an unpredictable revelation for guidance in the conduct of life, but are instead in a situation vis-à-vis moral truths that is essentially similar to that of God. Both stand in a cognitive relation to the good—the *bonum intellectum*—and in both cases this good is independent of their wills. Neither makes anything good by willing it or choosing it; for both, the goodness of an end is certified by a rational insight into its relationship to the nature of the being whose end it is. God's knowledge is, of course, perfect as man's is defective and partial; but man is subject to the will of God only as this is understood to be ordered to the ends proposed by his intellect, and these ends are in some degree apprehensible by the human intellect as well. If God loses his absolute autonomy by this submission of his will to his intellect, there is a compensating gain in moral intelligibility for man. Eventually, however, this subordination, which had been held by some theologians to place effective restrictions on the power of God, also came to be felt as a limitation on the moral freedom of human beings. In that feeling, a powerful movement of reaction against Thomistic intellectualism was to find one of its strongest motives.

The subsequent evolution of intellectualism in the modern period and the immense influence it has exerted over the development of ethical theory as a whole are too well known to require further comment here. One seventeenth century statement of its central thesis is so striking, however, that it must be noted:

. . . moral good and evil, just and unjust, honest and dishonest (if they be not mere names without any signification or names for nothing else, but willed and commanded, but have a reality in respect of the

Gentiles, Bk. 1, ch. 84. (The English version is taken from the Dominican translation published in London: Burns, Oates, and Washburne, 1923–24.)

11

persons obliged to do and avoid them) cannot possibly be arbitrary things, made by will without nature; because it is universally true that things are what they are, not by will but by nature. As for example, things are white by whiteness, and black by blackness, triangular by triangularity, and round by rotundity, like by likeness, and equal by equality, that is, by certain natures of their own. Neither can Omnipotence itself (to speak with reverence) by mere will make a thing white or black without whiteness or blackness . . .

And since a thing cannot be made anything by mere will without a being or nature, everything must be necessarily and immutably determined by its own nature, and the nature of things be what it is and nothing else. For though the will and power of God have an absolute, infinite and unlimited command upon the existences of all created things to make them to be, or not to be at pleasure: yet when things exist they are what they are, this or that, absolutely or relatively, not by will or arbitrary command, but by the necessity of their own nature.[9]

The interest of this passage is increased by the fact that its author, Ralph Cudworth, who was himself a Platonist, was consciously arguing against a radically anti-intellectualistic view of the divine will which had been worked out during the interval that separates him from St. Thomas, and which he imputes to certain "Occamite wranglers." A position that in its essentials is very close to Cudworth's was defended in the mid-eighteenth century by Richard Price.[10] After a substantial eclipse during the nineteenth century, intellectualism was once again restored to a position of influence within ethical theory by the two moral philosophers whose work has been the cornerstone of twentieth century ethics on the continent of Europe and in the English-speaking world: Max Scheler and G. E. Moore.[11] Their role in

[9] Ralph Cudworth, *Treatise Concerning Eternal and Immutable Morality* (New York: Andover, Gould and Newman, 1838), Vol. 2, pp. 373-74. A most illuminating discussion of this passage and of Cudworth's place in the development of ethical theory is contained in Arthur Prior, *Logic and the Basis of Ethics* (Oxford: Clarendon Press, 1949), ch. 2. Cudworth's influence on Price is shown in John Passmore, *Ralph Cudworth; an Interpretation* (Cambridge: Cambridge University Press, 1951).

[10] Richard Price, *A Review of the Principal Questions in Morals*, ed. D. D. Raphael (Oxford: Clarendon Press, 1948). See especially ch. 1, sec. 3, and ch. 5. In the latter chapter there is a forceful attack on doctrines that assign primacy to the will over the intellect within God's nature.

[11] G. E. Moore, *Principia Ethica* (Cambridge: Cambridge University Press, 1903) and Max Scheler, *Der Formalismus in de Ethik und die materiale*

stimulating the further development of ethical theory will be discussed in Chapter IV.

II

While one form or another of intellectualism has continued to command widespread acceptance among modern writers on ethical theory, perhaps its most important influence has been to call forth strong negative reactions that have moved ethical theory in new directions. It is not too much to say that innovation in modern moral philosophy has typically assumed the form of criticism directed against a tenaciously surviving intellectualism. Sometimes this reaction has been purely negative, and has issued in a comprehensive skepticism. But while a skeptic like Montaigne may despair of the possibility of finding stable moral truths, he does not usually challenge in principle the propriety of talking about truth and falsity in moral contexts. Indeed, nothing testifies quite so eloquently to the influence of intellectualism as the skeptic's assumption that there are no alternatives to it that do not plunge the whole subject of morality into an irremediable disorder.[12]

Skepticism, however, is hardly a new kind of ethical theory. Among the constructive reactions to intellectualism, the best known is probably the "ethic of sentiment" that was worked out by Hume and later given systematic form by Bentham and his school.[13] This view rejects the prime intellectualistic assumption that moral predicates denote independent attributes of the things

---

Wertethik (4th ed.; Bern: Francke, 1954). An earlier figure in this revival of intellectualism was Franz Brentano, whose most important work on ethics is *Vom Ursprung sittlicher Erkenntnis* (4th ed.; Hamburg: Meiner, 1955).

[12] For an estimate of Montaigne's skepticism, see R. Popkin, *The History of Skepticism from Erasmus to Descartes* (Assen, The Netherlands: Van Gorcum, 1960), ch. 3.

[13] The most important texts illustrating this movement in moral philosophy—those of Shaftesbury, Hutcheson, and later, Adam Smith—can be found in L. A. Selby-Bigge (ed.), *British Moralists* (Oxford: Clarendon Press, 1897). The influence of Hutcheson on Hume is described in N. Kemp-Smith, *The Philosophy of David Hume* (London: Macmillan Co., 1941), ch. 2.

evaluated, and holds instead that the assignment of such predicates implies no more than a capacity for producing certain feelings in human beings. If we abstract from the occurrence of such feelings, there is (so the argument goes) no sense in which moral judgment can be said to be true or false. On the other hand, these predicates *can* apply to such judgments if they are considered simply as predictions of what kinds of things will tend to produce agreeable and disagreeable feelings in human beings. When the further assumption is made, as it was by Bentham and his followers, that *only* these feelings can be the object of human desire, the way is open to the development of a type of ethical theory that differs fundamentally from intellectualism in its conception of the nature and subject matter of moral knowledge but, at the same time, subordinates individual choice to the notion of moral truth quite as strictly as the most rigorous intellectualism ever did.

There is still another mode of reaction against intellectualism that is significantly different from both skepticism and the "subjectivism" outlined above. While the latter saves the concept of truth for morals by transferring it to statements about the so-called "tertiary" qualities, and the former treats it as an ideal that is, unhappily, unrealizable at least in moral contexts, a third position raises, as the others do not, the more radical question about the underlying assumptions of intellectualism, and in particular its unquestioning application of the concepts of truth and falsity to moral principles. For the vocabulary of cognition which the intellectualist applies to the description of the moral life, it proposes to substitute a new set of concepts of which the most important is choice. The most familiar label for this tradition or counter-tradition in moral philosophy is "voluntarism."[14] The central meaning of the term, as it will be used in this study, lies in the assumption that moral principles are principles of action

[14] The term "voluntarism" was apparently first used by Ferdinand Tönnies in the late nineteenth century. A discussion of the long-standing antithesis of intellect and will within Western philosophy is to be found in H. Heimsoeth, *Die sechs grossen Themen der abendländischen Metaphysik* (Berlin: Junker und Dunnhaupt, 1922), ch. 6; also, David Pole in his *Conditions of Rational Inquiry* (London: University of London Press, 1961) devotes ch. 2 to a discussion of voluntarism in contemporary ethical theory.

to which the concepts of truth and falsity do not properly apply, and that while they certainly may guide individual choice, they are also, in a deeper sense, dependent upon choice. More specifically, a voluntaristic ethical theory denies that individual choices are subsumptions of particular cases under moral principles whose truth is independently established. It also denies that choice is psychologically or logically tied to some "natural" object, whether this be defined in terms of desirable feeling-states or in terms of some non-psychological form of teleology. Positively, voluntarism may be said to amount to a demand that moral phenomena be comprehensively redescribed in a vocabulary that explicitly recognizes the decisional and logically autonomous character of moral judgment.

Since the term "voluntarism" has often been used to characterize psychological or metaphysical doctrines of will, it is not altogether satisfactory as a term of reference for this set of theses in ethical theory. It has, however, the advantage of reminding us of the affinities such an ethical theory has with the conceptions of evaluation and action that are characteristic of a long line of theologians and philosophers who successively worked out a distinctive alternative to intellectualism and laid the foundations of a view of morality that is often supposed to be peculiarly modern. There can be little doubt that the first major statement of a "voluntaristic" position that is directly relevant to the concerns of ethical theory is to be found in certain movements of thought in later medieval theology that were to find expression also in the thought of the Protestant Reformers of the sixteenth century.[15] Later, voluntarism was transformed by Kant and others into a philosophical (as distinct from a theological) theory of ethics. It has often been remarked that Kant's ethical theory, as well as some contemporary views that bear the mark of its influence, have a distinctly Protestant flavor. In fact, this is what one would expect if, as I shall argue, philosophical voluntarism is in good part a transference to the sphere of human action of certain theses with respect to the relation of God's will to his intellect,

---

[15] Perhaps the best treatment of medieval voluntarism is to be found in the article by P. Vignaux, "Nominalisme," in the *Dictionnaire de Théologie Catholique* (Paris: 1903–50), Vol. 11 (1), pp. 717–84.

which are more characteristic of Protestant theology than of the main stream of Catholic thought.

The main argument of Part I of this book will be that existentialism, considered in its ethical aspect, is descended from this voluntaristic tradition in theology and philosophy. Whatever its merits and demerits as an ethical theory, it has an undeniable historical interest if only because it presents a conception of human action that is prefigured in the earlier phases of this tradition, but that had never before been isolated from the more or less adventitious religious and philosophical assumptions with which it was previously associated. The idea of a counter-tradition in reaction against intellectualism is, to be sure, not new; but it seems fair to say that the unity and pattern of development of the specific counter-tradition that is based on the concept of choice has not always been fully recognized, at least in the English-speaking philosophical world.[16] Existentialism as a whole has many sources, and no claim is made here to give an exhaustive genealogy for it. But ethical voluntarism is certainly one of the main traditions of thought on which existentialism has drawn; and a brief account of the stages through which that tradition has passed should be a useful preliminary to an analysis and appraisal of its most recent formulation.

A word must be said here about the implications of the view I am proposing of voluntaristic and existentialist ethical theory as a dialectical reaction to other theses about the nature of value which have to be understood if their denial is to have any point. If such a view were accepted, what effect would it have upon the broader human relevance and interest that such doctrines claim to possess? If the existentialist treatment of moral phenomena is intelligible only within the context of the Western philosophical tradition, presumably it will have something important to say only to those who are familiar with, and in some measure influenced by, that tradition. After all, what is the significance of a reactive thesis when there is nothing to react against, if only be-

16 One of the few books in which a review of the voluntaristic tradition is attempted is Herbert Spiegelberg, *Gesetz und Sittengesetz* (Zürich: M. Niehans, 1935), although Spiegelberg is more interested in the notion of morality as taking the form of laws than he is in will as the basis of morality.

cause (as is surely the case even for the overwhelming majority of educated persons), Platonic intellectualism is at best an ill-remembered relic of a college course in philosophy, and even more often a mere form of words to which no meaning at all is attached? To this question, the only justifiable answer might well seem to be flatly negative; and one might be tempted to go on to conclude that the widespread interest aroused by existentialism is due to a series of misunderstandings based on certain adventitious features of that doctrine, and can be expected to disappear when those confusions are dissipated. This conclusion could be avoided only if the intellectualism against which existentialism is a reaction proved to be not just an intra-philosophical phenomenon, but to have deeper roots in Western culture and life. In the latter event, a critique of intellectualism such as that undertaken by the existentialists *could* justifiably lay claim to a wider relevance. Whether or not this condition is satisfied is a question that must be postponed until the final chapter of this book.

CHAPTER II

THEOLOGICAL VOLUNTARISM

In the last chapter, it was suggested that ethical voluntarism can profitably be regarded as a transference to the sphere of human action of views with respect to the nature of value that were first put forward as theses about the relation of intellect to will within the moral personality of God. In the light of the close historical relationship between moral ideas and systems of religious belief, there is nothing surprising about this order of progression. Indeed, one would expect that just as the intellectualistic view of St. Thomas was stated in the form of a theory about the composition of God's moral personality, so a competing view would assume the form of a revision of that theory. Historically, the first stage in the development of ethical voluntarism was in fact predominantly theological in character. In this chapter, an attempt will be made to bring out some of the more important features of a voluntaristic moral theology, and to suggest ways in which such a position in theology may influence our understanding of evaluation and choice as human functions.

I

Theories that make the will of God the ultimate basis of morality are often classified by philosophers under the rubric of "theological naturalism."[1] In the sense which the term "naturalism" bears in current ethical theory, and in this particular use, it designates all interpretations of moral predicates like "good" and

[1] See, for example, C. D. Broad, *Five Types of Ethical Theory* (New York: Harcourt, Brace and Co., 1930), pp. 257–59. This terminology is discussed in D. A. Rees, "The Ethic of Divine Commands," *Proceedings of the Aristotelian Society*, N.S., Vol. LVII (1956–57), pp. 83–106.

"right" which make them logically equivalent to a set of predicates whose applicability can be determined by some procedure of verification. Thus, a hedonistic theory is naturalistic if it asserts that "good" and "tending to maximize pleasure" are synonymous and interchangeable expressions, and if there is some generally acceptable method for determining what actions in fact produce the greatest amount of pleasure. The only peculiarity of the theological variant of naturalism, from this standpoint, would be the fact that the criterial properties that stand in this relation of mutual entailment with "good" or "right" are not natural in any sense that implies amenability to empirical verification, and require instead another mode of apprehension. Nevertheless, if this difficulty is passed over,—and it has no importance for our purposes—the only difference between an ethical theory based on the will of God and a paradigmatic case of naturalism such as hedonism, lies in the criterial properties that establish goodness or rightness. In both cases, a "fact"—whether it be "x is pleasant" or "x is willed by God" makes no difference—has, as a necessary consequence, that "x is good." Viewed in this light, "will of God" theories of ethics might not seem to be very different from the intellectualistic views discussed in the last chapter, since they recognize a mode of cognition that provides conclusive answers to moral questions.

While this analysis of theological voluntarism is perfectly accurate as far as it goes, it completely misses what is truly distinctive and interesting in such theories. It does so because it confines itself rigidly to the point of view of those beings, human and otherwise, who are morally subordinate to God and for whom God's having willed x is in fact a necessary and sufficient condition of x's being good. Because the similarity between the situations of subordinate moral beings as understood by intellectualism and by this theological version of voluntarism is allowed to dominate our view of these theories, we miss the much more important difference between them which has to do with their conception of the moral personality of God. While the intellectualist recognizes the existence of an immense gap separating God and man in point of knowledge and goodness, he conceives God's nature as a moral being to be a perfected form of what is present in man in

20

an imperfect and fragmentary state. Both man and God thus have an essentially cognitive relation to their own essences and to the goodness that is implicit in these natures. The innovation of the voluntarist is to introduce the conception of a moral personality—God's—that cannot be described in intellectualistic terms at all. The voluntarist's God does not stand in a cognitive relationship to moral essences. His will is not coerced by what he knows, and what he knows does not provide a morally relevant standard by which the rightness of what he wills can be established. To be sure, what he wills constitutes a norm to which all subordinate beings must conform their wills since God is the moral being *par excellence*. But for just this reason, the voluntaristic reinterpretation of his nature is all the more significant. It amounts to saying that while superficially, from the standpoint of subordinate moral beings, morality is a matter of knowing, its ultimate basis is in the will of God and this is a will that is subject to no causal or logical constraints. On the voluntaristic view, morality is not a matter of "knowing" at all in the case of God, except in the trivial sense that God necessarily knows, reflexively, what he wills. For human beings, of course, it *is* a matter of knowing (i.e., knowing what God wills) ; but it is impossible in principle for them to know what is right in the sense of grasping the rational necessities on which God's commands rest, since these do not exist.

Now, among the doctrines that are classifiable as forms of theological voluntarism it is in fact possible to distinguish between those that place their principal emphasis on the moral personality of God, and those that are mainly concerned with the situation of subordinate moral beings under a God whose will is subject to no rational controls. As an example of the former, one can cite the conception of God's moral nature that was worked out by William of Ockham as not only the most radical and ruthlessly consistent view of its kind, but also as one that has the added interest of being a direct counter-statement to the Thomistic doctrine already considered. As an example of the second, man-centered kind of theological voluntarism, the thought of Sören Kierkegaard is probably without a peer. Together these two very different thinkers offer paradigms of the two aspects of theologi-

21

cal voluntarism that illustrate rather clearly both the internal dialectic and the final limitations of this mode of thought.

II

The crucial difference between Ockham's God and the God of St. Thomas is that the former does not have a nature in the sense of a real essence composed of universal attributes that can be apprehended by the intellect.[2] This is simply an application to God of Ockham's general thesis that only particulars exist and that such traditional distinctions of reason as that between God's essence and his existence, or between his will and his knowledge, are conceptual distinctions for which there is no counterpart distinction in God himself or in any object at all. God's nature, like that of all individuals, is absolutely simple and unitary; and the force of this thesis, as shown by the use Ockham makes of it, is to deny the possibility of any order of priority of intellect over will within the divine personality. The object of God's knowledge is particular things, not universal essences. The conception of a mediation and control of God's will in relation to particular things by the ideas contained in his intellect is rejected by Ockham as is also the cognate view that the being of a thing comprises a natural end which it strives to realize. The result is that God's acts of will are subject to no controls, whether logical or causal, be-

[2] Although a complete edition of Ockham's works is planned, there has been no modern edition of his *Commentary on the Sentences of Peter Lombard* in which his views on ethics are most extensively stated. Extensive selections from this work are presented in S. U. Zuidema, *De Philosophie van Occam in zijn Commentaar op de Sententiën* (Hilversum: Schipper, 1936); briefer excerpts are presented in translation in S. Tornay (ed.), *Ockham: Studies and Selections* (La Salle, Ill.: Open Court Publishing Co., 1938), and in P. Boehner (ed.), *Ockham: Philosophical Writings* (Edinburgh: Nelson, 1957). The most important recent work dealing with Ockham's moral philosophy is Georges de Lagarde, *Ockham: La morale et le droit*, Vol. 6 of the author's *La naissance de l'esprit laïque au déclin du moyen âge* (Paris: Presses universitaires de France, 1948). For the developments in medieval ethical theory that led up to Ockham, see Jean Rohmer's excellent study, *La finalité morale chez les théologiens de St. Augustin à Duns Scot* (Paris: J. Vrin, 1938), and also E. Gilson, *Jean Duns Scot* (Paris: 1952), especially ch. 9, "La volonté."

cause there is no moral order antecedent to the exercise of his will. The content of the latter is not derivable from his essence, nor from the essence of created beings, because God's will and his essence are one and the same thing. The divine will is thus constitutive of what is good and right; while God knows what he makes right and good by willing it, this knowledge is inseparable from the act of will itself, and is in no sense something in the mind of God by which the will is guided. The only limit set to the divine will by Ockham is that it cannot involve an internal contradiction; and he makes it very clear that this does not mean that God cannot change his will and make an action right that was previously wrong. By this very significant interpretation of the principle of non-contradiction as it applies to ethical predicates, which incidentally anticipates certain developments in contemporary ethical theory, Ockham in effect commits himself to the view that these predicates do not denote "qualities" in any normal sense of the term, and that their applicability is not susceptible of any normal epistemic certification.[3]

While God enjoys this total autonomy, he is the only "moral

---

[3] This point is made in A. Garvens, "Die Grundlagen der Ethik Wilhelm's von Ockham," *Franziskanische Studien*, Vol. 21 (3–4), pp. 243–73 and pp. 360–408. As Garvens points out, "ein innerwesentlicher realer Zusammenhang zwischen ontologischem und moralischem Sein besteht in Ockham's Weltbild nicht," (p. 267). The author also quotes the following passage from Ockham's *Commentary IV*, q. 9, S: "dico quod peccatum nec est ens reale nec rationis sed sicut alias dictum est de bono, vero et aliis connotativis conceptibus quod habent quid nominis et non quid rei nec rationis." This analysis of ethical predicates as "connotative concepts" to which no fixed "ens reale" attaches, rather clearly foreshadows modern views that deny descriptive meaning to ethical predicates and focus attention on the operation of the ethical *words* themselves. (See for example C. L. Stevenson, *Ethics and Language* (New Haven, Conn.: Yale University Press, 1947), pp. 20 ff; and A. Hägerström, *Inquiries into the Nature of Law and Morals* (Uppsala: Almqvist and Wiksell, 1953), pp. 142–64.) Quite consistently, Ockham associates with this interpretation of moral predicates the psychological doctrine that the will is not bound to any natural end, and that it can in fact make anything its end. Thus, in *Sent.* IV, q. 14 D, Ockham argues that "voluntas pro statu isto potest nolle ultimum finem, sive ostenditur in generali sive in particulari—dico quod intellectu indicante hoc esse finem ultimum potest voluntas illum finem nolle. Voluntas tamquam potentia libera est receptiva nolle et velle respectu cuiuscumque objecti." This passage recalls Kant's statement that human beings "can will anything," and it is worth noting that Ockham and Kant also agree that only acts of will can be good or bad.

agent" that does, according to Ockham; and the situation of subordinate moral beings is very different. The older view had been that since God's action is a function of his ideas, a degree of imitation of the divine essence is possible for subordinate moral beings. A rejection of this view has the effect of making insight into God's "reasons" impossible in principle. For inferior beings, "right" action *means* action that is commanded by God; and for them this formula also shows how they should set about discovering what they should do. (As previously noted, this equivalence would hold in a trivial sense for God, too, but it could not in his case provide a method for determining *what* to do.) The basis of morality is thus the *potentia absoluta* of God, his unfettered and continuing freedom to determine what actions are right and wrong. With this notion traditionally there have been associated disagreeable images of arbitrary personal despotism, which partly explain the unfavorable reaction that Ockham's views have usually encountered. Correctly understood, however, the point he is making is simply that at its highest level—in God—morality does not belong to the order of knowing, but consists in a spontaneous creativity that expresses itself in commands by God through which his creation is to be ordered, and in which rational beings are to find the constitutive principles of right and wrong. No moral principle—not even the highest—can claim any sort of necessary truth. God might have ordered his world otherwise than he has, and the content of his will with respect to human beings might have been very different. All moral principles are therefore at best conditionally valid, and the condition is conveyed in the phrase, *stante ordinatione divina quae nunc est.* God is subject to no obligations, and any uniformity that may characterize his commands is self-imposed and can be terminated at his pleasure.

It is often argued that when all moral principles are treated as dependent upon an uncontrolled divine will, morality in any usual sense becomes impossible because the relative stability and predictability presupposed by a code of moral rules are missing. In considering this sort of argument, the example of Ockham may be instructive. Just as the ultimately arbitrary character of even the highest moral principles may be said to be symbolized within his system by the idea of God's *potentia absoluta,* so the relative stability of these principles, which is a condition for the existence of a moral code in any familiar sense, finds its place through the notion of God's *potentia ordinata.* It is just a fact that God condescends to regulate his will so that what is right one day is not wrong the next; and it is upon this conditional uniformity of his will that human morality is based. Accordingly, Ockham is able to speak of a *recta ratio* that is the standard for human action and to continue to make use of a great deal of "intellectualistic" terminology in his account of human morality.[4] He can even recognize a form of natural law, and declare its propositions to be necessarily true. But this necessity is itself conditional, being derived from the contingent premise that God wills such and such actions to be done, together with the rule that right action consists in obedience to the will of God. He can also insist that only those commands of God that are explicitly cast in universalized form constitute obligations for all human beings and thereby meet another objection that is frequently brought against voluntaristic ethical theories.[5] What he cannot say, and what his whole theory in fact seems designed to deny, is that there can be any necessary truths in the sphere of morals that could be used to determine what one ought to do without any appeal to the will of God.

What emerges from this brief survey of Ockham's ethical theory is an extraordinary combination of the most absolute autonomy and an equally complete heteronomy of the will at different levels of the system. Looking up from the human level, the system is indeed a form of theological naturalism in which the human will has no share in determining what is right except, perhaps, in matters with respect to which there is no divine ordinance. Looking down from the top—from the God's-eye-view—there is no moral order at all that does not depend from moment to moment on the unrestrained will of God. De-

---

[4] Numerous passages illustrating this somewhat peculiar usage are cited in G. de Lagarde, *Ockham,* chs. 2, 3. For another interpretation of Ockham's doctrine of the *recta ratio,* see F. C. Copleston, *A History of Philosophy* (Rev. ed.; Westminster, Md.: Newman Press, 1960), Vol. 3, ch. 7.

[5] See Lagarde, *ibid.,* pp. 125 ff.

pending on the level in question, Ockham's ethics represents extremes of arbitrary individual fiat and rigid deontologism. Ockham was able to maintain this antithesis because autonomy and heteronomy were, on his view, attributes of numerically distinct persons, i.e., God and human beings. In the long run, however, it has proved difficult to prevent such a conception of the moral personality of God from modifying our view of subordinate moral personalities as well. If only by virtue of being subject to a completely autonomous will, human wills come to participate vicariously in the very autonomy that is denied them; and, as I have already suggested, it is tempting to see in theological voluntarism a preliminary sketch of a conception of autonomous *human* personality which in good Hegelian fashion has to be stated in a projected or externalized form before it can be applied to the understanding of self. In any case, when these levels come to be thought of as internal to one individual or at least to a community composed of human beings, the tension between the autonomy characteristic of the one and the heteronomy of the other is more likely to be felt as an out-and-out contradiction than is the case when the different levels are represented by different persons.

III

Ockham's radically voluntaristic conception of God's moral personality was never to be stated in its full rigor again.[6] There is, of course, much in the thought of the Protestant Reformers of the sixteenth century and particularly in their theory of justification that depends upon a contrast between God's *potentia absoluta* and *potentia ordinata*.[7] For Luther, as for Calvin, there is no

[6] Except by Descartes, who held that even the truths of mathematics are dependent on God's will. For a discussion of Descartes' voluntarism, see the most interesting essay by Jean-Paul Sartre, "La liberté cartésienne," in *Situations I* (Paris: Gallimard, 1947), pp. 314–35. This essay is particularly valuable for the light it casts on Sartre's own views.

[7] Detailed accounts of the ethical views of Luther, Calvin, and Melanchthon are given in O. Dittrich, *Geschichte der Ethik* (Leipzig: Meiner, 1926–32), Vol. 4. This work is also valuable for its discussions of the history of ethical thought during the medieval period.

statable set of conditions such that to satisfy them guarantees salvation. God's will is therefore a "hidden" will, in the sense that it cannot be bound by any body of rules by which human beings might orient themselves.[8] But it is not altogether clear whether this hidden will has a rationale that human beings are hopelessly incapable of understanding, or whether Luther subscribes to the full Ockhamistic doctrine of a divine will that is subject only to the restraints it condescends to accept and is therefore not even comprehensible in principle. In practice, there is little difference between these views when the intellectual incapacity of man in a state of sin is as complete as Luther and Calvin conceive it to be. Nevertheless, because the Reformers fail to expound a clear doctrine of the relationship of God's will to his intellect, they cannot be classified as radical voluntarists. Their focus of interest is on the problem of finding a proper relation to an autonomous and omnipotent person—God—rather than on the problem of what it is to *be* such a person.

At the same time, however, this very preoccupation with the situation of subordinate moral beings who must attempt to conform their wills to that of an incomprehensible God has made a rich contribution to the development of the ethical tradition we are studying. When the focus of attention is shifted from God to the description of human action, and when the human will is conceived, as it is by the Reformers, to be the passive instrument of God's will, any characterization of the latter will tend to color the coordinate concept of the wills that are subordinate to it. More specifically, the discontinuities and freedom from rational restraints that are peculiar to God's will, whether or not these are thought to be a function of our limited understanding, tend to pass over into the account that is given of human action. The significance of this evolution lies in its implications for the philosophical treatment of human action even after the theological assumptions that underlie it are dropped.

[8] This doctrine of God's hidden will is most clearly expressed in Luther's *The Bondage of the Will.* For a good discussion of this aspect of Luther's thought and of the subsequent interpretations of it, see J. Dillenberger, *God Hidden and Revealed* (Philadelphia: Muhlenberg Press, 1953). B. Gerrish, *Grace and Reason* (Oxford: Clarendon Press, 1962) gives a general account of Luther's view of the power and scope of human reason.

27

Nowhere is the effect of a voluntaristic conception of God's personality upon the description of human action as clear as it is in the case of Kierkegaard.[9] He is, to be sure, a voluntarist not in the sense of holding some doctrine of the relationship of intellect to will in God, but in the sense (just noted in the case of the Reformers) of rejecting all traditional claims that the content of God's will can be "known" by human beings in the form of universal principles. At the same time, there can be no question but that for Kierkegaard conformity to the will of God is still the proper end of man. Necessarily, therefore, the human response to God's commands will run the risk of appearing as anomalous and unjustifiable by the standard of a universalistic rule-ethic, as do these commands themselves. Since God is not bound by even the highest moral rule, the knight of faith who would do his will may, according to Kierkegaard, be called upon to violate generally valid moral rules as Abraham was in fact prepared to do. Kierkegaard speaks of this as passing beyond the sphere of the ethical, but by that he means beyond the sphere of the general moral rules by which men justify particular actions to one another. The familiar phrase Kierkegaard uses to describe Abraham's case—the "teleological suspension of the ethical"—can be somewhat misleading if it is not understood that the ethical that is transcended or suspended is the morality of general rules, and that the real effect of Kierkegaard's views is to expand the sphere of morality to include the requirement of obedience to God's particular commands. Kierkegaard is saying that it can be our duty (to God) to do what we cannot justify to other human beings by subsumption under a general principle. There is nothing Abraham can *say* in defense of the action which is nevertheless his duty, as Kierkegaard points out;[10] and it follows that our duties

[9] Kierkegaard's numerous treatments of ethical themes are scattered throughout his works, but the most important discussions are to be found in *Fear and Trembling* (Princeton, N.J.: Princeton University Press, 1941); in *Either/Or* (Princeton, N.J.: Princeton University Press, 1946), Vol. 2, pp. 133–278; and in *Concluding Unscientific Postscript* (Princeton, N.J.: Princeton University Press, 1941), Part II, chs. 1–3. Jean Wahl's *Études Kierkegaardiennes* (2d. rev. ed.; Paris: J. Vrin, 1949) is still perhaps the most useful of the secondary works on Kierkegaard, and offers analyses of his relationship to Hegel that are particularly helpful.

[10] *Fear and Trembling,* pp. 176 ff.

and our moral lives as a whole are not coextensive with the sphere of the universalizable and the communicable. In the upper reaches of the moral life, "the individual as a particular is higher than the universal and is justified against it, is not subordinate but superior."[11] As human action conforms itself to the *potentia absoluta* of God, the ethic of universal principles sinks to the status of just one element in the moral life as a whole, and becomes at least as much of an obstacle in the way of the realization of our highest end as it is itself an advance on "life's way."

Kierkegaard's use of the concept of choice gives perhaps the best evidence of the way his whole conception of human action has been modified. The central feature of the account he gives is that choice is *free* in the sense of being a self-transcending act by which the individual makes himself by choosing himself. This activity is conceived as going on outside the framework of any objective or public moral rationality. Kierkegaard was passionately convinced that to treat the moral life of the individual as simply the acting out of something that is already anticipated in the implicit logic of the world spirit was to make it too easy a thing. Indeed, he seems to have felt that the special quality of moral choice required that it be a kind of free and unsupported flight—a "leap"—that could not be subtended by any justificatory syllogism at all. Not only do we choose ourselves but we also choose to choose, i.e., to construe the world in terms of alternative courses of action that are really incompatible and to one of which we, as individuals, must commit ourselves. While the knight of faith who transcends the morality of general rules altogether acts on faith, as Kierkegaard says, that very faith is a kind of choice that is wholly unsupported by anything that would make it reasonable in the eyes of the world. To designate this non-cognitive, non-inferential movement of choice that is always particular and always logically gratuitous, Kierkegaard adopted the term "existence"; and just as he says of God that he "does not think (but) creates,"[12] so he says of man that his existence is irreducible to thought or logic or to an essential nature. Whatever ambiguities his choice of this term may generate, "existence," as

[11] *Ibid.,* p. 82.
[12] *Concluding Unscientific Postscript,* p. 296.

Kierkegaard uses the word, is just the rationally unsupported moral creativity that is the core idea of the voluntaristic tradition.

It would be going too far, however, to claim that Kierkegaard abandons all the apparatus of intellectualism in his treatment of the moral and religious life. The influence of Hegel which he unmistakably shows for all his passionate resistance to the "System" was doubtless too strong to permit such a radical reorientation. Thus, we find Kierkegaard summarizing his views in the cryptic declaration that "truth is subjectivity," even though the whole point of his characterization of ethical subjectivity seems to rest on a contrast with every familiar form of knowledge, and by implication, with every familiar sense of "truth." But even here one may be permitted to conjecture whether Kierkegaard in saying that "truth is subjectivity" is not really stressing the transcendent human importance of what he calls "becoming subjective." This last notion is itself somewhat difficult to interpret since the relevant sense of the polar term "objective" is specifically Hegelian. Nevertheless, it seems clear that under the label of "objectivity" Kierkegaard is condemning every attempt to redescribe individual choice in an idiom that incorporates it into some independent metaphysical structure to which we are then supposed to stand in a cognitive or contemplative relationship. This interpretation is strongly supported by Kierkegaard's insistence that, while "the objective accent falls on *what* is said, the subjective accent is on *how* it is said," and that this 'how' "refers to the relationship sustained by the existing individual, in his own existence, to the content of his own utterance."[13] Just to the extent that that relationship loses the character of an act—an individual act for which "I" alone am responsible—and is assimilated to the status of an element in some system of history or human nature, it no longer "carries its teleology within itself" and loses its distinctively ethical character. Conversely, if I do not *know* myself as a paragraph in the "System" but *choose* myself in and through my actions, I thereby achieve the truly ethical mode of life; but I also move into a sphere in which the notion of truth, if it survives at all, has been so fundamentally transformed

[13] *Ibid.*, p. 181.

as to render inapplicable all traditional conceptions of the justification of choice through subsumption under independently established and necessarily true principles.

IV

I have used Ockham's theology as an example of a voluntaristic
conception of God, and Kierkegaard's account of the ethical life
as an example of the way in which the situation of subordinate
moral beings under such a God is likely to be conceived. Deriva-
tively, i.e., by participation in the autonomous ethical activity of
God through obedience to his will, the moral life of human
beings comes to be described as a series of logically free choices to
which an external standard of truth is irrelevant. By way of substantiating this claim, it may be pointed out that in Protestant
"neo-orthodox" theology, an ethic of divine command that approaches Ockham's in its rigor has produced its counterpart in a
theory of human action in which the central importance of
choice is even more explicit than in Kierkegaard. In the work of
Emil Brunner, for example, the gap between the "ought" and the
"is" is interpreted as a result of original sin.[14] Man's disobedience
has destroyed the nature with which he was originally endowed,
and from that broken nature it is impossible to read off ethical
directives in the form of general principles that can guide conduct. Indeed, the attempt to erect a self-sufficient rational ethic is
explicitly condemned as sinful. Only the will of God can span the
gap between the "ought" and the "is"; and there can be no question of knowing beforehand what God will require. To turn the
divine command into a law from which subordinate laws can be
deduced breaks "the sense of responsibility for decision" and
gives "a false sense of security to the moral decision."[15] Everything, therefore, depends upon the reception of the divine command, for it is only by listening to it that I can find out "the one

[14] Brunner's most important work on theological ethics is *The Divine
Imperative*, trans. O. Wyon (Philadelphia, Pa.: Westminster Press, 1947). My
summary of his views is based on Bk. II, sec. I of this work, in which Brunner
analyzes the basis of ethics in the "divine command."

[15] *Ibid.*, p. 136.

and only one thing" that I am really bidden to do. Only the believer who acts "in God" escapes the heteronomy of the law and shares, as it were, in the autonomy of the divine personality. As Brunner says, action taken under these auspices is at once a discovery of what God bids me to do—a discovery I cannot anticipate by reason—and a decision for which I am responsible. The reverse or human side of the arbitrariness of the divine command is thus explicitly identified with individual moral decision.

It is in this strange fusion of activity and passivity within the concept of moral action that the difficulties of theological voluntarism come to a head. Is a decision that I cannot make unless God tells me what to decide really mine? In what sense am *I* responsible for what I do under the guidance of God? Alternatively, if *I* decide to do God's will, must I not share in the kind of autonomy he enjoys; and will I not in some sense escape the status of a subordinate moral being that theological voluntarism assigns to me? But then what becomes of the doctrine that the only "doer of good deeds" is God? These are the paradoxes which ultimately make it impossible to maintain an absolute separation of autonomy and heteronomy as attributes respectively of God's moral personality and of that of his creatures; and it is on this separation that theological voluntarism depends. Fortunately, there is no need to resolve these paradoxes here or even to show that they are in principle unresolvable. For our purposes, it is enough to have shown that a radical difference separates a thorough-going espousal of moral freedom from a doctrine that recognizes true autonomy only in one case, and treats the autonomy of other beings either as merely specious or as authentic only to the degree that the latter participate in the unique autonomy of God through a total submission of their individual wills to his. Many ethical theories that are currently described as existentialist are, in fact, of this type; but this classification obscures the fact that these theories differ from the more radical forms of voluntarism in ways that are even more important than those in which they resemble them. In a general way, these theories may be said to belong to the Kierkegaardian tradition of existentialism, and the more radical forms of voluntarism to the Nietzschean tradition. The latter, as I argued in the Introduction, represents the most thorough-going and consistent application of voluntarism to the analysis of *human* moral personality. The writers whose views will be considered in Part II are those that belong to that Nietzschean tradition, and an account of its philosophical origins must now be presented.

CHAPTER III

PHILOSOPHICAL VOLUNTARISM: FROM KANT TO NIETZSCHE

As a philosophical thesis, voluntarism has stood for a great many quite different doctrines, most of which have little or no relevance to this study. There have been philosophers like Descartes, who have argued for a metaphysical priority of will over intellect; others have conceived of will as a cosmic force, of which even physical nature is merely one expression. Sometimes these doctrines have been associated with an ethic or an ethical attitude, whether of renunciation of the volitional life in favor of the contemplative, as in Schopenhauer's case, or of indefinitely expansive self-assertion as in the case of Fichte. As often as not, the thesis of the metaphysical priority of the will has not been given a sense that is closely relevant to ethical theory as distinct from ethical attitudes; or, if it has, these hints have remained undeveloped.

From the standpoint of historical continuity, it is a fact of some interest that the philosophers who have contributed most heavily to the development of ethical voluntarism and on whose work twentieth century existentialism has built are the German idealists. It has often been noted (by Heine and by Santayana, among others) that German idealism is a kind of continuation of Protestantism by other means; and there can, in fact, be little doubt that the general ethos of nineteenth century idealism was significantly influenced by the Protestant religious culture out of which it grew. Nowhere is this more obvious than in the pervasive idealistic attempt to understand mind as an autonomous creative activity, and the "objectivity" of the worlds of nature and of culture as the dialectical issue of that activity. The philosophical extravagances to which this conception led in its application to nature has unfortunately brought the whole idealistic undertaking into disrepute; as a result, the profoundly suggestive character of much of what the idealists had to say about culture and history is rarely appreciated in the English-speaking philosophical world. It was, in fact, in the area of ethical thought that their hypothesis of mind as activity, together with their principled rejection of external authority in all its forms, found its most plausible application.

For the purposes of this study, there is no need to claim that a direct and historically demonstrable line of influence connects the working-out of ethical voluntarism as a philosophical position with its earlier theological forms.[1] It is enough to show a general affinity between the conceptions of the moral personality of God and of human beings that are characteristic of these two versions of voluntarism. If, on the other hand, an historical thesis with respect to the actual genesis of philosophical voluntarism were to be advanced, the intellectual history of the eighteenth century, particularly in Germany, offers a mass of evidence on which a defense of such a thesis could be based.[2] Nothing is more characteristic of that period than a pervasive dissatisfaction with both the traditional Protestant distinction between God and his sinful and helplessly dependent creatures, and the prevailing rationalistic Natural Law conceptions of the basis of moral obligation. A principal theme of an immense body of imaginative and critical literature was the pressing need to restore to human nature the prerogatives of moral and aesthetic creativity that had wrongly been reserved to an inaccessible and alien divinity. The literature of German classicism can, in fact, be regarded as one great expression of this search for a conception of man that would do justice to the integrity and autonomy of his natural capabilities. But, as a number of students of the period have shown,

[1] For an interesting side light on the whole question of the theological derivation of contemporary ethical theory, see G. Anscombe, "Modern Moral Philosophy," *Philosophy*, Vol. 33 (1958), pp. 1–19. The "Protestant" character of contemporary existentialism has been noted by a number of writers, among them W. Frankena. See his essay, "Obligation and Motivation in Recent Moral Philosophy," in A. I. Melden (ed.), *Essays in Moral Philosophy* (Seattle, Wash.: University of Washington Press, 1958), p. 64.

[2] In this connection, see E. Cassirer, *Freiheit und Form* (2d rev. ed.; Berlin: Cassirer, 1918), and H. Korff, *Geist der Goethezeit* (4th ed.; Leipzig; Koehler and Amelang, 1957–64).

this same problem of the moral freedom of human beings preoc-
cupied the philosophers of the time quite as much as the literati,
and inevitably brought both into conflict with orthodox religious
views of the man-God relationship. In a very clear sense, the
idealistic philosophy of the late eighteenth and early nineteenth
centuries was a response to an essentially religious question, and
it was a response that decisively modified our conception of the
relation of man to God, by assigning to the former a full measure
of the intellectual and moral autonomy that had previously been
reserved to God.

Within the limits of this study, it is not possible to undertake a
general survey of the history of eighteenth and nineteenth century idealism as it bears upon the evolution of ethical voluntarism. In place of such a review, it has seemed best to select for detailed scrutiny two philosophers—Kant and Nietzsche—who
stand, respectively, at the beginning and at the end of that evolution; and to notice only very briefly the contributions made by
such intermediate and (for our purposes) secondary figures as
Hegel and Schopenhauer. There is inevitably something paradoxical in the association of the names of Kant and Nietzsche under
any common rubric, because in most respects they are as different
from one another as it is possible for two philosophers to be. Nevertheless, while it is certain that Kant would have been horrified
by Nietzsche's conception of morality, they were both effective
and immensely influential critics of intellectualism and there is a
sense in which Nietzsche may be said to have traveled farther—
very much farther—on a road that Kant was perhaps the first to
enter upon and that was eventually to lead to the ethical theory
of existentialism. In the case of Nietzsche, the affinity with contemporary existentialism is obvious and has often been analyzed,
notably by Jaspers and Heidegger in two long studies.[3] I have already noted the existence of a Nietzschean, as distinct from a
Kierkegaardian tradition within existentialism. Nevertheless,
since there are important differences between Nietzsche and even

---

[3] K. Jaspers, *Nietzsche: Einführung in das Verständnis seines Philosophie-
rens* (Berlin: W. de Gruyter, 1936) , and M. Heidegger, *Nietzsche* (Pfullin-
gen: Neske, 1961) , 2 Vols. For a more compact statement of Heidegger's
interpretation of Nietzsche, see his "Nietzsche's Wort: 'Gott Ist Tot'," in
Holzwege (Frankfurt-am-Main: V. Klostermann, 1950) , pp. 193–247.

his closest existentialist followers, it has seemed wiser to treat him as a precursor of existentialism rather than as one of the primary representatives of the ethical theory we are studying.

I

Kant's moral philosophy is often presented as an extreme form of rationalism. In so far as this interpretation simply asserts what is true—that Kant defines a procedure for determining what actions are morally right and believes that this procedure is capable of providing a conclusive answer to the question "What should I do?"—there can be no ground for criticism. At the same time, it is important to remember that Kant attributes these powers to practical reason as distinct from theoretical reason, and that he was a determined and acute critic of all attempts to apply theoretical reason to the solution of ethical problems. Furthermore, what Kant meant by the attempt to make theoretical reason yield substantive ethical truths is, in fact, indistinguishable from the ethical intellectualism described in Chapter I. His criticism of intellectualism therefore deserves careful attention, as do the distinctive features of his conception of practical reason. In one sense, of course, this is a distinction without a difference, since Kant was just as confident as Wolff and Baumgarten—the intellectualists he criticized—that uniquely valid answers to moral questions were available. From another point of view, however, the changes that he effected were momentous, if only because Kant obtained the old results via a new set of concepts—in particular, the concept of autonomy. These concepts were to reveal an astonishing capacity for development once certain limitations imposed on them by Kant had been dropped by later writers to whom they seemed arbitrary. Specifically, the concept of autonomy, to which Kant first gave a central place within the moral life, was to reach full fruition in Nietzsche's doctrine of the creation of values, and from there it was just a step to twentieth-century existentialism.

One principal reason for the widespread failure to understand Kant's role in this development is that too often his doctrine of freedom as autonomy is not clearly distinguished from what he has to say about freedom as spontaneity.[4] By the latter, Kant means the power to originate a causal series; and he argues that it is legitimate to postulate that the noumenal will is free in this sense, though it cannot be known to be so. Autonomy, by contrast, consists in legislating for one's self, or in being subject only to those obligations that one has created oneself. Its opposite, heteronomy, is being subject to a law of which one is not the creator. As it turns out, spontaneity and autonomy are closely interdependent, but the net effect of the distinction is a significant amplification of the kind of freedom that is a necessary presupposition of morality. Kant is saying that morality requires not merely causal freedom, but also what might be called logical freedom. If the moral law were delivered to us from some outside source, we would, to that extent, not be free. This would be the case, for example, if the moral law were just God's command to us, even if we were free in the sense of being able to obey or disobey that command. Freedom as autonomy means that the principle of our action must not itself be derived from any external source whatsoever, and that all action under principles that have such an external origin must be viewed as being under a special kind of constraint.

Using this standard, Kant summarily dismisses all principles that are based on empirical knowledge of human nature and on the tendency of different types of action to produce satisfaction. At the same time, he considers whether there are any rational (i.e., non-empirical) principles of morality. If there were, they would presumably satisfy the condition of autonomy that Kant has laid down, since they would be worked out by the understanding without any dependence upon external materials. In

[4] This distinction is made in L. W. Beck, *A Commentary on Kant's Critique of Practical Reason* (Chicago: University of Chicago Press, 1960), pp. 194–203. It is closely related to another distinction between *Wille* (in the sense of what I have been calling the rational, or moral, will) and *Willkür*, which is precisely the power of spontaneous self-determination. The relation between *Wille* and *Willkür* and their significance for Kant's ethical theory are most interestingly discussed by John Silber in "The Ethical Significance of Kant's *Religion*," Part II of the Introduction to Kant's *Religion within the Limits of Reason Alone*, trans. T. M. Greene and H. Hudson (2d. rev. ed.; La Salle, Ill.: Open Court Publishing Co., 1960).

fact, there are no such principles that are at once necessary truths and non-tautological. Either they turn out to be analytic, and thus provide no differential guidance for conduct (i.e., are not moral principles at all), or substantive content is smuggled in from empirical sources, in which case the condition of autonomy is not met.[5] The conclusion can only be that the moral will does not derive its principles of action from the senses or from theoretical reason at all, but must somehow find the principle within itself. It also follows that the concepts of good and evil are not antecedent to, and independent of, the concept of will, as they would be if they were concepts of a certain perfection toward which our natures tend, but involve instead an essential reference to will. Instead of its being our duty to will what is good, the morally good is that which can be willed *in a certain way;* and it is the will itself that by willing establishes the duty to which it is then subject.

The will that creates obligations is, of course, the "rational will"; and it is Kant's conception of the nature of rational will that rules out any element of arbitrariness or choice in the determination of what is right.[6] Kant seems to have thought of the relationship of the rational will to impulse and desire as essentially similar to the action of the understanding upon the materials of

[5] At the end of sec. 2 of his *Fundamental Principles of a Metaphysic of Morals,* Kant classifies the "heteronomous" principles of morality as either "empirical" or "rational." The "rational" principles are further divided into those that involve the "ontological conception of perfection" and those based on "the theological conception which derives morality from a divine, absolutely perfect will" that is independent of human will. Interestingly enough, Kant is decidedly critical of the latter view which is equivalent to what I have been calling theological voluntarism, and he expresses a preference for the "ontological" doctrine of perfection. At the same time, however, he declares that this doctrine is empty and circular. These criticisms are stated in greater detail in the *Lectures on Ethics,* trans. L. Infield (London: Methuen, 1930), pp. 24–27.

[6] As Silber points out, there is a sense in which by virtue of Kant's doctrine of *Willkür,* or radical spontaneity, human beings may be said to choose to be moral (i.e., to obey the moral law), just as they may choose to be immoral; both of these choices are authentic expressions of freedom for which we may be held responsible. But Kant also holds that we can judge our actions only in accordance with the moral law; thus there is no sense in which the moral law, considered as the norm by reference to which our actions are judged, could be said to be chosen. (See Silber, n. 2 above, pp. ciii–cxiv.)

sense. As the latter are organized through the imposition of the categories which are the forms of human thought, so the maxims of proposed actions are tested by the standard of their capacity for universalization. According to Kant, this requirement is an expression of the nature of rational will itself. The will is rational only to the extent that it is consistent with itself; a maxim which on universalization proved to be self-contradictory or self-destructive would therefore have to be rejected by a rational will. Kant of course makes the further assumption that universalizability is not just a necessary, but a sufficient condition for determining the rightness of an act. While much critical discussion of his ethical theory has traditionally addressed itself to the issues raised by this assumption, his conception of rationality itself is perhaps of greater long-run significance. On this interpretation, the will is rational not by virtue of accepting and translating into action moral truths that the intellect apprehends, but by actualizing its own peculiar virtue of consistency. The novelty of this view resides in the fact that the rational or logical controls over the will have been introjected into the will itself, so that any maxim of conduct that the will can accept while remaining faithful to its essential nature becomes *ipso facto* morally right.

At first sight, this innovation may not seem very important. After all, what is the difference between a will that is guided by an intellectual intuition of independent and substantive moral truths, and a will that is independent of theoretical reason but so intellectualized by virtue of a special interpretation of its inner nature that it *can* will only the uniquely right course of action in any situation? The action of a will such as Kant describes may well be felt to possess only the kind of freedom that is required to vote in an election in which there is only one slate of candidates. This reaction is justified to the extent that it warns us against exaggerating Kant's affinities with the more radical forms of voluntarism. It must be made absolutely clear that the autonomy of which Kant speaks is not only reconcilable with the recognition of general principles, but strictly requires such principles as a guarantee of the will's independence of external and "pathological" influences. Once the will cleaves to its own essential rationality, it proceeds, so to speak, "under orders," and the only choices it

41

faces are choices between courses of action that have been shown by the criterion of universalizability to be morally right.

Nevertheless, Kant's shift from the intellectualistic model to a conception of will as creating moral laws is a momentous one for the future development of moral philosophy, because even this highly restrictive conception of will as the basis of morality makes an important break with intellectualism; and because, by transferring the moral enterprise from the theoretical intellect to the will, it facilitates the development of a conception of morality as a whole that would hardly have been possible without this change of venue. The fact is that while Kant's ethical theory is still in a sense a theory of human nature, it drastically narrows the basis in human nature on which the edifice of morality is supposed to rest. Instead of a theory of the real essence or nature of human beings that would comprehend the whole range of human functions as these are revealed in experience, the moral essence of man is now concentrated in the will, and it is exclusively by reference to the "real essence" of the will (i.e., its consistency with itself), that the rightness of actions is to be determined. Of course, it could be argued with some cogency that Kant has no right to be such a confident teleologist in his treatment of the rational will and at the same time to write off all empirical evidence of natural human tendencies as merely "pathological" and irrelevant for the purposes of morals. Still, the effect of his views, as they stand, is to exclude any possibility of a justification of particular volitional acts on the ground of their appropriateness in the light of a comprehensive conception of human nature, and to require that such justification be sought in the nature of rational volition itself, with which human nature is now identified. The point I wish to make is that the dissolution of all logical bonds between morality and "human nature" in the broader and more traditional acceptation of that term, together with the notion of the will's realizing its own nature as a criterion of the rightness of its acts, is at least as important a feature of Kant's view as the specific view he took of what that nature consisted in.

In Chapter I, the intellectualistic thesis was identified as the view that evaluative judgments are susceptible of being true and false; and that, when true, they represent cognitive apprehensions of qualities or relations inherent in the objects to which they refer. It has already been shown that Kant rejects this analysis of ethical judgments. It might seem plausible to go further and to conclude that because Kant presents all moral principles in the form of imperatives, he has simply abandoned the notion of truth as applied to such judgments. This would be a mistake, however, since Kant explicitly declares the categorical imperative or highest moral principle to be a synthetic a priori *truth*. What he does say with respect to the truth of such principles is that it cannot be made out on the strength of the concepts themselves that are used in the categorical imperative (or in any of its specifications). Instead, a "third thing" is always required to link the concepts together, and this is the concept of freedom. If the will in question is a free will (i.e., one that is not subject to external influences), then it is analytically true that the only law such a will imposes upon itself is the law of its own nature which is (assumed to be) that of consistency and universalizability. Here, once again, the significant novelty of Kant's position lies at least as much in his denials as in his affirmations. When he denies that the autonomous moral will is subject to any limitations other than the laws of its own nature, it is hard to see how "true" (as applied to specific ethical judgments) can convey anything more than their consistency with those internal requirements. The notion of truth as correspondence to independent moral fact has been dropped; with this notion of truth as correspondence, a major obstacle to a recognition of the decisional character of moral judgments is removed. I have already pointed out that Kant's conception of the nature of the rational will is such as to make the kind of volitional act that is involved in the determination of what is right a peculiarly limited one that can hardly be called a choice. But it is surely quite as important that a decisional element at the highest level of moral deliberation has been admitted at all; and it is clear that any modification of Kant's conception of the essential nature of the moral will might well have the effect of accentuating the volitional character of moral judgment and expanding its scope. As it turned out, Kant's claim that universalizability was a sufficient condition for the rightness of a maxim of conduct never gained wide acceptance, and its place was to be taken by other interpretations of the essential nature of will; these, in turn, generated new criteria for judging particular volitional acts by the degree to which they realize that essential nature.[7]

II

Kant's moral philosophy was to influence the thought of his immediate successors in both a negative and a positive sense. It was widely held that the test Kant had proposed as a sufficient condition of the moral rightness of acts yielded, at most, a necessary condition thereof; and that the excessively formalistic character of his ethical theory must be offset by the introduction of some material criteria of rightness. At the same time, however, Kant's doctrine of autonomy had made an indelible impression on the minds of his critics; and as they attempted to work out a conception of the moral will that would incorporate some of the substance of human preference and desire, they sought in one way or another to attribute to that enriched moral will an effective independence of external sources of moral knowledge along Kantian lines. This notion that not just the form of the moral will but its content and substance as well should be regarded as autonomous expressions of human freedom was to lead ethical theory in two quite different directions. On the one hand, there were those who, like Hegel, felt that what they held to be the sterile formalism of Kant's moral philosophy could be offset only by transferring the concept of autonomy, which Kant had associated exclusively with the volitional acts of individual human beings, to the historical community to which these individuals belong and on which they are (it was argued) dependent for their ethical substance. The other line of revision which was initiated by Schopenhauer, and fully developed by Nietzsche, led to an abandonment or radical modification of the criterion of universa-

[7] For a brief but valuable discussion of Kant's conception of the will and its relationship to contemporary existentialism, see O. Bollnow, "Existentialismus und Ethik," *Actas del Primer Congreso Nacional de Filosofía*, Univ. Nacional, Cuyo, Vol. 12 (1949), pp. 974–997. Also published in *Die Sammlung*, Vol. 4 (1949), pp. 321–35.

lizability itself. This line of criticism was often inspired by the feeling that such a test involved a concession to a public and impersonal conception of the self and to a social demand for uniformity that were incompatible (so it was thought) with true individuality.

In spite of these sharp divergencies from Kant's position, both Hegel and Schopenhauer, in their different ways, testify to the continuing influence of his conception of autonomy. The case of Hegel is particularly interesting, for not only was he a most determined opponent of the Kantian conception of the moral autonomy of the individual person, but he has been identified since the time of Kierkegaard as the great adversary of all the intellectual tendencies that culminate in existentialism.[8] In fact, however, the case is not so straightforward. For while Hegel relentlessly pushes the individual moral consciousness toward a recognition of its lack of ultimate sovereignty and self-sufficiency, he conceives its self-conscious acceptance of the social matrix, on which it is dependent in any case, as a progressive resumption and internalization of powers of ethical creativity that had been alienated through projection into personal and "objective" institutions and laws. To be sure, the "self" that recognizes the latter as the precipitate of its own activity is a supra-individual self; and it can be argued that in its final systematic elaboration, Hegel's treatment of moral phenomena recognizes only a collective autonomy which, from the standpoint of the individual, must seem rather unreal. Nevertheless, *The Phenomenology of Mind* contains brilliant descriptions of the way in which the moral consciousness liberates itself from the condition in which it is oblivious to its own prerogatives, and automatically concedes to custom and tradition a normative authority to which it is not conscious of making any contribution of its own. Eventually, this moral con-

---

[8] Hegel's most trenchant formulations of his objections to Kantian ethical theory appear in his *Philosophy of Right*, trans. T. M. Knox (Oxford: Clarendon Press, 1942), pp. 86 ff. Also, in the *Phenomenology of Mind*, trans. J. B. Baillie (2d ed. rev.; London: Allen and Unwin, 1931), pp. 613–627. The famous Preface to the *Phenomenology* is probably the best account of the way in which, according to Hegel, autonomy is achieved by a progressive internalization of the various forms of objectivity in which absolute spirit expresses itself.

45

sciousness comes to recognize itself as a purely negative power of reducing to mere external fact institutions and practices which had previously been apprehended as infused with an unchallengeable moral authority. To be sure, this stage does not represent true autonomy according to Hegel, but his account of this purely negative kind of moral freedom has exerted nevertheless a profound influence on the French wing of existentialism.[9]

By contrast with Hegel, Schopenhauer made no very significant contribution to voluntarism considered as a theory of moral choice, and was indeed heavily committed to a deterministic theory of character that can be reconciled with moral freedom only at a supra-individualistic level. The bulk of what Schopenhauer has to say on the subject of moral judgment takes the form of an extremely critical commentary on Kant's ethical theory.[10] He derides Kant for his emphasis on universal moral principles, and stigmatizes his whole doctrine as a denial of genuine moral freedom that differs from the older forms of ethical rationalism only in subjecting the will to an internal tyrant-conscience instead of to an external master, God. Nevertheless, Schopenhauer gives credit to Kant for the first statement of his own principal philosophical thesis, i.e., that noumenal reality is will; and he recognizes that the essential merit of Kant's ethical theory consisted in its identification of man's nature and his freedom. Kant's position can, he says, be understood as a reinterpretation of the Scholastic dictum *operari sequitur esse* which makes our "being" or "nature" metaphysically prior to our actions. What Kant does, according to Schopenhauer, is to "lead us out of the error that consists in assigning necessity to being [*esse*] and freedom to ac-

---

[9] The influence of Hegel upon French existentialism was mediated by the lectures of A. Kojève on the *Phenomenology of Mind,* now published as *Introduction à la Lecture de Hegel* (2d rev. ed.; Paris: Gallimard, 1947). Another work that is important for an understanding of the character this influence assumed is J. Wahl, *Le Malheur de la conscience dans la Philosophie de Hegel* (Paris: Rieder, 1929). See also J. Hyppolite, *Genèse et Structure de la Phénoménologie de l'Esprit de Hegel* (Paris: Aubier, 1946).

[10] Schopenhauer's criticism of Kant as well as his statement of his own ethical theory are presented in his *Über die Grundlage der Moral,* Sämtliche Werke, ed. Hübscher (Leipzig: 1937–39). Vol. 4. Schopenhauer's ethical views are discussed at some length in P. Gardiner, *Schopenhauer* (Baltimore, Md.: Penguin Books, Inc., 1963). ch. 6.

tion," and to make us understand that "freedom is located in our very being."[11] In other words, we *are* what we make ourselves be, and it is for being "as the result of our actions, just such a person and no other that we feel responsible."[12] This appreciation of Kant's achievement is the more interesting since it attributes to Kant a view of the relationship between "nature" and "action" that is virtually identical with the later existentialist thesis with respect to essence and existence. It also indicates an acceptance by Schopenhauer—on his own philosophical terms, of course—of what I have represented as one of the two major theses of Kant's moral philosophy: that morality is the affair of an autonomous self-legislative will. This thesis Nietzsche was to espouse in turn, but his (and Schopenhauer's) repudiation of the other pillar of Kant's moral philosophy—the doctrine of universalizability—was to blind him to the reality of the debt he owed, through Schopenhauer, to Kant.

III

The true significance of Nietzsche's contribution to moral philosophy can be understood only in the context of his general theory of truth and its special application to the area of values.[13] In spite of a great many extreme statements that make it sound as though he had no use for truth in any form, the real thrust of

[11] "Durch Kant's Theorie werden wir eigentlich von dem Grundirrtum zurückgebracht, der die Notwendigkeit ins Esse und die Freiheit ins Operari verlegte, und werden zu der Erkenntnis geführt dass es sich gerade umgekehrt verhält." Schopenhauer, *ibid.*, p. 177.

[12] "Dass . . . (der Mensch) wie es sich aus seiner Handlung ergiebt, ein Solcher und kein Anderer ist—das ist es wofür er sich verantwortlich hält, hier im Esse liegt die Stelle welche die Stachel des Gewissens trifft." *Ibid.*, p. 177.

[13] The interpretation of morality and of moral phenomena generally may be said to be the theme of almost all Nietzsche's works, although *The Genealogy of Morals* and *Beyond Good and Evil* are perhaps most directly concerned with these topics. Of even greater interest, however, especially from the "meta-ethical" standpoint of this study, are the writings of Nietzsche's last period, some of which are known under the title of *The Will to Power* but which have been arranged and edited with great skill by K. Schlechta in the third volume of his edition of Nietzsche's *Werke* (München: C. Hanser, 1956).

Nietzsche's argument is against dualistic or "copy" theories of truth. In particular, he rejects the notion of "things in themselves," and with it the view that truth must consist in a relation of correspondence to the latter. But if our ideas and beliefs are not to be described as reflections of a self-subsistent order of things, then (he argues) they must be thought of as products of our own devising which we, in some sense, impose upon our experience of the world. All of our intellectual apparatus must be in the nature of a construction or interpretation by which we actively organize and dominate the world in a certain way. Even the law of contradiction, Nietzsche argues, represents a condition that is set by us and not an ontological truth that is read off from the nature of things.[14] Nietzsche's term for this general view of the conceptualizing function is "perspectivism," and it clearly has many points of affinity with the pragmatism of William James and others. Like the pragmatists, Nietzsche believes that all of our knowledge and our modes of conceptualizing experience involve an evaluative component and represent a decision to construe the world in a certain way. The "will to power" is simply Nietzsche's shorthand label for the aggressive character of the relationship of human subjectivity to the world that it subjects to its categories.

At the same time as he reinterprets the general notion of truth in this pragmatic spirit, Nietzsche also recognizes a fundamental distinction between establishing the truth of a factual statement and the volitional acts by which an end, i.e., a value, is freely posited.[15] The difference is that verification involves a certain passiv-

[14] Nietzsche, *Werke,* pp. 537, 538. "Kurz, die Frage steht offen: sind die logischen Axiome dem Wirklichen adäquat, oder sind sie Maszstäbe und Mittel, um Wirkliches, den Begriff "Wirklichkeit," für uns erst zu *schaffen?* . . . Um das erste bejahen zu können, müsste man aber, wie gesagt, das Seiende bereits kennen; was schlechterdings nicht der Fall ist." Heidegger discusses this passage and the Aristotelian doctrine on which Nietzsche is commenting in *Nietzsche,* Vol. 2, pp. 595–616. An insightful comparison of Nietzsche's views on these and other subjects with those of L. Wittgenstein can be found in E. Heller, "Ludwig Wittgenstein," *Encounter,* Vol. 13 (1959), pp. 40–48.

[15] Das *Feststellen* zwischen "wahr" and "unwahr," das *Feststellen* von Tatbeständen ist grundverschieden von dem schöpferischen *Setzen,* vom Bilden, Gestalten, Überwältigen, Wollen, wie es im Wesen der *Philosophie* liegt. Einen

ity in relation to what is external to the self, although Nietzsche's general doctrine of mind requires that even here *some* element of activity be present. By contrast, evaluation is a purer expression of the human power of legislating for oneself, of assigning values and meanings without any dependence on, or need for, a supporting value-quality in the things evaluated themselves. On this distinction rests what may fairly be termed the central thesis of Nietzsche's ethical theory. This is that any conception of evaluation that makes it an apprehension of truth in the sense of a verification of some state of affairs, whether empirical or metaphysical, distorts its nature and ultimately denatures the evaluative function itself. By this emphatic repudiation of all conceptions of evaluation as knowing, and by his insistence that evaluation must be understood as a volitional act, Nietzsche aligns himself with the voluntaristic tradition against all forms of intellectualism and naturalism.

Throughout his works, but especially in the writings that were to be edited posthumously under the title of *The Will to Power*, Nietzsche repeatedly drives home this point. He declares that philosophers, i.e., moralists, must be legislators, but first the confusion of the moralist with the scientist must be dispelled. "As though values were inherent in things so that all one had to do were to keep a grip on them!"[16] In another passage, Nietzsche lays down as his first principle that "there are no moral phenomena but only a moral interpretation of these phenomena."[17] Evaluative judgments are "active" and the "value of the world lies in our interpretation."[18] To transform this interpretative, evaluative function into "predicates of being," "to demand that our human interpretations and values should be general, and perhaps even constitutive values, belongs among the hereditary idiocies

---

Sinn hineinlegen—diese Aufgabe bleibt immer noch *übrig*, gesetzt, dass *kein Sinn darin* liegt . . .

Die noch höhere Stufe ist ein *Ziel setzen* und daraufhin das Tatsächliche einformen: also die Ausdeutung der Tat und nicht bloss die begriffliche *Umdichtung*. (*Ibid.*, p. 552.)

[16] Als ob die Werte in den Dingen steckten und man sie nur festzuhalten hätte! (*Ibid.*, p. 447.)

[17] *Es gibt keine moralischen Phänomene, sondern nur eine moralische Interpretation dieser Phänomene.* (*Ibid.*, p. 485.)

[18] Der *Wert der Welt* (liegt) in unserer Interpretation. (*Ibid.*, p. 497.)

of human pride."[19] As a form of practical shorthand, it may be admissible to treat values as properties; but we must not forget that they are properties of a kind to which the concept of knowledge does not apply.[20] The properties to which it does apply are quantitative in character, and value properties are merely the pseudo-objective coloring-off on the world of evaluative judgments which thus penetrate the sensuous quality of things instead of being determined by it.

A certain ambivalence runs through Nietzsche's account of the human tendency to substantialize value. In some passages he declares that "to impress the character of being upon becoming is the highest form of the will to power."[21] If the stability of being is an illusion, particularly in the case of "value properties," then a sovereign indifference to the falsity involved in such substantialization might indeed be expressed by one who had seen through the illusion and still continued to reify values; and this kind of indifference is something that Nietzsche greatly admired. But when this ontologizing of value is not the expression of a self-conscious will to impose one's evaluation upon the world at large, as of course it is not in the great majority of cases, Nietzsche condemns it in the severest terms. It indicates a weakness of the will, an incapacity for autonomous ethical creativity which typically passes over into nihilistic despair when its support is removed. "The belief that the world as it should be really exists is a belief of those unproductive persons who do not wish to create a world as it should be . . . The will to truth is the incapacity of the will to create."[22] Here Nietzsche is breaking new

[19] . . . Zu verlangen, dass diese unsre menschlichen Auslegungen und Werte allgemeine und vielleicht konstitutive Werte sind, gehört zu den erblichen Verrücktheiten des menschlichen Stolzes. (*Ibid.*, p. 914.)

[20] Aber alles, wofür das Wort "Erkenntnis" Sinn hat, bezieht sich auf das Reich, wo gezählt, gewogen, gemessen werden kann, auf die Quantität: während umgekehrt alle unsre Wertempfindungen (d.h. eben unsre Empfindungen) gerade an den Qualitäten haften, d.h. an unsren, nur uns allein zugehörigen perspektivischen "Wahrheiten," die schlechterdings nicht "erkannt" werden können. (*Ibid.*, p. 914.)

[21] Dem Werden den Charakter des Seins *aufzuprägen—das ist der höchste Wille zur Macht.* (*Ibid.*, p. 895.)

[22] Der Glaube, dass die Welt, die sein sollte, *ist,* wirklich existiert, ist ein Glaube der Unproduktiven, die *nicht eine Welt schaffen wollen,* wie sie sein

ground. Intellectualism is no longer just a philosophical error, but a symptom of a moral tendency in human beings that is positively bad. A certain conception of evaluation is thus intimately connected with a style of life, and it is not surprising that Nietzsche also believed that his own conception of evaluation could, by itself, yield a positive ethic.

It has often been pointed out that the positive ideal toward which humanity is to reorient itself is, in fact, only very obscurely delineated by Nietzsche. This is true, and it might be added that such specificity as his proposals acquire through the imagery of ruthlessness and violence with which they are associated distorts his meaning in a way that has proved immensely prejudicial to a correct understanding and balanced appraisal of his views. At the same time, this very vagueness may be taken as a sign that Nietzsche is at least as interested in changing our conception of ourselves as evaluative beings as he is in proposing the substance of a new moral ideal. The "transvaluation of values" is not, in the first instance, a repudiation of old values in favor of new ones. Instead, it is a new conception of evaluation as a human activity, and a resultant transformation of the style and temper of that activity itself. To use the current jargon of analytical philosophy, Nietzsche is the prophet not so much of an ethical revolution as of a "meta-ethical" revolution. As was noted above, he certainly believed that once human beings fully comprehended their own capacity for being a law unto themselves, an immense change would be effected in every area of human life. He also projected a vision of what that change would consist in, which, in spite of its indistinctness, most people find repellent. But the crux of his ethical thought is the question as to the nature of evaluation itself, and it is his answer to that question which places him squarely in the voluntaristic tradition.

If Nietzsche is thus in fundamental agreement with Kant in situating the ethical in the province of will and in denying that the theoretical intellect can legislate for human action, he breaks sharply with Kant in his conception of that will itself, and he has a quite different view of how the will must realize its own distinc-

soll. . . . "Wille zur *Wahrheit*"—*als Ohnmacht des Willens zum Schaffen.* (*Ibid.*, p. 549.)

51

tive virtue. He rejects the view that an action is right only if it would be right for every other human being in the same situation, and he repudiates the cognate conception of morality which makes its chief task the harmonious adjustment to one another of a community of wills. There is, of course, a clear connection between the Kantian view that universalizability is a necessary and sufficient condition of an action's rightness and the view that morality is at bottom a guidance of conduct by principles that *everyone* could accept. For this ethic of reciprocity, Nietzsche reserves his most scornful epithets, and the violence of his denunciation of the principle of equivalence implicit in such a conception of morality has often blocked an understanding of the logical considerations on which Nietzsche bases his attack on universalizability. Consistently with his pragmatic theory of concept-formation, Nietzsche argues that the concept of the "same action" on which the whole idea of universalizability and reciprocity rests presupposes the adoption by the person who uses it of certain criteria of sameness.[23] It is, in fact, we who create these equivalences of one action with another, and Nietzsche's point is that this assimilation itself expresses a moral *parti pris*. Such a classification of actions as equivalent cannot therefore be treated (as it is by Kant) as the deliverance of a rational will that brings cases under general rules without thereby "pre-evaluating" them. Instead, it is itself a primary, and perhaps decisive, evaluative act.

More important, however, is Nietzsche's belief that a truly conceived morality is concerned not with the compatibility of individual wills with one another, but with the creation and realization of ideals. These ideals are comprehensive styles of life that express a preference that is not justifiable by any standard except itself. They are pre-eminently the expression of individual choice and preference, and they make no claim to universal validity or acceptance. It is characteristic of such ideals that they make demands on those who espouse them to which others are not subject; and the value of what one does at the behest of such an ideal resides, in great part, in this very uniqueness. This claim is no longer felt to be a command for others—a *"du sollst"*—but an *"ich will,"* and ultimately, an *"ich bin"*—an expression of what

[23] *Ibid.*, pp. 476, 670.

the individual chooses and of what (by virtue of his choices) he is. Nietzsche's great example of this free morality of self-creation was the Greeks. Christianity represented in his eyes precisely the opposite: a morality that combines a lack of inner freedom with a regulation of life by universal principles and the tame virtues of which the mass of people is capable.

This insistence on the central role of ideals in the moral life is perhaps Nietzsche's main contribution to ethical theory. With it is associated a new conception of autonomy which, as he says, consists in not being "locked into a system of purposes" and in being one's own moral lawgiver. The will realizes itself, not by laying down laws that are to be valid for everyone, but in projecting a unique ideal of the self and in living by that ideal. It is a freedom to "re-evaluate all values" in the light of one's own ideal. The autonomy of a will that can act only when the maxim of its action has been shown to enjoy a universal validity is simply a new form of the old subjection to an external master, although that master is no longer God but one's fellow men or "society." Whether "social morality" in the sense of a universal code based on the idea of reciprocity could have a subordinate place, even within an ethic that recognizes the distinctive character of ideals, is not absolutely clear. What Nietzsche often seems to be saying is not that ideals will replace the discipline of social morality, but that the relationship between the two must be understood in a new way. Instead of social morality determining what ideals are to be admissible, the ideals of a controlling elite must give direction to a society as a whole and, in cases of conflict, take precedence over the demands of the "universal" moral code. Nietzsche always assumes that this distinction between the morality of social rules and the morality of ideals will be duplicated by a distinction between the passive majority and a certain ruling elite; and much of the unpopularity of his views has its basis in the images of harsh and tyrannical domination that he associated with this notion of a class that creates and lives out an ideal. In practice, of course, even an elite needs rules of reciprocity quite as much as society as a whole does, so it may be reasonable to view "ideals" and "social rules" as two aspects of morality, neither of which can claim to be the whole of morality by itself. In any case, what is genuinely important in Nietzsche's discussion of ideals and rules is not any simplistic assumption that some class or individual can dispense entirely with the one or the other, but rather his reversal of the more usual view that only those ideals are valid that are compatible with the rules of universal morality. Moral obligations to others will henceforth have to be authenticated by reference to ideals, and not the other way around; and this exactly formulates the most serious problem that the existentialists who follow Nietzsche were to encounter.

In support of the interpretation proposed above, it may be noted that there is much in Nietzsche's own writings that is hard to reconcile with the customary view that he is an extreme individualist in ethical theory. To begin with, the ideals he speaks of are the ideals of some group that is smaller than the whole society, but certainly cannot be confined to a single individual. Nietzsche, in fact, often speaks with contempt of moral individualism, and insists strongly on the importance of tradition and continuity and a sense of responsibility for the future of man as a whole.[24] Indeed, he often seems to be arguing that the harsh domination of society as a whole by the ideal of an elite is in the interest of the human race as a whole, whatever hardships it may entail. It might also be said that in his view, such an elite would be legislating for all men, since it is insisting that its style of life shall be the one that dominates and shapes society as a whole (and for its ultimate good) even though it is not one in which the mass of human beings can directly participate. It is interesting to note that when the existentialists speak of choosing for all men in choosing for one's self, they often use the language of Kant to whom they in fact appeal, but they have not always made clear that they understand how sharply this conception of universalizability breaks with the views of Nietzsche. To choose for all men in the Kantian sense is to choose that which every rational being must recognize to be right; but to choose for all men in the Nietzschean sense is to choose for one's self and one's class and thereby to create a world in which others must live, willy-nilly.

To trace the line of descent of contemporary existentialism to

[24] Sharply critical comments on "individualism" can be found throughout the *Nachlass*. (See for example, *ibid.*, pp. 474, 605, 907.)

both Kant and Nietzsche is thus to expose a centrally important ambivalence in its ethical theory. With respect to the independence of the moral from the theoretical intellect and the necessity for treating moral legislation as an autonomous function of the will, both Kant and Nietzsche are in agreement; and this dual ancestry poses no problem for present-day existentialists for whom a rejection of all forms of "natural" morality has become an agreed upon starting-point. But when Kant and Nietzsche separate, as they do, on the issue of the internal controls to which the moral will is subject, a serious problem *is* posed for anyone who stands in the same voluntaristic tradition as they. *Either* he must hold with Kant that there is a single test—or set of tests—that every rational being must apply to proposals for action and by the outcome of which he must be guided; *or* he must, with Nietzsche, abandon the notion of strict universalizability as a criterion of rightness and adopt the view that standards and ideals of conduct are ineradicably plural, and universal only in the sense that the ideals of the dominant class are imposed upon everyone and "willed for them."

Now it is often supposed that contemporary existentialists have unambiguously opted for Nietzsche and against Kant on this issue.[25] This is, in fact, not the case. They have, it is true, often criticized the morality of general rules, but they have done so not on the grounds that the ordering of conduct by reference to such rules is incompatible with moral autonomy, but on the more restricted grounds that such rules too often serve as substitutes for the decisions we are unwilling to face. The existentialists often sound like Nietzsche, but they also often sound like Kant, so it is hardly surprising if they are charged with not having a clear doctrine of universality as an element in moral judgment. In Part II, I shall attempt to show what views they do hold, and what development those views would permit. It is enough to point out here that to attribute an extreme antinomian particularism to the ethical theory of the existentialists is not justified. Critics who have done so have correctly located the fundamental issue for that

---

[25] See for example, E. Gellner, "Ethics and Logic," *Proceedings of the Aristotelian Society*, N. S. Vol. 55 (1955), p. 157. No evidence is presented from any existentialist writings in behalf of this interpretation.

theory, but as is so often the case, they have too quickly identified existentialism with an extreme and one-sided position on that issue.

One final observation: in spite of all the obvious affinities between Nietzsche and existentialism, it would not be difficult to make a case for treating Nietzsche as a representative of a quite different type of ethical theory. He was, after all, a severe critic of all attempts to isolate "morality" from its biological and psychological matrix; and he insisted that moral judgment must be understood as an expression of underlying biological forces, rather than as an apprehension of a self-subsistent realm of moral truths. At times he went so far as to see in moral activity nothing more than a kind of epiphenomenal symptom of the vital self-assertiveness of a given individual or society. From this position, it would seem to be just a step to the view that moral judgments are translatable into statements that describe the direction and intensity of whatever biological drives these judgments serve to express. Nietzsche never quite took this step, however, and it seems clear that he did not think that moral judgments are intended, or understood by those who make them, as descriptions of their own biological or psychological state, even though they might profitably be so viewed by the psychologist of morals. In practice, if not in theory, Nietzsche does treat the moral life as a distinctive human function that cannot be reduced to a merely symptomatic expression of vital drives. Indeed, it is tempting to see in Nietzsche's "biologism" no more than an addendum, inspired by the Darwinism of his day, to his main account of morals.[26] Nevertheless, this naturalistic tinge to his ethical thought does set him apart from the existentialists who, in constructing their even more radical doctrine of autonomy, were to reject all of Nietzsche's dubious biological metaphors.

[26] Heidegger's rejection of the "biologism" imputed to Nietzsche is stated in his *Nietzsche,* Vol. 1, pp. 590–616.

CHAPTER IV

THE EMERGENCE OF EXISTENTIALISM

Many accounts have been given of the successive stages by which existential philosophy has reached its present level of development. In these accounts, due note is usually taken of many of the "forerunners" in the nineteenth century and earlier, who were discussed in the preceding chapters. Nevertheless, the relationship in which Heidegger and Sartre stand to these earlier figures often remains quite obscure, largely because the distinctive form assumed by their thought under the influence of Edmund Husserl is treated as an almost adventitious intrusion of alien modes of thought into the highly personal and idiosyncratic philosophical world of Nietzsche and Kierkegaard. To the degree that Husserl's philosophy makes a positive contribution to existentialism, it does so, in the view taken by many commentators, exclusively as a conception of method which the existentialists have freely adapted to their own purposes.[1] Inevitably, this denial of any closer or more organic connection between Husserl's doctrines and existentialism leaves the co-presence of elements drawn from such radically disparate sources within one system of thought pretty much of a mystery.

In this chapter, I hope to remedy this defect of most existing accounts by arguing that the leading existentialists did not simply borrow a conception of method from Husserl that would permit them to generalize a view of human life which they were developing from other sources. Instead, it would appear that something much more like the reverse of this sequence took place. I

---

[1] See for example, Barrett, *Irrational Man,* p. 213. Heidegger is said to make "use of an instrument, phenomenology, borrowed from his teacher, Edmund Husserl; but in adopting the instrument he gives it a different sense and direction from Husserl's."

mean that a group of philosophers, reared in the tradition of critical idealism and deeply versed in the phenomenology of Edmund Husserl, which was its twentieth century version, came face
to face with what they took to be a breakdown of that mode of
thought on an issue of crucial importance; and that in this situation they began to draw on ideas elaborated within the voluntaristic tradition with a view to dealing by these new means with
features of the human relationship to the world that found no
adequate expression within Husserl's philosophy. This interpretation which I propose does not, of course, entail that these philosophers did not have an antecedent and independent interest in
the earlier writers whom they were to lay under such heavy contribution, nor that they abandoned Husserl's doctrine *in toto* because it had turned out to be fatally misconceived in one respect.
I am asserting simply that the issues to which existentialism is a
response can be shown to have developed within the inner *Prob-
lematik* of Husserlian phenomenology, and that this circumstance offers a more profitable way of understanding the nexus of
disparate philosophical strands within existentialism than does
the more familiar kind of account.[2]

I

There is, to begin with, an element of paradox in the relationship of twentieth century existentialism to the earlier forms of
ethical voluntarism that have been considered so far. These have
all been, in one way or another, denials of the intellectualistic
view that man has a morally determinate nature by reference to
which questions of conduct are at least in principle resolvable.
Particularly in some forms of theological voluntarism, this lack of
a nature has been treated as a defect or privation, and it has been
explained by reference to the destructive effect of sin upon the
nature with which man was originally endowed. In Kant and

[2] I have tried to analyze the complicated relationship between Husserl's
philosophy and existentialism in much greater detail in my essay, "A Central
Theme of Merleau-Ponty's Philosophy," a contribution to a volume devoted
to existentialism and phenomenology, and scheduled for publication in 1967
by the Johns Hopkins University Press.

Nietzsche, on the other hand, a clear tendency appears to treat the morally autonomous will as the central element in human personality, rather than as a mere lack of an antecedently defined nature. It is this tendency that comes to full expression in contemporary existentialism which is therefore properly described as "ontological voluntarism." Man's "nature" (or being) is now explicitly asserted to consist in his *not* having a nature in the traditional sense of the term in which a nature is at once an object of knowledge and a source of principles of action. In place of the intellectualistic ontology of moral determinacy, the existentialists have attempted to construct an ontology of moral freedom, i.e., an analysis of those structural features of human being by virtue of which moral knowledge in the intellectualistic sense becomes impossible, and autonomous choice an inescapable necessity of the human condition. What the intellectualist and the existentialist have in common, however, is the assumption that philosophers must have a theory of real (as distinct from linguistic, or nominal) essences if they are to explain in a satisfactory way either the possibility or the impossibility of moral knowledge.

In the next chapter, an attempt will be made to find a workable interpretation for the ontological vocabulary in which the existentialists' doctrines are formulated. Here, I wish merely to point out one important result of their recasting of voluntarism into an ontological form. Whatever else "ontological" may turn out to mean in this context, it means at least "non-psychological"; and it follows that existentialism is not to be understood in any sense as a thesis about the will considered as a mental faculty. If Kant and Nietzsche, as was noted earlier, in their different ways came close to an "ontological" view that identifies will as the essence of man, their conceptions of the will nevertheless retained a strongly psychological and mentalistic flavor. By contrast, the existentialists are emphatic in their desire to disassociate their doctrines from any conception of the will as one faculty of the mind among others; and they are unanimously opposed to the whole basically Cartesian theory of mind as a mental substance that typically underlies such views.[3] Although

[3] Heidegger's critique of Descartes occurs in *Sein und Zeit* (8th ed.; Tubingen: Niemeyer, 1957), pp. 24, 25, and pp. 89–101. An even more

one of the commonest misinterpretations of existentialism represents it as an extreme form of romantic subjectivism, in fact it has been distinguished by a strong insistence that no account of either knowledge or evaluation can be given in purely mentalistic terms, and that the vocabulary of mental substances with their faculties and affections must be given up in favor of a quite different account of our relationship to the objects of these activities. Existentialism is not a doctrine of the inner life, and it cannot be accurately understood as a set of theses with respect to the relationship to one another of faculties of the human mind. If human subjectivity generally is not reducible to a sort of intramental activity, then neither can voluntary human action be so treated. Action and choice must instead be defined as a certain relationship to the world, and as a function of that dimension of human being by virtue of which it reaches out beyond itself. The case is not that the notion of will has dropped out of existentialist thought. Instead it has been developed within the framework of a general conception of human subjectivity that defines the latter not in terms of internal states but rather as a certain relationship to the world.

In the light of this resistance on the part of the existentialists to a psychologistic formulation of their theses, it is not surprising that the phenomenology of Edmund Husserl should have provided the philosophical matrix within which twentieth century existentialism was to develop.[4] Profound differences of ethos and methodology separate Husserl from the "existential" phenomenologists who were later to reject much of his teaching; but that fact does not cancel out their profound indebtedness to his conception of philosophical inquiry. Both Heidegger and Sartre began as phenomenologists and both, in their early work, looked to Husserl as the master of their discipline. They made extensive use of technical phenomenological concepts; and even

---

powerful attack on Descartes is mounted by Merleau-Ponty in Pt. III, ch. 1, of *Phénoménologie de la Perception* (Paris: Gallimard, 1945).

[4] By far the best study of the underlying philosophical motives for the evolution of existential phenomenology out of Husserl's transcendental phenomenology is H. Dreyfus's Harvard doctoral dissertation, *Husserl's Phenomenology of Perception* (1964). See also H. Spiegelberg, *The Phenomenological Movement* (The Hague: Nijhoff, 1960), 2 Vols.

when they broke with Husserl on central points of phenomenological method, they presented these departures, at least at first, as modifications of phenomenology from within. Whether either of them is properly described as a phenomenologist in the light of his later philosophical development is a question that need not be answered here; but there can be no doubt that it is this affiliation with Husserl that explains why ontological voluntarism came to be stated in the form of a theory of consciousness, or conscious human being. It also provides a second important distinction between Heidegger and Sartre, on the one hand, and the other two major "existentialists" of the present day, Jaspers and Marcel. Neither of the latter has ever presented himself as a phenomenologist, and neither has developed his own views in any close association with those of Husserl. This circumstance, together with the fact, already noted, that these philosophers stand in a Kierkegaardian rather than in a Nietzschean tradition of existentialism, seems to offer ample justification for a separate consideration of Heidegger and Sartre and their followers.

II

It is not possible within the limits of this study to present anything like an adequate summary of the main theses of Husserl's philosophy.[5] It is, as was noted above, a philosophy of consciousness; and it rests on the assumption that the characteristic structures of consciousness can be isolated and described without settling one way or another any ulterior questions about the independent or "transcendent" reality of its objects. As a philosophy of human subjectivity, phenomenology builds on the earlier achievements of Descartes and Kant; but it abandons the ontological dualism of mental and material substances that was ex-

[5] Only two of Husserl's major works have been translated into English: *Ideas: General Introduction to Pure Phenomenology*, trans. W. B. Gibson (London: Allen and Unwin, 1931), and *Cartesian Meditations*, trans. D. Cairns (The Hague: Nijhoff, 1960). The translation of *Ideas* is incomplete, but the second and third parts are now available in German as *Ideen zu einer reinen Phänomenologie u. phänomenologischen Philosophie II & III, Husserliana*, Vols. 4 and 5 (The Hague: Nijhoff, 1952).

plicit in the former and implicit in the latter. Instead, it takes its stand within the situation of conscious beings and undertakes a rigorously exact description of the world, as it appears in its various modes of objectivity to human consciousness. To the different types of object that compose this phenomenal world— material objects, other persons, etc.—there correspond those intentional acts of consciousness by which these objects are, as Husserl says, constituted. But just as Husserl scrupulously avoids all the idioms by which an action upon consciousness from without is suggested, so the intentional acts of which he speaks are not to be thought of as imposing categorial form upon an alien material in the manner set forth by Kant. While it is true that in Husserl's own case the methodological suspension of all affirmations with respect to extra-phenomenal reality passed over into a transcendental idealism that denies the very possibility of there being anything wholly independent of consciousness, he maintains, within the conscious situation, a strict parallelism of intentional acts and intentional objects. Whatever view he may have come to hold with respect to the ultimately spiritual character of all being, Husserl's whole doctrine of "constitution" is developed within the limits of a strict correspondence theory of truth, with the result that no implication of volitional freedom attaches to the constitutive activity of the transcendental self.[6] Husserl's emphasis always falls upon the structures of meaning by which our experience is articulated. He insists that all conscious activity—theoretical, evaluative, and practical—must derive its validity from the intuition of such structures which together compose the intentional object that we call a "world." Most important, there is and can be no breach in this system of meanings, "no point," as Husserl says, "at which the life of consciousness might be pierced and at which we might attain a transcendence

[6] This point is made and supported by ample textual evidence in A. De Waehlens, *Phénoménologie et Vérité* (Paris: Presses Universitaires, 1953) , Pt. I. It has been argued persuasively by E. Fink in his "Les concepts opératoires dans la philosophie de Husserl," *Colloque philosophique de Royaumont sur Husserl et la phénoménologie, Cahiers de Philosophie, No. 3* (Paris: Editions de Minuit, 1959) , pp. 214–230, that certain basic notions of which Husserl makes use, such as concepts of "constitution" and "act," to which volitional overtones inevitably attach. were never satisfactorily worked out by Husserl.

that could have any meaning other than that of an intentional unity appearing in the very subjectivity of consciousness."[7] To put the same point in non-Husserlian language, the human world is defined and constituted by our systems of meaning, and there is no sense that can be attached to the idea of a confrontation and comparison of these systems with anything else on which they have not already left their mark.

This thesis of a seamless continuity and hermetic self-sufficiency of mental activity is associated with another assumption of great importance for phenomenology generally and for its theory of value in particular. This is the view that all intentional acts involve the entertaining of propositions and are therefore susceptible of being judged by the standard of truth and falsity.[8] All predicates that figure in such propositions must accordingly designate some property or relation in the intentional object, and all statements are to be treated as reports of what is so given to intuition. When applied to the analysis of ethical phenomena, this assumption has implications that clearly commit Husserl to an intellectualistic theory of evaluative judgment which he never fully formulated.[9] The available evidence indicates, however, that he regarded evaluative consciousness as amenable to the same kind of analysis into object and act that he applied to other modes of mental activity. To every evaluative intuition, there must accordingly correspond an intentional object—in this case, a value essence of some kind. Consistently with his own interpretation of phenomenological method, Husserl is not

[7] "Es gibt keine erdenkliche Stelle wo das Bewusstseinsleben durchstossen und zu durchstossen wäre und wo wir auf eine Transzendenz kämen die anderen Sinn haben könnte als den einer in der Bewusstseinssubjektivität selbst auftretenden intentionalen Einheit." *Formale und Transcendentale Logik, Jahrbuch für Philosophie ünd Phenomenologische Forschung* (Halle: Niemeyer, 1929) Vol. 10, p. 208.

[8] In *Ideen II* (The Hague: 1952) Husserl argues that all forms of intentional acts, such as for example aesthetic and evaluative experience, can be converted into "theoretical acts" in which, as he says, "das Gegenständliche theoretischer Gegenstand wird, d.i. Gegenstand einer aktuell vollzogenen Seinsetzung in der das Ich lebt und Gegenständliches erfasst, als Seiendes fasst und setzt." (p. 11)

[9] Some of Husserl's hitherto unpublished lectures on ethics are now available in A. Roth, *Edmund Husserls Ethische Untersuchungen* (The Hague: Nijhoff, 1960) .

interested in any transcendental reality such values may have, but he does want to describe the mode in which values present themselves. His answer is that "without further effort on my part, I find the things before me furnished not only with the qualities that befit their positive nature, but with value characters such as beautiful and ugly, pleasant and unpleasant and so forth."[10] Again, "these values and practicalities belong to the constitution of the actually present objects as such, irrespective of any turning or not turning to consider them or indeed any other objects."[11] Finally, "the valuing consciousness constitutes over against the mere world of positivity the typically new 'axiological' objectivity, a 'being' of a new region."[12] Even these brief quotations make it quite clear that in spite of all his terminological innovations, Husserl was an intellectualist and an intuitionist in ethical theory. There are value essences, and there is a distinction between adequate and inadequate apprehensions of these essences. There can thus be axiological objectivity and evaluative truths, although Husserl never gave any indication of the precise way in which he would deal with ethical disagreement. In all these respects he was defending a position to which the voluntaristic tradition and its existentialist progeny were in the most pronounced opposition.

In spite of these major differences, it would be an error to represent the relation of the existentialists to the phenomenological position in ethical theory as purely negative. Indirectly, Husserl and, to an even greater extent, Max Scheler, whose conception of value is essentially similar to Husserl's, contributed to existentialist ethical theory by clearing the ground for it.[13] While both Hus-

[10] "Ohne weiteres finde ich die Dinge vor mir ausgestattet wie mit Sachbeschaffenheiten, so mit Wertcharakteren, als schön und hässlich, als gefällig und misfällig, als angenehm und unangenehm, u. dgl.," Husserl, *Ideen*, Vol. 1, p. 59.
[11] "Auch diese Wertcharaktere und praktischen Charaktere gehören konstitutiv zu den 'vorhandenen' Objekten als solchen, ob ich mich ihnen und den Objekten zuwende oder nicht." (*Ibid.*, p. 59.)
[12] "Das wertende Bewusstsein konstituiert die gegenüber der blossen Sachenwelt neuartige 'axiologische' Gegenständlichkeit, ein 'Seiendes' neuer Region." (*Ibid.*, p. 290.)
[13] Scheler's *Der Formalismus in der Ethik und die materiale Wertethik* was probably the most influential work in the field of ethical theory to be written

serl and Scheler treat evaluation as a form of cognition, they also insist strongly on the distinctive and autonomous nature of ethical knowledge. Scheler, in particular, argues at length against virtually all of the conceptions of ethical knowledge which found wide acceptance during the nineteenth century, and which seek to assimilate it to some recognized mode of rationality. He rejects all evolutionary and utilitarian conceptions of value; and while he recognizes that Kant contributed greatly to the understanding of the autonomy of ethics, he argues that Kant fails to grasp the distinctive nature of the intuition of values, because he confused this intuition with the subjective experience of pleasure and pain. Finally, Scheler dismisses all forms of historicistic ethical theory which tie the concept of value to some schedule of social or cultural development in the manner of Hegel and Marx, on the ground that they fail to do justice to the independent character of ethical understanding.

It is perhaps worth noting that the relationship in which Brentano and Husserl and Scheler stand to the existentialists is very similar to that of the intuitionists in the English-speaking philosophical world to the emotivists and prescriptivists who were to follow them. What G. E. Moore accomplished in *Principia Ethica* was to discredit ethical naturalism in all its varieties, in the eyes of several generations of philosophers, and to establish the autonomy of ethics on the basis of arguments which seemed unanswerable. Those philosophers who accepted Moore's refutation of naturalism and its corollary, the autonomy of morals, in many cases came to conceive the nature of that autonomy in ways very different from Moore's.[14] Instead of treating evaluation as a distinctive

---

on the Continent during the first quarter of the twentieth century but remains untranslated and virtually unknown in the English-speaking world. In that work, Scheler himself notes the similarity of his position to that of G. E. Moore. The one major study of Scheler's philosophy is M. Dupuy, *La Philosophie de Max Scheler* (Paris: Presses Universitaires de France, 1959) , 2 Vols., in which Pt. 6, Vol. 2 is devoted to his ethical theory.

[14] I have in mind, of course, both the emotive theory as represented by C. L. Stevenson, *Ethics and Language* (New Haven: Yale University Press, 1944) , and prescriptivism of the type represented by R. M. Hare, *The Language of Morals* (Oxford: Clarendon Press, 1952) . For a brief survey of the development of ethical theory in Britain during the twentieth century, see M. Warnock, *Ethics Since 1900* (London: Oxford University Press, 1960) .

and autonomous form of knowledge, they have interpreted its autonomy as being due to the fact that it is not a form of cognition at all. Nevertheless, it is difficult to imagine the development of noncognitivistic conceptions of evaluation without the preceding criticisms of naturalism from an intuitionistic standpoint. Similarly, without Scheler's and Husserl's criticism of all attempts to provide psychological and biological foundations for ethics, it seems doubtful whether the existentialist conception of the autonomy of ethics could have emerged in quite the form it took.

III

But this pattern of fundamental disagreement and incidental agreement in matters of ethical theory is of secondary importance for an understanding of the complex dialectical relationships between existentialism and phenomenology. Existentialism is, in the first instance, a philosophical account of the structure of human "being-in-the-world" that developed out of the Husserlian doctrine of transcendental subjectivity or pure consciousness. The crucial issue, therefore, concerns the character of the revision effected by Heidegger and Sartre in the Husserlian conception of a consciousness that stands in a relationship of perfect correspondence to its own milieu, and never encounters anything that is radically independent of it. It is, of course, well known that this revision took the form of a rejection by the existentialists of the phenomenological reduction as conceived by Husserl through which the sphere of pure consciousness and its intentional correlates was to be isolated. Both Heidegger and Sartre after him insist that a purely phenomenalistic treatment of external objects is impossible, and that the transcendent being of things is always implicitly recognized.[15] Sartre even offers what he

---

[15] Heidegger never directly criticizes Husserl's conception of the phenomenological reduction but very significantly such a reduction plays no role in his own phenomenologcal practice and he makes it very clear that a characterization of human existence that "bracketed off" the essential reference it makes to the being of what he calls "das innerweltlich Seiende" would

takes to be a strict "ontological proof" that the intentional object of consciousness *must* transcend that consciousness.[16] But if things have a mode of being of their own that is unassimilable to that of consciousness, it becomes necessary to give a differential characterization of the nature or being of consciousness by contrasting it with the mode of being of things. The ontological turn taken by phenomenology under the influence of first Heidegger and then Sartre is thus best understood as an effort to break out of the monistic and idealistic ontology that was implicit in Husserl's philosophy, and to construct a more adequate ontology that would at least permit the making of a radical distinction between the being of things and the being of consciousness. What is now called existentialism is the outcome of that effort.

The most important feature of conscious human being, in this pluralistic ontology, is its referential and self-transcending character. This assumes two principal forms, and an understanding of existentialism, both generally and in its specifically ethical aspect, is largely dependent upon a correct grasp of both the distinctness and the inter-relatedness of these modes of self-transcendence. First, since the phenomenological reduction cannot be carried out, and "things" stubbornly resist assimilation to the status of meanings or mind-constituted objects, consciousness must be characterized as referring beyond itself and the circle of its meanings to that which exists independently of its being known or experienced or thought of, i.e., to being-in-itself. The existentialists insist that this being of things is not to be understood on the model of Kantian things-in-themselves, and that no appeal to

---

be self-defeating (cf. *Sein und Zeit*, pp. 61, 164, 183). Beginning with the distinction between immanence and transcendence or reference to what exists independently of consciousness, Husserl progressively assimilated the latter to the former as what he calls "transcendence within immanence" with the result that the possibility of extra-conscious being is not just disregarded for methodological purposes but denied. In Heidegger, by contrast, the notion of immanence is not used and the notion of being, while it is problematic in the sense of requiring philosophical analysis, is assumed from the outset to have two principal uses, one applying to "things" and the other to conscious human existence. Neither is to be reduced to the other. See, also, Heidegger's characterization of "phenomenology" and the concept of the "phenomenon" in *Sein und Zeit*, pp. 28–39.

[16] This proof is given in *L'Être et le néant*, pp. 27–29.

representational theories of perception or to a causal interpretation of the relation of things to consciousness is intended by them. Some of the difficulties connected with this conception of an encounter with being will be taken up in the next chapter. The relevant point here is that being-in-itself is understood to be set over against the whole human apparatus of perception and conceptualization. While the latter thus addresses itself to a mode of being that is radically distinct from it, nothing can really be said about being-in-itself except that it is. Whenever we go beyond that simple statement, according to Sartre, what we say inevitably makes an implicit reference to the structures of human subjectivity. Indeed, what we call the "world," as distinct from being-in-itself, is no more than those structures themselves, described as one might say in the material mode rather than in the language of conscious activity. As one critic has pointed out, Heidegger describes human subjectivity largely in terms of this objective equivalent—the world—of the conscious activity in terms of which Sartre carries out his analyses.[17] Whichever method of description is adopted, being-in-itself remains that which appears within the intentional framework of human subjectivity, but which cannot be identified with any of our intentional acts, nor reduced to the status of an intentional object.

At first sight, it might not seem that the introduction of the notion of being-in-itself could have any very profound effect upon Husserlian phenomenology. After all, apart from the one statement that being-in-itself *is*, everything else one might go on to say would presuppose the constitutive activity of human consciousness and its distinctive modes of conceptualization. Nevertheless, this innovation is of decisive importance for the emergence of existentialism, because it modifies in a fundamental way the distinction, within conscious activity, between those intentional acts that

[17] This contrast is made by F. Jeanson in his *Le problème morale et la pensée de Sartre* (Paris: Editions du Myrte, 1947). "On peut donc poser *qu'à toute structure essentielle de la conscience correspond une structure existentielle du monde,*" p. 64. "Si . . . nous mettons l'accent sur le *vécu* des significations, nous aurons la tendance existentielle de la phénoménologie: pour celle-ci, représentée par Heidegger, c'est dans chaque cas la structure existentielle du monde qui sera interrogée . . ." (p. 65).

are primarily addressed to things-in-being and those that are not primarily so addressed. The former are characterized by a special and uneliminable passivity—the passivity of the cognitive, fact-stating mode; and it is to them that the kind of truth that consists in the correspondence of a judgment with a state of affairs is appropriately attributed. By parity of reasoning, to the degree that intentional acts are not confined to an apprehension of things-in-being, they will quite naturally be thought of as enjoying a degree of spontaneity and freedom that is denied to those that are. It is precisely this freedom associated with the absence of anything to which such acts are to conform themselves, or to which they are to be true, that was to be of fundamental importance for the existentialist view of ethical judgment.[18] In place of Husserl's conception of a continuum of intentional acts, *all* of which had their own relation of correspondence to an immanent intentional object and to no other kind of counterpart at all, the existentialists adopted a dichotomous treatment of mental activity that breaks this continuum into two main segments. Within one of these—the properly cognitive segment—any constitutive activity attributed to the transcendental ego is heavily qualified by the requirement of referential fidelity to an object that is more than just the shadow cast upon the world by our own conceptual operations. At the same time, this reinforced passivity attaching to mental acts directed upon objects that transcend them has the effect of lightening, through contrast, and indeed, of cancelling altogether our sense of a relationship of correspondence in the case of those forms of intentionality that *do* exhaust their "objects." While for Husserl pure transcendental consciousness was equally active in its constitutive function through all the spheres of its activity, and therefore (as one might be tempted to suggest) not truly originative or spontaneous in any of them, the existentialist will in-

[18] Heidegger's doctrine of the dependence of "truth" (in the traditional sense that turns on the notion of correspondence to that which *is*), upon "freedom" conceived in terms of a reference beyond what is, is stated most clearly in *Vom Wesen des Grundes* (3rd ed.; Frankfurt-am-Main, 1955), pp. 43 ff., and in his *Vom Wesen der Wahrheit* (3rd ed.; Frankfurt, 1959). See also De Waehlens, *Phénoménologie et Vérité*, ch. 8.

sist on a special freedom that attaches to one dimension of conscious activity by virtue of its referring not to being-in-itself but beyond it.

This second type of self-transcendence is that by which human consciousness goes beyond itself, but in this case, toward what is merely possible, and not (at least currently) actual. As will be shown more clearly later, these possibilities are possibilities of action on the part of the individual whose "projects" they are. Here, however, the important point is that at the same time as it addresses itself to being-in-itself, human consciousness carries within itself a reference to what is not actual that is just as primitive and just as irreducible to any combination of intramental acts or states as was the reference to being-in-itself. The two forms of transcendence are, in fact, inseparably linked and are distinguishable dimensions of all conscious activity instead of being attributes of numerically distinct acts. It is, in fact, only because being-in-itself is thus invested with a "halo of non-being" that it is apprehended as contingent, i.e., as emerging "absurdly" from a circumambient nothingness. But if "truth" is in that sense dependent upon freedom, every expression of that freedom issues out of a situation of fact that is apprehended under a certain description, and while that situation can impose no limitations upon the particular possibility toward which human consciousness transcends itself, it nevertheless contributes an essential element to the sense of the choices we make.[19]

Although both of these forms of transcendent reference are to be conceived as forms of activity which, taken together define human being, it is the second—the reference to possibility or non-being—that breaks most sharply with the intellectualistic presuppositions of Husserl's philosophy, and accordingly calls for a genuinely novel characterization. It is precisely here, in the

[19] The interdependence of "practical" and "theoretical" attitudes is very clearly stated in *Sein und Zeit*, p. 69:

> Das "praktische" Verhalten ist nicht "atheoretisch" im Sinne der Sichtlosigkeit, und sein Unterschied gegen das theoretische Verhalten liegt nicht nur darin, dass hier betrachtet und dort *gehandelt* wird, und dass das Handeln, um nicht blind zu bleiben, theoretisches Erkennen anwendet, sondern das Betrachten is so ursprünglich ein Besorgen, wie das Handeln seine Sicht hat.

characterization of this second type of transcendence, that the influence of the voluntaristic tradition makes itself felt upon contemporary existentialism. Historically, the evidence seems to indicate that once Heidegger had made his initial break with Husserl, by recognizing the inadequacy of the latter's account of mental activity in terms of act-object correspondence, he proceeded to use as his models for the understanding of human being (or *Dasein*) the conceptions of human subjectivity that he found in Nietzsche and in Kierkegaard, and that Heidegger's concept of *Dasein* itself is at bottom a scholastic reworking, in the technical vocabulary of phenomenology, of ideas he drew from these writers and from the tradition from which they derived.[20] This set of ideas

[20] Heidegger's estimate of Kierkegaard as a philosopher is not very favorable and the latter's influence upon Heidegger's thought, while important, appears to have made itself felt largely in the analysis of "Angst" and "Sorge." See *Sein und Zeit*, p. 235 fn. For a similarly critical judgment by Sartre, see *Critique de la raison dialectique*, pp. 18 ff. The influence of Nietzsche is in every way more important. While Heidegger's lectures on Nietzsche were given in the thirties, and thus postdate *Sein und Zeit*, several references to his thought in *Sein und Zeit* indicate that Heidegger was aware of the affinity between them—an affinity that is explored in great detail in his *Nietzsche* (1961). These lectures are based mainly on the writings grouped together under the title "The Will to Power" and Heidegger concentrates his attention on Nietzsche's "new principle of value-positing" and the related problem of truth that was central to his own earlier work. While it is a legitimate question to ask to what extent Heidegger's interpretation of Nietzsche is a projection of his own ideas upon Nietzsche's philosophy, there are many passages in the *Nachlass* that can be seen, without any forcing, to anticipate Heideggerian positions; and in the light of Heidegger's known interest in Nietzsche at the time of the writing of *Sein und Zeit* and his later detailed analysis of just those aspects of Nietzsche's thought that are most relevant to the concerns of that book, it seems legitimate and indeed unavoidable to assign a considerable influence to Nietzsche in the emergence of the Heideggerian version of existentialism. The passages from the *Nachlass* in which the parallelism with Heidegger's conception of *Verstehen* (see ch. 5) is particularly striking, may be cited:

Das "Was ist das?" ist eine *Sinnsetzung* von etwas anderem aus gesehen. Die *"Essenz,"* die *"Wesenheit"* ist etwas Perspektivisches . . . Zugrund liegt immer "was ist das für *mich?*" (Für uns, für alles, was lebt, usw.) . . . Man darf nicht fragen: *"Wer* interpretiert denn?" Sondern das Interpretieren selbst, als eine Form des Willens zur Macht, hat Dasein (aber nicht als ein "Sein" sondern als ein *Prozess*, ein *Werden*) als ein Affekt (p. 487). Unsere Werte sind in die Dinge *hineininterpretiert*. Gibt es denn einen *Sinn* im An–sich? Ist nicht notwendig Sinn eben *Beziehungs*-Sinn und Perspektive? Aller Sinn ist Wille zur Macht (alle Beziehungs–Sinne lassen sich in ihn auflösen (p. 503).

that thus filled the breach made in Husserl's system had been primarily inspired by reflection on the nature of action and value, rather than by the typically phenomenological concern with a rigorous ideal of scientific knowledge. Furthermore, the concept of evaluation implicit in them was radically incompatible not only with the general "scientific" spirit of Husserlian phenomenology, but to an even greater degree with Husserl's views on the subject of value and evaluative judgment, which, as we have seen, were characterized by a fairly orthodox Platonizing intellectualism. In any case, the result of this crossing of such diverse philosophical strains was that certain conceptions of a primarily *moral* subjectivity were pressed into service as characterizations of human subjectivity generally. It is scarcely surprising that the existentialist ontology should, as the result of this *generatio aequivoca,* have become permeated with concepts of ethical origin, nor that at the same time its principal architects should have been able to deny in good faith that they were putting forward an ethical theory. They had, in fact, so thoroughly transformed a theory of moral personality into a general account of human being that it is only by a subsequent analysis that the nature of their ethical theory in the more restricted sense can be exhibited.[21]

This last citation may be compared with Heidegger's statement that "Sinn ist ein Existential des Daseins, nicht eine Eigenschaft, die am Seienden haftet . . . Sinn hat nur Dasein . . . nur Dasein kann daher sinnvoll oder sinnlos sein." (*Sein und Zeit,* p. 151.) With regard to the earlier forms of voluntarism and Heidegger's knowledge of them, it is interesting to note that Heidegger is the author of a study of Duns Scotus, *Die Kategorien und Bedeutungslehre des Duns Scotus* (Tübingen: Mohr, 1916), in which the great medieval voluntarist is praised for having expanded the Aristotelian table of categories to include non-being and is interpreted as having made a contribution of great value "durch (sein) Zurückgehen auf eine fundamentale Probemsphläre der Subjecktivität (p. 231). There is no discussion in Heidegger's study of Scotus's theory of value and morality but it is clear that Heidegger saw a close connection between Scotus's philosophical preoccupations and his own. See especially pp. 228 ff.

[21] Heidegger's views on the relationship of ontology and ethics are briefly stated in *Sein und Zeit,* p. 167; and like Sartre's in *L'Être et le néant* (p. 720), they emphasize the independence of ontology from ethics and the ethical neutrality of the former. In his *Über den Humanismus,* however, Heidegger appears to conceive the connection as being a much more intimate one; and he says that "dasjenige Denken, das die Wahrheit des Seins als das

If voluntarism loses its specifically ethical character through being transformed into an ontology of human being, the continuing directive influence of its main theses within this new context is unmistakable. Not only is a distinctively human experience of the world henceforth to be thought of as a mode of action; it is also action that is not guided by any natural ends, or regulated by any a priori moral truths. It is "free," not only in the sense that its fundamental patterns of meaningfulness have no prototypes in being-in-itself which is their ultimate reference, but also in the sense that the direction and goals of human action must be self-generated. Because human consciousness transcends itself toward things-in-being on the one hand and toward non-being on the other, its two fundamental modalities are knowledge and action. With the former is associated the whole apparatus of terms of cognitive appraisal, in particular the notions of truth and falsity.[22] These are inapplicable to the other modality of human consciousness which is defined precisely as a reference beyond the sphere in which these notions are at home. Even if, as Heidegger sometimes seems to suggest, nothingness has an ontological status that is independent of the being of consciousness, the relationship to possibility that is implicit in human action necessarily involves an element of selection or choice that is *toto coelo* distinct from the discipline of truth conceived simply as the patient effort to say what is the case. The existentialists are united in holding that this effort itself presupposes the context of a mode of being characterized by a going-beyond what is, through action and choice. But within the comprehensive unity of what they call "being in the world," they maintain a distinction between cognition and evaluation that is coordinate with their distinction between being-in-itself and non-being and is, in its way,

anfängliche Element des Menschen als eines existierenden denkt, (ist) in sich schon die ursprüngliche Ethik," p. 41.

[22] Sartre's discussion of "la connaissance" in Pt. I, ch. 3, of *L'Être et le néant* is a detailed exploration of the "mode d'être ek-statique du pour-soi" that knowledge presupposes. Heidegger treats scientific inquiry as a modification of our normal practical concern with the world that is motivated by a desire to allow things to emerge as merely "vorhanden," or by what he calls a "Defizienz des besorgenden Zu-Tun-Habens mit der Welt." See *Sein und Zeit*, pp. 59–61 and pp. 66 ff.

every bit as rigid as the parallel distinction often made by positivists between value and facts, or between cognitive and emotive meaning.

IV

There are many questions that could be raised about the position that has just been briefly summarized. In particular, one might well question whether the existentialists can do justice to the passivity of the fact-stating, reality-oriented mode when, on their analysis, every statement about the "world" involves the application of categories that are related to the structure of human subjectivity. Some of these questions will be taken up in later chapters. Here, it is necessary only to avoid one possible misunderstanding of the contrast between the two modes of transcendence which has just been presented. This contrast is not intended by the existentialists as a denial that in our ordinary experience "fact" and "value" are much more intimately entangled in one another than this distinction suggests. Indeed, Heidegger is particularly insistent on the degree to which the human world is dominated by the instrumental and action-oriented character of "things"; and he recognizes this *Zuhandenheit* as the primary and pervasive modality of our apprehension of our natural environment.[23] Just as in the common sense view of the world, no distinction is made between the degree of objectivity assignable to "fact" and to "value." Indeed, if there is a priority, it might seem to go to the latter. At the same time, however, this human world, shot through with purpose and intention, is firmly contrasted with being-in-itself to which none of the peculiarly human categories of temporality or value or negation are held to be applicable. In this way, the existentialists maintain a double perspective on evaluative activity: the one, emphasizing its constitutive role in the familiar "world" of human experience; the other, its abso-

[23] See *Sein und Zeit*, pp. 66 ff. Heidegger's concept of the "world" is expounded at length in Pt. I, ch. 3, of that work, and also in *Das Wesen des Grundes*, sec. 2, with interesting historical comparisons. Heidegger's views on this matter are analyzed in W. Biemel, *Le concept de monde chez Heidegger* (Louvain: E. Nauwelaerts, 1950).

lute independence of everything that can, in the strict sense, be said to be "known." It is the latter that provides the basis for the distinctively existentialist doctrine of individual moral autonomy. The former, if fully developed, would presumably include the whole of what may be called the public, or institutional side of the moral life.

The tension between these two views of evaluative activity runs through the whole of the existentialist literature. Unfortunately, what might have proved to be a most valuable explanation of the relationship between individual choice and the impersonal and public morality of codes and institutions has been distorted from the beginning by a strong moral bias on the part of the existentialists themselves. There is a conspicuous irony in the fact that a philosopher such as Heidegger, who declares himself to be quite uninterested in developing any ethical implications latent in his thought, should have presented the social and "objective" dimension of morality solely as a denial and antithesis of individual responsibility and choice, and should have interpreted his doctrine of the primacy of the individual human project in such a way as to exclude, in principle, any possibility of a shared morality that is not based on mystification and a motivated suppression of one's own "true" nature as a moral being.[24] In the case of Sartre, there is no such pretention to ethical neutrality, but at least in his earlier works, it seems to be assumed that the function of philosophical analysis is not just to exhibit the role of human freedom and

[24] See the discussion of "Das 'Man'" and 'Mitsein" in *Sein und Zeit*, Pt. I, ch. 4, in which "Das *Man*" is defined as "das *Niemand* dem alles Dasein im Untereinandersein sich je schon ausgeliefert hat," p. 128.
In spite of the strongly condemnatory tone of his discussion of "Das Man" and "Das Gerede," Heidegger insists that it has a "rein ontologische Absicht" and has nothing to do with a "moralisierende Kritik des alltäglichen Daseins." (*Sein und Zeit*, p. 167.) While Heidegger was to reject French existentialism precisely because, as he made clear in his *Über den Humanismus* (Frankfurt: Klostermann, 1949), it was animated by moral and humanistic intentions, it may be doubted whether Heidegger has himself been faithful to the distinction between ontology and ethics. Certainly, in his *Die Selbstbehauptung der deutschen Universität* (Breslau: Verlag Wilhelm Gottlieb Korn, 1934), he seemed to associate his philosophy closely with the National Socialist program. The question of Heidegger's relation to the Nazi movement is discussed from different points of view in A. De Waehlens, "La philosophie de Heidegger et le Nazisme," and E. Weil, "Le cas Heidegger," *Les Temps Modernes* (1947), pp. 115–38.

choice in the constitution of the familiar moral world, but also to restore that freedom to its pristine individual state by dissolving the specious unities by which it is obscured.[25] The result of this interpretation has been an exacerbated moral individualism which has often—and justly—been criticized on the ground that its proponents have not made it clear how any kind of moral consensus or community could be reconstituted in a manner compatible with the view they hold of the primacy of individual choice.

It would appear that the analysis of evaluative phenomena carried out by the existentialists is animated by two distinct, and often conflicting, motives. One of these is a specifically philosophical motive: a desire to exhibit, by isolating it, the evaluative component in the whole structure of our relationship to things-in-being, and more specifically, to the more restricted domain of public values and social rules. The other is a strong disposition to condemn, and if possible, to eliminate, the pseudo-objective and inauthentic mode of moral being in which the individual fraudulently connives at the reification of his own moral personality. Unfortunately, in the case of Heidegger (and to some extent the early Sartre as well) moral consensus was too often treated as being *necessarily* a form of inauthenticity; in these circumstances, the two forms of analysis noted above virtually coalesced, with unhappy results. To be sure, even in Sartre's early work, there were strong indications that this did not represent his final view, and that a moral community could, in his view, be constituted on the basis of a recognition of the ultimate moral sovereignty of the individual. These hints remained largely undeveloped, until the appearance of the first volume of the *Critique de la raison dialectique*. While that work is certainly intended to correct the exces-

---

[25] The notion that morality is by its essence a piece of mystification is one which Sartre has always been strongly disposed, with at least part of his mind, to accept; but even in his most strongly individualistic period he did not deny the possibility of a universally valid ethic. See, for example, the last section of the last chapter in *L'Être et le néant*, significantly entitled "Perspectives Morales" in which he poses the questions about value and ethics that emerge from his work and promises to deal with them in "un prochain ouvrage" which, at least in the form projected, has never appeared. For Sartre's present view of his earlier attitude toward the political and social aspects of ethical questions, see his essay, "Paul Nizan," in *Situations* (New York: Fawcett Publishing Co., 1966) , pp. 82–123.

sive individualism of Sartre's earlier writings, some critics feel that it may have swung so far in the opposite direction as simply to cancel out the most distinctive features of Sartre's earlier mode of dealing with questions of ethical theory. As I will try to show in Chapter VIII, I believe this interpretation is mistaken, although the issue will remain in doubt until the *Critique* is finished. What can be said with assurance is that only in the work of Maurice Merleau-Ponty was there a recognition from the beginning that moral community and shared evaluative standards have a place in a just characterization of the moral life, and that their role and importance can be acknowledged without prejudice to the doctrine of the primacy of choice.[26]

[26] Merleau-Ponty's most important statement on the subject of value and choice is to be found in Pt. 3, ch. 3, of *Phénoménologie de la Perception,* and it is cast in the form of a critique of Sartre's theory of freedom.

CHAPTER V

AN INTERPRETATION OF EXISTENTIALISM

The most serious obstacle in the way of an understanding of what the existentialists have to say in matters of ethical theory, and in other matters as well, is the special philosophical terminology in which they set forth their views. Among the concepts they employ, those that give the greatest difficulty are precisely those that are ontological in character (i.e., the concepts of being, of the different modes of being, of non-being, and of the relationship between being and non-being.) These are the concepts that the existentialists use for the purpose of elucidating the nature of human subjectivity; and if the way in which they are to be understood remains fundamentally obscure, as it has to many readers of Heidegger and Sartre, the philosophical theses formulated by means of these concepts will be correspondingly unintelligible. Fortunately, there is reason to think that this difficulty can be met, and that a method of interpretation can be found for the ontological vocabulary of the existentialists that facilitates an understanding of their general position and yet does not require the philosophical commitments which that vocabulary imposes in its present form. Some of the obscurity of which readers complain is, of course, due to the fact that the main existentialist writers use key terms in different ways; and even more must be attributed to the habit, which they all share in varying degrees, of writing in a rather Orphic style that makes great demands upon the reader. Difficulties of this kind can be removed, if at all, only by the authors themselves; but they can be expected to lose much of their power to block comprehension when a clearer insight has been gained into the nature of the philosophical procedures that underly them. In this chapter, I will outline an interpretation of the ontological mode adopted by the existentialists, and I will also

79

try to show how this interpretation might be applied to some of their leading concepts.

I

In an earlier chapter, it was suggested that one principal effect of the ontological mode of statement which the existentialists use is to "de-psychologize" the theses they defend with respect to the nature of moral freedom. The latter had been explained by the earlier voluntarists as internal powers peculiar to the human—as distinct from the animal—soul. This soul was of course temporarily situated in a natural milieu to which its relationship was that of one (mental) substance to other substances; but the freedom, both causal and logical, of the soul was conceived to be entirely independent of this relationship to the natural milieu in which it happened to find itself. By contrast, the existentialists argue that, so far from its being the case that moral freedom or any other distinctive feature of conscious human being is an internal power independent of the human situation vis-à-vis the being of things, its nature and reality can be understood only within the context of that situation.[1] It follows from this view that a philosophical analysis of freedom requires a general theory of conscious human being and of its relationship to "things," i.e., what the existentialists call an "ontology." A question still remains as to whether this ontology represents the same kind of philosophical undertaking as the classical systems of philosophy that bear that name. More specifically, may there not be some way of interpreting the ontological theses of Heidegger and Sartre that would preserve their non-psychological character while at the same time avoiding the difficulties attendant upon ontologies of the classical type?

A basis for an affirmative answer to this question is suggested by some evident differences between the existentialist conception of ontology, and the classical conception that is best exemplified

---

[1] This point is repeatedly made by Heidegger as, for example, when he declares that "Dasein ist nie 'zunächst' ein gleichsam in-seins-freies Seiendes, das zuweilen die Laune hat, eine 'Beziehung' zur Welt aufzunehmen." *Sein und Zeit*, p. 57. See also pp. 60–62.

by Aristotle. As Aristotle defines it, ontology is the science of being and it comprises all the propositions that are true of a thing—any thing—simply by virtue of the fact that it *is*. Such propositions obviously enjoy an unrestricted universality since they hold for everything that exists; and the first ontological "truth" that Aristotle produces is the law of non-contradiction: "The same attribute cannot at the same time belong and not belong to the same subject and in the same respect."[2] In addition to unqualifiedly universal truths such as this one, Aristotle's ontology also comprises a concept of the nature of what exists as such. By an analysis of the different senses in which being may be predicated of a thing, he arrives at the conclusion that there is a mode of being that is presupposed by all the other modes of being, e.g., by qualitative and relational being. This is substantial being. Whatever is, either is a substance or is dependent for its being upon substance, and substance is what remains the same through time and is the bearer of attributes. In Aristotle's ontology, there are thus both a concept of what is as such—the concept of substance—and universal truths concerning what is. Within the category of substance, there are also all of the concepts of the different natural kinds (man, horse, etc.) into which individual substances are classified; and with each of these, there is associated a body of truths, the scope of which is restricted to things of that particular kind. These truths hold for those things, not simply by virtue of the fact that they *are,* but by virtue of the fact that they belong to a certain natural kind within the category of substance. Such truths are necessary; but they are not ontological truths in the strict sense Aristotle stipulated.

[2] *Metaphysics* iv. 3.1005^{b}18.
Once again, I must point out that my account of Aristotle's views by-passes difficult issues of interpretation which are not of central importance for my purposes. Two recent essays may be noted, however, both of which make interesting points about Aristotle's conception of ontology: D. M. MacKinnon, "Aristotle's Conception of Substance," and G. E. L. Owen, "Aristotle on the Snares of Ontology," both in R. Bambrough (ed.), *New Essays on Plato and Aristotle* (London: Routledge and Kegan Paul, 1965).
The former would seem to be in general agreement with the interpretation outlined here; while the latter questions in effect whether Aristotle ever held a view of ontology according to which "being" designates a common genus of some kind.

81

Ontology, in this monistic and universalistic sense, is at best an ideal in the writings of the existentialists. Sartre has explicitly declared that a unitary concept of being (which would be comparable to Aristotle's concept of substance) is unachievable; and while Heidegger still clings to the idea of a general ontology, he has never gone on to write the second part of *Sein und Zeit* in which he had proposed to construct one.[3] Unlike Aristotle, both writers make the initial assumption that there are at least two fundamentally different kinds of being; and both treat the possibility of an over-arching concept of being as a problem that must be postponed until one or both of these subordinate kinds of being has been subjected to a detailed examination. Furthermore, the kind of being that both choose to use as a clue to the nature of being in general is conscious, human being. While it is true that the conception of human being which the existentialists then elaborate can be fully understood only through a contrast with their conception of the being of things, it is also a fact that when they have attempted to go beyond these two sub-ontological concepts and such "regional" truths as may be coordinate with them, they have either lapsed into a mystical and incommunicable intuition of being as such, in the manner of the later Heidegger, or like Sartre, they have been led to the conclusion that a general ontology is impossible. In these circumstances, it seems plausible to suggest that what the existentialists have done is not to elaborate an ontology in the traditional sense just described, but rather to work out a concept of "human being" together with its polar concept "thing"; and that their writings should be read and judged as essays in the analysis of these concepts. To the extent that the existentialists' ontology remains irreducibly pluralistic, whether by intention or by default, its emphasis will inevitably fall on the differentiating features of human being. This

---

[3] See *L'Être et le néant*, pp. 711–720. ". . . il est impossible de passer de la notion d'être-en-soi à celle d'être-pour-soi et de les réunir en un genre commun . . . C'est cet échec qui explique le hiatus que nous rencontrons à la fois dans le concept de l'être et de l'existant." (p. 717) The use of the phrase "le concept de l'être" should be noted.
In his *La philosophie de Martin Heidegger* (Louvain: 1948), A. De Waehlens argues that it would in fact be impossible for Heidegger to construct a general ontology on the basis of his analysis of *Dasein*. See especially pp. 302 ff.

fact, by itself, makes it unlikely that the outcome of such analyses will be so purely "ontological" as to abstract entirely from the familiar characteristics by which human beings are identified. If so, and if a selection of certain traits as those that differentiate human being from other modes of being has to be made out of the common stock from which concepts of human being or human nature are normally drawn, it seems reasonable to expect that the novelty of such a reinterpretation would be due not to the introduction of wholly new and unfamiliar elements of human nature, but to the salience and delineation accorded to aspects of that nature with which we were, to be sure, antecedently familiar, but the centrality and importance of which we had not grasped.

To suggest that what the existentialists are proposing is a revised concept of human being may sound far-fetched to anyone who is even slightly familiar with the differences of ethos and methodology that separate the existentialists from the philosophers who describe their own work (and philosophy as a whole) as "conceptual analysis." The existentialists, after all, have been at great pains to distinguish the kind of thing they do from anything that could be characterized in the manner I have proposed; and they have had some harsh things to say about the practitioners of conceptual analysis.[4] Nevertheless, even in the face of these very serious objections, a case can be made for adopting this interpretation which associates two groups of philosophers with one another a good deal more closely than may be congenial to either group.

First, to the extent that this objection stems from an assumption that ontological questions are radically distinct from questions about the nature of our concepts it is itself highly vulnerable to criticism, for it is not just self-evident that "modes of being" and the familiar garden-variety of attribute are as radically different as it appears to be assumed.[5] If I contrast a stone

[4] In his recent autobiographical work, *Les Mots* (Paris: Gallimard, 1964) Sartre declares that he prefers detective stories of the "série noire" to Wittgenstein.

[5] Two works that cast light on the relation between ontology and conceptual systems are W. V. Quine, "On What There Is," in *From A Logical Point of View* (Cambridge, Mass.: Harvard University Press, 1953), pp. 1–19, and P.

with a human being, there are many obvious differences between them; and some of these will be derivable from the concepts "stone" and "human being." On the other hand, if for some reason I am not satisfied with this kind of contrast by means of observable properties, and propose to go deeper and contrast the "mode of being" of the one with that of the other, how am I to proceed? If a distinction not previously noticed is produced, how will it differ in principle from the other distinctions between the two kinds of object that are enshrined in the respective concepts, and why should it not be incorporated into those concepts? What finally is the relationship between the attributes normally used for identifying a thing, and those more elusive features which differentiate its *being* from the being of some other kind of thing? To these questions, the traditional distinction of being and essence on which the existentialists somewhat incautiously rely provides no answer since the notion of being has to be explained by contrasting the fact *that* a thing is with *what* it is (i.e., by contrasting its being with every possible attribute or essence that it might have). In these circumstances, to ask how the being of one kind of thing differs from that of another is to subvert the very distinction between being and essence itself because it amounts to asking for the essence of what by definition has no essence or attributes of any kind. It seems to follow that the existentialists are the victims of an elementary logical confusion, and that the inquiry that they initiate under such unhappy terminological auspices is condemned to failure from the very start.

Occasionally some existentialists have indicated an awareness that there is something peculiar about asking for the "essence of being," and have seemed to recognize that they are asking a question which is unanswerable, simply by virtue of their own way of defining the terms in which it is posed.[6] Significantly, however,

---

Strawson, *Individuals* (London: Methuen, 1959). The Introduction of the latter work is a defense of what Strawson calls "descriptive metaphysics," but metaphysics understood in this sense corresponds much more closely to what the existentialists call "ontology" than it does to the traditional metaphysics of which they disapprove.

[6] Both Heidegger and Sartre distinguish between "being" and the "meaning" or "sense" (*Sinn* and *sens*) of being. Thus Sartre declares that "c'est n'est pas dans sa qualite propre que l'être est relatif au pour-soi, ni dans

this awareness does not lead them to abandon that question. Instead, by making a distinction between being and the "meaning" or "sense" of being as it figures in human experience, they contrive to evade—at least verbally—the paradox noted above. While this maneuver may not have any great intrinsic merit, it does suggest that the paradox itself may be the result of a misleading description by the existentialists of what, in fact, they are doing when they ask questions about types of being. To ask a question about the mode of being of a thing would thus not really be a request for a characterization of what is in principle uncharacterizable, nor would a distinction between kinds of being be something utterly different from a conceptual distinction. Instead, I would argue that what the existentialists call an ontological distinction is simply a conceptual distinction which, either by reason of its importance, or a tendency to confuse it with others—or both—deserves special designation and separate treatment. Thus, many of the "structures" which these philosophers regard as fundamental to human being, such as our ability to make reference to past and future events for example, are not very naturally thought of as "attributes" or "properties" of the kind that typically appear in an inventory of what is contained in a concept. More generally, when we construct a list of the "attributes" that compose human nature, we may very well be influenced, without knowing it, by certain paradigms of attributehood which limit attributes to distinct, readily observable traits. The existentialist's point in describing such features of human being as "ontological" would thus be to remind us of the great

---

son être . . . mais c'est dans son "il y a," puisque dans sa négation interne le Pour-soi affirme ce qui ne peut s'affirmer, connait l'être tel qu'il est alors que le 'tel qu'il est' ne saurait appartenir à l'être." Similarly, when Heidegger says that his investigations are addressed to being itself, he significantly adds "insofern es in die Verständlichkeit des Daseins hereinsteht." (*Sein und Zeit*, p. 152.) About being as such neither philosopher has much to say and neither tries to give any definition of its "qualité propre" or "essence." About the "sense" of being, i.e., the structures distinctive of the human apprehension of being, they say a very great deal. In this connection, one should note Heidegger's reference to the "Abhängigkeit des Seins, nicht des Seienden, vom Seinsverständnis, das heisst die Abhängigkeit der Realität, nicht des Realen." (*Sein und Zeit*, p. 212.) This surely *sounds* as though "Sein" and "Realität" were being treated more like concepts than "predicates of being."

difference between the kind of attribute of human being in which he is interested, and the paradigm cases of attributehood which, for most of us, are probably colors or shapes.[7] There is, to be sure, a price to be paid in confusion when our attention is drawn to this distinction by contrasting a certain feature of human existence with all of the "essential" properties that a thing might have when, in fact, both are repeatable or sharable characteristics of human beings. A judgment on the validity of such a terminological strategy must depend in the end on the interest and elucidatory power of the conceptual revisions in which it issues.

One further point: the fact that the structures of human existence are repeatable, and in that sense universal characteristics, is amply demonstrated by the fact that they constitute the mode of being peculiar to a certain *kind* of being that the existentialists are interested in. If it were the being of particular individual existents that concerned them, they would have no reason to think that any set of conclusions that might emerge from their ontologizing would have a range of application wider than the one individual they had analyzed. In fact, the importance that these philosophers attach to their results, and their belief that these are applicable to *all* human beings, and are in fact definitive of what it is to be a human being, are quite inconsistent with any such interpretation of what they are doing. But if the "structures" of human being are to be thought of as defining a class of entities—human beings—then there can be no valid objection to saying that they form part, at least, of the concept of human being, and that the analysis of such structures is a form of conceptual analysis.[8]

[7] Heidegger often makes pointed contrasts between the structures of human existence and the ordinary philosophical notion of properties (*Eigenschaften*). See *Sein und Zeit*, pp. 42, 83, 133.

[8] For an explicit recognition of this element of universality in his analyses of "la réalité humaine," see *L'Être et le néant*, p. 533, where Sartre speaks of the "invariables structures (qui) constituent la réalité humaine." See also *L'Existentialisme est un humanisme*, pp. 67–69, for a discussion of what Sartre calls the "universalité humaine de condition" as distinct from an "essence universelle qui serait la nature humaine." Heidegger's views on "apriorisch-ontologische Verallgemeinerung" are stated in *Sein und Zeit*, p. 199; further discussions of "das Wesen" of *Dasein* and of man can be found on p. 42 of that work, and in *Über den Humanismus*, pp. 14, 15.

In this connection, it may be useful to take note of an apparent inconsistency in the thought of the existentialists to which I will have occasion to return later. There is scarcely any traditional metaphysical doctrine to which the existentialists are more strongly opposed than the Aristotelian theory of natural kinds, which was discussed in an earlier chapter. This is the view that every substance has a nature in the sense of a central core of characteristics that make it the thing it is, quite independently of the conventional criteria of identification that may be laid down in our language. Against this view, the existentialists have defended a strongly pragmatic account of the way in which human beings classify and identify elements in their environment; and they have presented this capacity for shifting from one method of identification to another as fundamental to human being.[9] When

[9] One of the most significant steps in the development of existential phenomenology is the dropping of Husserl's theory of essential intuition (*Wesenschau*) and of the language that is suggested by that theory. Husserl had held not only that particular objects are the bearers of universal essences that can be grasped as such through a particular mode of intuition but also that the fact that a certain quality is the essence of a certain object is independent of and prior to the system of classification reflected in our language for talking about such objects. (See "Philosophie als Strenge Wissenschaft," *Logos*, Vol. 1 [1910–11], pp. 289–341, especially p. 305 and pp. 314–19.) Merleau-Ponty's comments on this doctrine can be found in his "Phenomenology and the Sciences of Man," *The Primacy of Perception*, ed. J. Edie (Evanston, Ill.: Northwestern University Press, 1964, pp. 64–78).

Heidegger, by treating our apprehension of "things-in-the world" as shot through with practical intentions which in turn reflect the self-determined interests and purposes of *Dasein*, substitutes what is in many respects a highly pragmatic account of our identification of things for Husserl's intellectualistic doctrine of prelinguistic essences. See Heidegger's characterization of the "Als-struktur" in *Sein und Zeit*, pp. 148 ff. "Die Auslegung von Etwas als Etwas wird wesenhaft durch Vorhabe, Vorsicht und Vorgriff fundiert. Auslegung ist nie ein voraus-setzungloses Erfassung eines Vorgegebenen." (p. 150) Sartre's conception of language which appears to be based largely on Heidegger's, places strong emphasis on both the role of language as the medium of intersubjectivity and on the constitutive function of the *Pour-soi* in relation to the meanings it employs. In his essay, "Aller et Retour," *Situations* I (Paris: 1947), pp. 189–244, Sartre conveys something of his view of language as, for example, when he says that "le langage peut me resister, m'égarer mais je n'en serai jamais dupe que si je le veux, car j'ai la possibilité de revenir toujours à ce que je suis, à ce vide, à ce silence que je suis, par quoi cependant il y a un language et il y a un monde." (p. 236) Other statements on the subject of language can be found in *L'Être et le néant*, pp. 596 ff., and in "Qu'est ce que la littérature," *Situations* II (Paris, 1948), pp. 59 ff.

it comes to determining criteria for the concept of human being itself, however the existentialists prove to be decidedly rigid about the centrality of these capacities that they propose to build into the concept of "human being," and, in fact, seem to be presenting something very much more like a real definition in the Aristotelian sense than would have seemed likely after their strenuous resistance to the "essentialism" implicit in such a doctrine. Once again, one may conjecture that what the existentialists have presented as a rejection of all attempts to define a human essence or nature is really a rejection of certain stereotypes that would construe human nature on the basis of a narrowly conceived model in which certain important human capacities find no really satisfactory representation. What they are most deeply interested in is a loosening-up of such stereotypes that would permit the formation of a more adequate concept of human being, and not a paradoxical denial that any such concept can be formed. This interpretation still leaves an unresolved question with respect to the manner—realistic or nominalistic or whatever—in which such determinations of this concept are to be understood. But it gives us what is sufficient at this point in the argument: A way of construing what the existentialists have to say in these matters that is not obviously self-contradictory and that establishes a relationship between what they do and familiar philosophical practice.

There is another important consideration that speaks in favor of the interpretation that I have proposed. It is sometimes supposed that the characterization the existentialists offer of human being has no empirical basis and that their "ontological structures" must be apprehended by a special mode of intuition that has no affinity with any other kind of knowledge that we may have of ourselves. While some passages in their writings may lend support to this interpretation, the actual practice of the existentialists reveals a much closer relationship between their ontological analyses and the "natural" activities and powers of human beings as these are known to everyday observation and to the sciences of man. Even when Sartre, for example, is most violently critical of the scientific method of studying human beings, he is objecting to what he regards as a positivistic refusal to recognize the fact that the value of scientific results is heavily dependent on the adequacy of the conceptual—he would say "ontological"—scheme, in terms of which they are stated.[10] On more than one occasion he explicitly presents the analyses of Husserl and Heidegger as providing a conceptual system that would be at once a corrective for the indiscriminate "empiricism," i.e. anti-conceptualism, of contemporary psychology and anthropology, and a superior instrument for use in further scientific inquiry. Certainly, in existentialism as a whole there is an anti-scientific bias that cannot be reduced to a criticism of current scientific practice for its alleged failure to do justice to the role of conceptual schemes in inquiry. Nevertheless, it remains true that what the existentialists speak of as the structures of our being are not the objects of an isolated quasi-mystical intuition, but the conceptual-ontological framework which, in their view, is best suited to the understanding and statement of what are called the empirical facts of human life.

There are also clear indications in the writings of Heidegger and Sartre and others that the conceptual scheme they propose is not only designed for the purpose of more effective re-statement of what we know about ourselves, but has empirical roots itself. In other words, it is a generalization or projection upon the whole sphere of human experience, of ideas that were first developed to deal with certain restricted areas of that experience, in which they still find their most natural application. To be sure, the existentialists do not all draw on the same sources for clues to the general character of human functioning. In Heidegger's case, it is unquestionably language that serves as the touchstone for human being as a whole, to the point where he is willing to say that "we are what we say to one another."[11] Language is the quint-

---

[10] See Sartre's *Esquisse d'une théorie des émotions* (2d ed.; Paris: Hermann, 1948), pp. 3–13.

[11] *Hölderlin und das Wesen der Dichtung* (München: Albert Langen/George Müller, 1937), p. 6. Heidegger's most important discussion of language and speech is in *Sein und Zeit*, pp. 160–170. On p. 161, he declares that "als existenziale Verfassung der Erschlossenheit des Daseins ist die Rede konstitutiv für dessen Existenz." He adds, later: "Der Mensch zeigt sich als Seiendes, das redet. Das bedeutet nicht, dass ihm die Möglichkeit der stimmlichen Verlautbarung eignet, sondern dass dieses Seiende ist in der Weise des Entdeckens der Welt und des Daseins selbst." (p. 165)

essentially human activity, and much of what Heidegger says about human existence is intelligible only if one keeps in mind that he is talking, in the first instance, about linguistic activity. Sartre, too, has often taken some feature of linguistic behavior as his point of departure as for example, in his long analysis of negation at the beginning of *Being and Nothingness*.[12] In his work, however, the role of perceptual consciousness as a model to be used for the understanding of human being in general is at least as important as that of language. Again, in the early writings of Maurice Merleau-Ponty the "primacy of perception" was unambiguously asserted.[13] These examples do not show that the leading concepts of these philosophers are validated simply by having an empirical model, since it is quite possible that the applicability of these concepts, even to the restricted area from which they are drawn, needs to be challenged. But their special relationship to such sub-areas of human experience does constitute strong evidence that they are put forward, not as special and unchallengeable intuitions, but as instruments for the description of the human fact. As such, they are deserving of the same kind of assessment as are the less ambitious extended-metaphors which have on different occasions turned out to be both intensely illuminating and profoundly misleading in the history of the natural and the humane sciences.[14]

Unfortunately, the existentialists themselves have not made it easy to interpret and appraise their ideas in this way. While there can be no doubt that their theses have often been suggested by—and applied retroactively to—matters of empirical fact, there are very few sign-posts on the logical route that leads from the one to the other. Instead of sign-posts, there are pictures—the meta-

---

[12] *L'Être et le néant*, ch. I, Pt. I, especially pp. 40–47.

[13] See his "Le primat de la perception et ses conséquences philosophiques," *Bulletin de la Societé Francaise de Philosophie,* Vol. 41 (1947), pp. 119–53. Also to be found in J. Edie (trans.) , *The Primacy of Perception* (Evanston, Ill.: Northwestern University Press, 1964) , pp. 12–42.

[14] Two recent studies in which the uses of metaphor in the natural sciences and critical theory respectively are explored are N. R. Hanson, *Patterns of Discovery* (Cambridge, Eng.: Cambridge University Press, 1958) , and M. Abrams, *The Mirror and the Lamp* (New York: Oxford University Press, 1953) .

phors that are strewn through the texts of these philosophers—
and these pictures pose as many difficulties of interpretation as do
the very abstract ideas which they are supposed to make more
perspicuous. Sartre, for example, describes what he calls the
"human reality" by means of a great variety of metaphors which
represent consciousness as a crevice, a mirror, and a "worm coiled
in the heart of being," to mention just a few. Heidegger, too, by
his heavy stress on the etymologies of abstract words establishes a
close connection between his ontological terminology and certain
highly specific images.[15] The suggestive power of these images,
which is often considerable, is due, of course, to the very concreteness and specificity that makes it difficult to extract from them
the distinguishing traits of the whole range of human activities
which they are evidently intended to sum up. Similar difficulties
sometimes arise in connection with the pictorial models used by
physical theories, but there, the theorist usually calls attention to
the metaphorical character of his description and points out
which of the implications that the picture may seem to carry are
adventitious and irrelevant to the special use to which it is being
put. Such directions are not provided by the existentialists who
rarely seem to be aware of the metaphorical character of many of
their ideas, and certainly are not in any way disturbed by it.

There is a deeper philosophical reason for this tendency to
apply to the structures of consciousness terms that are drawn
from our own vocabulary for describing concrete things and
events. Consistently with their commitment to the ontological
mode, the existentialists hold that the concepts of being and
non-being cannot be reduced to the status of logical operators
functioning within a language system, and must instead be

---

[15] The best example of this tendency is Heidegger's breaking-up of the term
"Dasein" to yield "Da-sein" which permits him to say such things as "(das
Dasein) ist in der Weise sein Da zu sein." Heidegger has also extended this
treatment to Greek words like "a-letheia" and "ek-stasis" and has been
severely criticized for seeking to suggest by these means that the early Greek
philosophers were expressing insights similar to his own. In *Sein und Zeit,*
this etymologizing is still under control, but in more recent works like
Einführung in die Metaphysik (Tübingen: Niemeyer, 1953) it has become
altogether too prominent a feature of Heidegger's style of writing and
thinking.

thought of as being themselves descriptive in nature, i.e., as having a counterpart *in re*.[16] This view may be quite innocuous so long as it is understood that it is precisely through our use of the concepts of existence and possibility and other cognate concepts that our commerce with their extra-logical counterparts is effected. Too often, however, philosophers who hold such views have yielded to the temptation to look for other, more direct, and above all, more dramatic characterizations of the referents of "is" and "not." This search for a description of being that bypasses the logical articulation of the concept of being produces metaphors of the kind noted above, which often have the effect of suggesting that our "encounter with being" has a quasi-perceptual concreteness about it of which the logical structure of the verb "to be" is at its best a very pallid and distant replica.[17] Too often, the existentialists have been guilty of undercutting their own best inspiration in this way, and have had to pay a high price in

[16] It should be pointed out, of course, that in the case of the existentialists the "counterpart" is the ontological structure of human existence and not, as in the case of the classical ontologists, the ontological structure of the things that language can be used to talk about, or at any rate not the latter in isolation from the former.

Sartre's views on this matter are clearly stated in *L'Être et le néant*, pp. 40–47. For him the decisive argument against a purely judgmental interpretation of negation is the fact that while a question is formulated in an "interrogative judgment" it is not itself a judgment. "C'est une conduite préjudicative; je peux interroger du regard, du geste; par l'interrogation je me tiens d'une certaine manière en face de l'être et ce rapport à l'être est un rapport d'être, le jugement n'en est que l'expression facultative." (p. 42)

Heidegger's conception of the relationship between logical functions of judgment and ontology are set forth in *Sein und Zeit*, pp. 153–60. Elsewhere in that work ontology is contrasted with both logic and the analysis of the conceptual structure of the different types of knowledge, and of course with the positive sciences themselves. (p. 10) See also, *Was Ist Metaphysik* (7th ed.; Frankfurt: Klostermann, 1955) where Heidegger unequivocally declares "das Nichts" to be "ursprünglicher als das Nicht und die Verneinung." (p. 28)

[17] The outstanding example of this attempt to convey the "experience of being" is undoubtedly Sartre's early novel, *La Nausée* (Paris: Gallimard, 1938), especially pp. 62–67. While Sartre's descriptions have an undeniable power, it is worth noting that he does feel the need to introduce explicitly philosophical notions such as that of contingency to interpret the experience he is seeking to render.

Heidegger's doctrine of *Befindlichkeit* moves along much the same lines. Various *Stimmungen*, such as fear and anxiety, are said to reveal both being and non-being. See *Sein und Zeit*, pp. 134–42, and pp. 189–91; also, *Was Ist Metaphysik*, pp. 28–35.

misunderstanding and hasty rejection of their views. There is a special irony in this, since it is in fact one of the achievements of existentialism to have drawn attention to and strongly emphasized precisely the "act" or "performance" aspect of language which is effectively suppressed when an exclusively descriptive theory of concepts is adopted.

It is always dangerous to claim to know how a writer or group of writers should ideally have formulated their own views, or to show that these were seriously distorted by the method they actually used. Nevertheless, it is the contention of this study that the adoption of the ontological mode has had a distorting effect upon the philosophizing of the existentialists, and that their position is better presented when its leading ideas are construed as a new mode of conceptual organization for the knowledge we already have about human beings, and not as descriptive of ontological counterparts whose activities are at best faintly manifested by those human activities to which we do have empirical access. What I am proposing is not that existentialism should drop all reference to being and existence, nor that it must explicitly translate all the propositions in which these terms occur into the "formal mode" (i.e., into statements about the concepts of "being" and "existence") ; but rather that it give up the hopeless task of providing an independent description of that which is denoted by these concepts. Even if these concepts are denotative or descriptive in character, it would be reasonable to assume that an analysis of the way they function and of the logical peculiarities that set them apart from other descriptive concepts would be a better guide to the "essence of human being" than any set of metaphors that by-passes language entirely or does only very partial justice to it. In any case it is clear that these pictures themselves are in need of interpretation and that they can be interpreted only in the light of the very concept of human being which they are intended to elucidate. It has been assumed too often, by both the existentialists and their commentators, that their key-metaphors are self-interpreting. The contention of this study, by contrast, is that only an interpretation that makes the concept of human being the central theme of Heidegger's and Sartre's thought, and assigns a strictly subordinate place to the metaphors

associated with the concept gives it a chance of holding its own in the face of serious philosophical criticism.

Fortunately, it is not necessary to put forward this interpretation of existentialist ontology simply as a forceful accommodation of alien modes of thought to an approved conception of philosophical method. In the writings of Maurice Merleau-Ponty, one finds a conception of human consciousness and action that in its essentials is very similar to that of Heidegger and Sartre, and yet remains largely unencumbered by the special ontological vocabulary of these writers.[18] To say that Merleau-Ponty was engaged in conceptual analysis would be to strain the meaning this expression has acquired in the English-speaking world. He certainly did not think that philosophical analysis should limit itself to sorting out the established meanings of words, and in this respect was much closer to that wing of the analytic movement that defines its objective as the revision of our conceptual system, rather than as the description of its present state. But if conceptual analysis is so defined as to permit innovation and revision, and if the subject matter of the analysis is not merely linguistic behavior in some highly restrictive sense, then there is no justification for any absolute distinction between this mode of philosophizing and much that is familiar in the English-speaking world. Most importantly, the standard Merleau-Ponty himself proposes for judging philosophical analyses is pragmatic and not ontological—"their richness, what they yield to us, the way they organize our field of thought."[19] Unfortunately, ethical theory is only very sparsely represented in the main body of his work, although even the brief remarks he makes are highly suggestive as there will be occasion to demonstrate in later chapters.

[18] This statement must be qualified somewhat in light of the fact that the fragments of the work Merleau-Ponty was working on at the time of his death, now published as Le visible et l'invisible (Paris: Gallimard, 1964) make clear his intention to supply the ontological foundations for his earlier phenomenological studies.

[19] This quotation is taken from Merleau-Ponty's comments on a paper by Professor Gilbert Ryle which was presented at a colloquium held at Royaumont in 1957. The papers presented to an audience of Continental (mainly French) philosophers have been published in La philosophie analytique, Colloque philosophique de Royaumont, Cahiers de Philosophie, No. 4 (Paris: Editions de Minuit, 1962). Merleau-Ponty's remarks are on pp. 93–96.

II

Against this background, it should now be possible to clarify certain features of the existentialist concept of human being. First, it needs to be pointed out that the account that Heidegger and Sartre give of human nature is ontological in a double sense.[20] They undertake to give a definition of the mode of being of man, and this mode of being is then characterized as a certain relation to being and non-being. In Heidegger's terminology, man is "ontic-ontological": he exists as a being who sustains a relationship to being. If the method of interpretation of ontological theses that I have been proposing is to be applicable, there must correspond to this doubly ontological definition of man a concept of human being which has, as its principal criterion of applicability, not a relationship to being but the possession and use of a concept—the concept of being. The concept of man that the existentialists are proposing thus emerges as the concept of a user of certain concepts, specifically the concepts of being and of non-being or possibility. What this comes to is the assertion that human nature is to be defined by reference to a specific feature of the conceptual system that human beings use, and that is judged to be of such fundamental importance for the understanding of that system as a whole and of the creatures that use it that we are justified in incorporating it into our concept of them. What Heidegger and Sartre express in the material mode by saying, respectively, that possibility is the fundamental existential trait of *Da-*

[20] "Das Dasein ist ein Seiendes, das nicht nur unter anderem Seienden vorkommt. Es ist vielmehr dadurch ontisch ausgezeichnet, dass es diesem Seienden in seinem Sein um dieses Sein selbst geht. Zu dieser Seinsverfassung des Daseins gehört aber dann, dass es in seinem Sein zu diesem Sein ein Seinsverhältnis hat. Und dies wiederum besagt: Dasein versteht sich in irgendeiner Weise und Ausdrücklichkeit in seinem Sein. Diesem Seiendem eignet, dass mit und durch sein Sein dieses ihm selbst erschlossen ist. *Seinsverständnis ist selbst eine Seinsbestimmtheit des Daseins.* Die ontische Auszeichnung des Daseins liegt darin, dass es ontologisch ist." (*Sein und Zeit,* p. 12.) "Certes, nous pourrions appliquer à la conscience la définition que Heidegger réserve au Dasein et dire qu'elle est un être pour lequel il est dans son être question de son être, mais il faudrait la compléter et la formuler à peu près ainsi: *la conscience est un être pour lequel il est dans son être question de son être en tant que cet être implique un être autre que lui.*" (*L'Être et le néant,* p. 29.)

sein and that human consciousness is nothingness, passes over into the conceptualistic mode as the statement that human beings are, by definition, beings that can make the contrast between what is (contingently) the case and what is not the case but might (possibly) become actual.

In saying that the relationship human beings sustain to being is to be interpreted as the possession and use of the concept of being, I am not forgetting the importance of perceptual consciousness as a model of that relationship. To be sure, the account that is given of perception by both Sartre and Merleau-Ponty portrays it as an encounter with something that is wholly unconceptualizable—an irreducible surd which stands over against human consciousness and can never be assimilated to the status of a term of thought. This sounds very much as though any attempt to analyze this encounter as an application of the concept of being would be ruled out in advance. In fact, however, the point Sartre and Merleau-Ponty are making is not that there can be no concept of being—for taken literally this would cut the ground out from under their own philosophical discourse about being—but rather that this concept does not lend itself to a reductive phenomenalistic analysis.[21] They are saying that any attempt to equate the being of a material object with the "possibility of sensation" or with the availability of sense-data must fail. Since they tend to think of concepts as terms of thought whose content can be spelled out in this way, they sometimes express this view by saying that existence cannot be conceptualized. But if the notion of a concept itself is not used in such a restrictive way, and if anything we can talk about is to that degree conceptualizable, it becomes not only permissible but important and true to say that human perceptual consciousness involves, whether explicitly or implicitly, a use of the concept of being.[22] It is important because the distinctive feature of human perceptual consciousness is not just awareness of objects—animals presumably have that—but of objects conceptualized in a certain way. They are perceived as what contingently exists and in contrast to what might (possibly) exist but in fact does not; and this is to say that even in

21 See ch. 4, n. 2.
22 See *Sein und Zeit*, p. 149.

96

the case of perception the human relationship to being is mediated by concepts. Human beings are thus the beings that are able to view things *sub specie possibilitatis*—that "possibilify" the world—and the capability for this kind of conceptualization is a condition of what the existentialists have in mind when they call human being a *Sein-können* or *pouvoir-être*.[23]

It is important to take note of a number of distinctions which Heidegger makes in connection with this "existential" sense of "possibility." It is not to be confused with logical possibility or the "merely possible," and the most obvious basis for this distinction is the fact that existential possibility is limited in various ways that have nothing to do with the presence of internal contradictions.[24] I interpret this to mean that what is existentially possible represents a certain sub-class of the actions that are consistently imaginable in a certain situation—the sub-class, namely, that includes those actions which there is some reason on the basis of what I know about the world to think I could accomplish. Out of the non-being with which everything that is is contrasted there emerge certain effective possibilities which are *mine,* and among which I have to choose. The possible is what I can do; and Heidegger's point may be expressed as the view that the use of "can" in statements of the form "I can . . ." is unique and irreducible to any set of hypotheticals in which the causal relation-

---

[23] There are many discussions throughout *Sein und Zeit* of the central importance of possibility to *Dasein*. The following statements are typical:

Das "Wesen" des Daseins liegt in seiner Existenz. Die an diesem Seienden herausstellbaren Charaktere sind daher nicht vorhandene "Eigenschaften" eines so und so "aussehenden" vorhandenen Seienden, sondern je ihm mögliche Weisen zu sein und nur das. (p. 42) Dasein ist nicht ein Vorhandenes, das als Zugabe noch besitzt, etwas zu können, sondern est ist primär Möglichsein. Dasein ist je das, was es sein kann und wie es seine Möglichkeit ist. (p. 143)

The role of the notion of possibility is thoroughly explored in W. Müller-Lauter, *Möglichkeit und Wirklichkeit bei Martin Heidegger* (Berlin: De Gruyter, 1960) . Sartre's most direct treatment of the concept of possibility is in *L'Être et le néant,* pp. 139–47. See also *L'Imagination* (Paris: Alcan, 1936.) , pp. 227–39.

[24] See, for example, *Vom Wesen des Grundes,* pp. 46–47. "Damit sind dem Dasein bereits andere Möglichkeiten—und zwar lediglich durch seine Faktizität—entzogen."

ships between certain types of events are set forth.[25] It is, of course, no part of the existentialist analysis of possibility to deny that "possibility" has a proper application to things, or to turn the causal powers of things into subjective inventions of the human mind. What both Heidegger and Sartre *are* saying is that the concept of (as they call it) modal or categorial possibility which applies to things as distinct from persons is ontologically posterior to the sense of possibility that applies to the person who makes this judgment with respect to things. This view is perfectly consistent with our being quite narrowly circumscribed in what we can actually do so long as there is in any given situation more than one action that we can take. In one sense, the effect of this view is to make certain important features of our conceptual system dependent on the fact that we are active creatures. On the other hand, the notion of activity that is being used here is one that cannot be explicated otherwise than by referring to the use we make of the concepts of possibility and reality. What this comes to is the view that the ability to make these distinctions is so closely bound up with our nature as human beings as to be consubstantial with it and that a being that did not (or could not) make them would be so unimaginably different from us that it could scarcely be regarded as human at all.

Human being, according to the existentialists, is "Being-in-the-world"; and they are at great pains to underline the very special sense of "in" that is used in this expression, and to distinguish it from the "in" of spatial inclusion that applies to physical objects.[26] In seeking for a positive interpretation of the sense in which human beings are in the world, many critics have been misled, by the figurative language the existentialists too often use, into imputing to them a doctrine that makes human consciousness a strange wraith-like or pneumatic being that curls itself

[25] For a treatment of "can" by an analytical philosopher which comes to conclusions that are in many respects similar to Heidegger's, see R. Taylor, "I Can," *Philosophical Review* LXIX (1960), pp. 78–89. Also of interest in this connection is J. L. Austin, "Ifs and Cans" in his *Philosophical Papers* (Oxford: Clarendon Press, 1961), pp. 153–80.

[26] Heidegger's discussion can be found in *Sein und Zeit*, pp. 52–62. It is not too much to say that the whole of this book is an explication of the sense of "in" that properly applies to human beings in their relation to the "world."

around the edges of the world. In fact, the sense in which human beings are "in" the world can be accurately explained only by reference to the use of the concepts of being and possibility by which the human apprehension of things is mediated. The "world" that human beings are "in" is not the Cartesian world of *res extensae,* although it is equally important to understand that they are not outside physical space either, in the way disembodied spirits may be supposed to be. The case is rather that human beings are in the world in the sense of being confronted with things, but they are not in the world in the way things are, since they are able to refer beyond things-in-being to what is not the case. Thus the human "world," in this special sense, is compounded of actuality and possibility and exists only for a being that uses these concepts. When the existentialists say that human being is different from the being of things, they are saying simply that it is human beings who set up the contrast between things—what is—and what is not but could possibly come to be, i.e., non-being. The "distance" that human beings get on things is not a real distance—the kind of distance that separates things from one another—and not even a spooky kind of non-physical distance, but rather the perspectival distance that is implicit in all objectification and conceptualization.[27] Human consciousness "holds itself out into non-being" or is itself non-being just in the sense that its fundamental mode of conceptualization, dominating all the endless ramifications of the classificatory schemes it elaborates for "things in the world," involves this contrast between what is contingently the case and what might possibly be the case. Man is the being through whom not just sin but being and possibility came into the "world."

From what has been said, it should be clear in what sense facticity and transcendence are the two poles of human existence. By the former term, Heidegger means to convey the fact that human consciousness opens upon a world of things that exist contingently, and that their contingency is final and irreducible.[28] Since

[27] Heidegger associates transcendence closely with objectification and what he calls "Thematisierung" although he denies that transcendence *is* either of these. Instead, it is presupposed by them. (See *Sein und Zeit,* p. 363.)

[28] "Der Begriff der Faktizität beschliesst in sich: das In-der-Welt-sein eines 'innerweltlichen' Seienden, so zwar, dass sich dieses Seiende verstehen kann als

this reference to contingent being is not an accidental or elimin-
able feature of conscious human being, the latter necessarily
shares the same status of "brute factuality" which it confers upon
things by its mode of conceptualization. But at the same time as
it opens upon a situation that just is what it happens to be,
human being transcends it by interpreting it in terms of the alternative possibilities it suggests. Since such possibilities are possibilities of human action, this transcendence is always temporally oriented toward the future in which these possible actions may be
carried out. Once again, this transcendence or "ecstasis" is not to
be understood as some mysterious ability to get out of the present
into another point in time, much less into an altogether timeless
world. Instead, it is simply the ability to see "facts" in a temporal
context, to refer to the future and the past, and to have in this
sense a temporal horizon that animals and God possibly lack.

Readers of Heidegger and Sartre are often puzzled by the fact
that they speak of human being or existence as though it were an
activity or on-going function of some kind. But if the distinctive
capability of human beings is a capability for using certain concepts, as I have argued, then this way of speaking loses a good
deal of its paradoxical quality. A deployment of this capability
through a continuous reading of the world in terms of the concepts of contingent being and possibility—what Heidegger calls
Verstehen[29]—may indeed be regarded as an activity of a kind al-

---

in seinem 'Geschick' verhaftet mit dem Sein des Seienden, das ihm innerhalb
seiner eigenen Welt begegnet." (*Sein und Zeit*, p. 56.)

[29] This very important Heideggerian concept should not be confused with
the type of *Verstehen* with which the name of W. Dilthey is inseparably
associated. The latter, which is often misunderstood by its critics, represented
Dilthey's conception of the way we understand the historical and social world
while Heidegger's *Verstehen* designates the fundamental human activity of
giving sense and meaning to the "world" and is a matter of choosing and
projecting goals rather than one of gaining intuitive insight into the patterns
of meaning in the life of another person.

Das Verstehen (hat) an ihm selbst die existenziale Struktur die wir den
Entwurf nennen. Es entwirft das Sein des Daseins auf sein Worumwillen
ebenso ursprünglich wie auf die Bedeutsamkeit als die Weltlichkeit seiner
jeweiligen Welt . . . Das Verstehen ist, als Entwerfen, die Seinsart des
Daseins, in der es seine Möglichkeiten als Möglichkeiten *ist*. (*Sein und
Zeit*, p. 145.)

though it is, of course, different in important respects from other activities such as, for example, doing calisthenics. The principal agency through which this activity is carried on is language as Heidegger is at great pains to make clear. He is even willing to go so far as to say that "speech as an existential condition of the openness of *Dasein* is constitutive of its existence."[30] This amounts to saying that distinctively human activity is discursive activity. Typically this conceptualizing activity takes the form of projecting relationships from what is to what might possibly be. Thus, we see a given object as a hammer, i.e., as something we might use to build a house, and the meaningfulness or intelligibility of things—what Heidegger calls their *Sinn*—is just the network of such projections which are fundamental to all types of discourse, both cognitive and evaluative, although, as will appear later, they function in importantly different ways in the two cases.[31]

There is one important qualification that must be associated with this conceptualistic version of existentialist ontology that I am proposing. I have already indicated that there is a substantial disagreement among philosophers as to the relation of concepts to the world and that the existentialists belong to the party that insists that there must be extra-logical counterparts for concepts like being and non-being. I have argued that this disagreement need not preclude the possibility of translating from one idiom into the other. There is another disagreement however, bearing on the nature of concepts that is closely relevant to the notion of "having a concept," and must therefore be touched on here. The question at issue is not so much whether "having a concept" is solely a matter of linguistic capability and performance as whether, to the extent that it is, it is susceptible of a purely behavioristic analysis. To both of these questions, Heidegger has given a resoundingly negative answer, although the question naturally arises for him as one about structures of human being, and not about anything that he is willing to call "concepts." The

---

[30] *Sein und Zeit,* p. 161.

[31] For a very eloquent evocation of the relational character of human existence, see M. Merleau-Ponty, *Phénoménologie de la Perception* (Paris: Gallimard, 1945) , p. 520.

view that the possession of a concept can be manifested in non-linguistic ways is one that is widely accepted and indeed obviously true; and it is worth mentioning only because both Heidegger and Sartre are apparently led to think that their ontological structures cannot be forms of conceptual organization by virtue of a one-sided interpretation of the nature of concepts from which it follows that anything that has pre- or extra-linguistic manifestations must be more than or different from a concept.[32] But even after this difficulty is removed, the fact remains that "having a concept" or using language generally is not, according to the existentialists, susceptible of a reductive behavioristic analysis. As Heidegger says, "philosophical inquiry must eventually decide to face the question about the mode of being that is proper to language . . . (whether) it is stuff (*Zeug*) that is at hand 'in the world' or whether it has the mode of being of *Dasein*."[33] The importance of this choice is due to the fact that if the second alternative (which

---

[32] It is an interesting fact that the term "concept" occurs infreqently in the writings of the existentialists who regularly prefer terms like "essence," probably because "concept" continues to have psychologistic connotations for them as it had for Husserl. (See *Ideas,* p. 89–90.) At the same time, they are eager to avoid the Platonistic commitments of "essence"; one wonders whether the intermediate notion they are seeking to enunciate is not very close to the non-mentalistic notion of a concept. To be sure, the natural habitat of a concept is a judgment; but the fact that, as Sartre points out, there can be non-judgmental modes of expressing, e.g., a negation does not seem to require that we adopt in place of "concept" a term like "essence," whose natural associations are in many ways directly antithetical to the point the existentialists are making. What that point is may be suggested by an early essay of Sartre's, "M. Jean Giraudoux et la philosophie d'Aristote," *Situations I* (Paris: Gallimard, 1947). After describing Jean Giraudoux as an "Aristotelian" dramatist whose characters all seem to have fixed "natural" essences, Sartre concedes that sometimes our experience of people and things does really seem to fit the Aristotelian picture of the world. Then he goes on to say that this is really an illusion, because "ce que je saisis sur les trottoirs, sur la chaussée, sur les façades des immeubles, c'est uniquement le concept de rue, tel que depuis longtemps déjà je le possède. Impression de connaître sans connaissance, intuition de la Necessité—sans necessité. Ce concept humain que la rue, que la soirée réfléchissent comme des miroirs m'éblouit et m'empêche de voir leur sens inhumain, leur sourire de choses, humble et tenace." Here, Sartre seems to be saying that what we tend to think of as natural and fixed essences are really so many conceptual configurations; and it is interesting to note that he denies that in perceiving these natures we are knowing anything other than ourselves.

[33] *Sein und Zeit,* p. 166.

is clearly Heidegger's) is taken, then the nature of language and linguistic activity can be understood only by applying to them the very ontological concepts which, I have argued, stand in need of clarification. Since this clarification is one that they can receive, on the view I have proposed, only by being understood as a very abstract rendering of our mode of linguistic and conceptual functioning, there is here a kind of vicious circle. The resistance of the existentialists to an interpretation of their theses through a non-ontological theory of language or conceptualization is due mainly to a belief that such a theory will turn out to be behavioristic in character; and virtually all of the existentialists are united in the belief that no such theory can satisfactorily construct, simply in terms of relationships between physical events, the dimension of intentional reference of words to objects. Nevertheless, while conceding that these differences of opinion as to the nature of concepts and the criteria of "having a concept" are important, one may also point out that there are many nonexistentialist philosophers who do not think that a completely behavioristic theory of intentional reference or of conceptual and judgmental activity generally is possible.[34] Furthermore, it would seem that questions about how the concept of human being should be constructed, and whether the criteria proposed by the existentialists are good ones are substantially independent of the question of what "having a concept"—any concept—is.

Perhaps this very rough sketch of the concept of human being that emerges from the analyses of Heidegger and Sartre will at least suffice to indicate the general way in which the method of interpretation I am proposing might be applied to some of their major theses. The great weakness that is common to the philosophical writings of both of these men is that they develop a new and difficult set of concepts for talking about human beings and their condition without taking sufficient care to explain the relationship between these new concepts and our more familiar ways of talking about these matters. They do, however, give indications of the more familiar and empirical human activities that

[34] See, for example, H. H. Price, *Thinking and Experience* (Cambridge, Mass.: Harvard University Press, 1953), chs. 6 and 11; and C. Taylor, *The Explanation of Behavior* (London: Routledge and Kegan Paul, 1964), ch. 3.

have served as models for their general concepts of human being, and I have argued that these clues can be developed in such a way as to yield an intelligible account of what these writers are doing. One might even go so far as to say that in one sense what they are saying about human beings is not only intelligible but obviously true. Neither Heidegger nor Sartre, after all, is defending any speculative thesis about human beings. They are merely focusing our attention on features of our common situation that are so primordially familiar that in the ordinary course of things they seem scarcely worth commenting on. It is, to be sure, another question whether these truisms are important truisms, or whether they have the implications that the existentialists think they have. Here, I have simply tried to show that there is a way of interpreting what these philosophers are doing in the philosophical idiom of conceptualism which they have, as I think, too hastily rejected, and which raises fewer problems of understanding than does the ontological idiom they have adopted in its place.[35]

[35] Sartre's and Heidegger's conceptions of metaphysics (as distinct from ontology) are significantly different. Sartre's view, which is well-stated in his early polemic against Marxism, "Máterialisme et Revolution," *Les Temps Modernes,* Vol. 1 (1946), pp. 1537–63, and Vol. 2, pp. 1–32, is based on fairly traditional objections to the absolutistic, "God's-eye point of view" of the metaphysician, as well as to the inherently unverifiable character of his theses. Heidegger, in *Was Ist Metaphysik?* and elsewhere characterizes metaphysics as concerned with "das Seiende als Seiende," i.e., with the most general traits of what is, and not with "das Sein des Seienden."

PART II

CRITICAL

CHAPTER VI

ACTION AND VALUE

In Chapter IV, the existentialism of Heidegger and Sartre was characterized as "ontological voluntarism," and it was argued that the distinctive achievement of these philosophers has been to introduce into the concept itself of conscious human being an interpretation of human action and evaluation which they derive from Nietzsche and from the voluntaristic tradition that culminates in his thought. By itself, this pedigree commits the contemporary existentialist to a rejection of all forms of the doctrine of ethical intellectualism. In fact, both Heidegger and Sartre emphatically deny that human beings can properly be said to *know* what is morally required of them in a way that is genuinely independent of their own individual choices; and they repudiate in principle the use of the concepts of truth and falsity in moral contexts.[1] It would be a mistake, however, to see in this rejection

[1] It must be understood that the "truth" which is inapplicable to evaluative and moral contexts is the traditional concept of truth as the correspondence of a judgment to a state of affairs. Heidegger argues that this kind of truth as correspondence is possible only within the framework of *Dasein;* and he seeks to convey the derivative status of judgmental truth by characterizing *Dasein* itself as being "truth" in a primary sense, and judgments as being true only in a secondary sense. While the "primary" sense of truth would of course be applicable throughout the spheres of both knowledge and action, this sense, whatever its merit may be, involves such an extreme extension of the ordinary sense of truth that in the interests of clarity I have avoided using it in my text. I have instead paraphrased the points Heidegger makes about *Dasein* as a presupposition of judgmental truth and have reserved the term "truth" itself for the correspondence relationship that Heidegger is criticizing. See *Sein und Zeit,* pp. 212–30 and *Vom Wesen der Wahrheit,* pp. 6–13. There are no comparable discussions of truth in Sartre's writings but to judge from his use of the term he appears to make a similar distinction between primary and derived senses of the term and there can be no doubt that in his view judgmental truth or what he is more likely to call "du connu" misses precisely the element of free transcendence of "situation" that is central to evaluation and action.

of intellectualism nothing more than a ratification of an inherited line of argument. Not only do the existentialists restate the case against intellectualism in their own philosophical idiom, but the version of that doctrine on which they direct their fire is, in certain respects, different from the versions that Kant and Nietzsche had in mind. It is unfortunate that this existentialist critique of intellectualism exists in the writings of Heidegger and Sartre only in fragmentary form. Nevertheless, its importance for any attempt to state the ethical theory implicit in their work is such that a detailed reconstruction of the argument must be undertaken.

There is a special reason why the existentialist critique of intellectualism should claim our attention. As many critics have remarked, there is not very much straightforward argument in the writings of Heidegger and Sartre in behalf of the conception of value which they defend. Instead, the latter is developed as a kind of dialectical consequence of the very general characterization of human being which I attempted to summarize briefly in the last chapter. To the external critic who may (or may not) accept that characterization, the existentialists might well seem to have little to offer in the way of persuasive grounds for accepting their views. It suggests itself that their failure in this respect is largely due to a feeling that the only alternative to the position they are defending is some form or other of intellectualism. Certainly, both Heidegger and Sartre think they have shown the untenability of that alternative. Their account of value is thus presented as one that must be true since the only alternative meta-ethical theory has been shown to be untenable. This demonstration is the task to which their critique of intellectualism is addressed; and for the extra-mural critic, it has a special importance, since it affords one of the rare opportunities for locating existentialist ethical theory by a species of triangulation from more or less familiar alternatives in the field with which it deals.

I

Before undertaking this reconstruction of the existentialists' critique of intellectualism, it will be useful to correct a particularly widespread misconception of their views on this matter. It is often assumed that the existentialists' rejection of all forms of intellectualism reflects a simple failure to recognize—much less account for—the *prima facie* independence of individual will that characterizes the moral qualities commonly attributed to various types of conduct.[2] This assumption is mistaken; and the full complexity of the ethical theory of existentialism cannot be grasped until its analysis of this *prima facie* objectivity and its reasons for rejecting the latter, finally, as specious have been appreciated. Whether those reasons are judged to be conclusive or not, it is important to understand that the decision to override "common sense" and to reinterpret the status of value has been taken in full awareness of the degree to which this reinterpretation violates many of our most "natural" assumptions about the relationship in which we stand to the moral quality of our own actions and those of others.[3]

It also needs to be emphasized that the existentialists have attempted to give an account of the way in which what they regard as the illusion of objectivity arises, and that they are far from regarding intellectualism as simply an inexplicably mistaken conception by common sense of the nature of its own moral judgments. This account, admittedly, presupposes that a conclusive

---

[2] This charge is very forcefully made against Heidegger in H. Reiner, *Pflicht und Neigung* (Meisenheim: Westkulturverlag A. Hain, 1951) , pp. 107–11. Reiner is one of the few commentators who recognizes the fundamental importance within Heidegger's philosophy of his critique of the theory of "values" and this book contains a long and highly critical discussion of Heidegger's views on the subject. (See pp. 145–161.)

[3] This is stated in so many words by Heidegger:

Die *Seinsart* des Daseins fordert daher von einer ontologischen Interpretation, die sich die Ursprünglichkeit der phänomenalen Aufweisung zum Ziel gesetzt hat, *dass sie sich das Sein dieses Seienden gegen sein eigene Verdeckungstendenz erobert.* Die existenziale Analyse hat daher für die Ansprüche bzw. die Genügsamkeit und beruhigte Selbstverständlichkeit der alltäglichen Auslegung ständig den Charakter einer ,*Gewaltsamkeit. Sein und Zeit* (p. 311) .

For an interpretation of Sartre's philosophy as a "réflexion purifiante" which realizes a "moralisation de l'être moral," see F. Jeanson, *Le problème moral et la pensée de Sartre,* pp. 329 ff. The effect of an acceptance of the insights contained in *L'Être et le néant* upon established moral attitudes is briefly considered on pp. 721–22 and on pp. 75–76 of that work.

case has been made against intellectualism. It follows that in arguing against intellectualism, the existentialists are not entitled to *assume* that our precritical sense of ethical objectivity is an illusion as they sometimes seem to do, but must instead refute the intellectualist thesis first and then go on to explain how common sense may have come to hold such a mistaken view of its own procedures of moral judgment. It is equally clear, however, that moral philosophy has no right to treat common sense views as incorrigible data that subsequent analyses must in no way undercut. Very often the main objection registered against existentialist ethical theory seems to be that its results are incompatible with the moral assumptions of common sense.[4] For example, it has been alleged that no such ethical theory can account for such phenomena of the moral life as self-condemnation, i.e., the fact that we sometimes choose to act in a certain way but at the same time judge our own conduct to be morally wrong. Certainly it is fair to ask that existentialist ethical theory deal with cases like this; but it cannot be assumed in advance that they are consistent with only one theory of ethical judgment, or indeed that we are clear about the kind of "objectivity" that has to be presupposed in order to make sense of such cases. They are most frequently presented in unanalyzed form as counter-instances to some existentialist thesis; but once they have done their work, one is given very little, if anything, in the way of a positive account of the status of moral qualities that they presuppose. The result is that they seem to support an extremely simplistic theory of moral objectivity which is allowed to benefit from the doubts raised about antiobjectivist position without ever having to present its own credentials. When the existentialists are criticized for not giving enough weight to the testimony of common sense and common usage, they can fairly reply that by itself such an attitude is no more tendentious than the opposite procedure of their opponents.

While the main task of this chapter is to set forth the existentialists' reasons for concluding that the objectivity of values is an illusion, it will be useful to note in passing the account given by the existentialists of the way that illusion arises, and of its under-

---

[4] See for example A. Plantinga, "An Existentialist's Ethics," *The Review of Metaphysics,* Vol. 12 (1958), pp. 235–256.

lying motives. Briefly, the existentialist view is that the objectivist "illusion" arises when one kind of stability which accrues to our evaluative judgments under certain specifiable conditions is confused with, and is expressed in the language appropriate to, the quite different kind of stability that is characteristic of fact-stating judgments.[5] This tends to happen whenever an individual treats someone else's evaluations as automatically valid for himself, and at the very least does not think of his appropriation of these evaluations as itself an evaluative act. The "someone else" may be a parent or a supernatural person—God—or perhaps a collective "person," i.e., the historical community of which one is a member. In any case, our sense of the objectivity of the moral

[5] Heidegger argues that interpreting one's personal existence on the model of "das innerweltlich Seiende" represents one of the two fundamental possibilities between which human beings have to choose; and he also says that "das Dasein hat . . . gemäss einer zu ihm gehorigen Seinsart die Tendenz, das eigene Sein aus *dem* Seienden her zu verstehen, zu dem es sich wesenhaft ständig und zunächst verhält, aus der 'Welt'." (*Sein und Zeit,* p. 15). This "losing oneself in the world" is closely associated with the anonymous, collective life of "Das Man" in which "die Aufgaben, Regeln, Maszstäbe, die Dringlichkeit und Reichweite des besorgendfürsorgenden In-der-Weltseins—je schon entschieden (ist) . . . Das Man verbirgt sogar die von ihm vollzogene stillschweigende Entlastung von der ausdrücklichen *Wahl* dieser Möglichkeiten." (p. 268) It is clear, too, that Heidegger sees a close connection between this inauthentic mode of understanding of self and the doctrine of "values" which are precisely "vorhandene Bestimmtheiten eines Dinges" and as such distorted, reified images of choice. For Heidegger's treatment of "values," see references in note 9.

Sartre's interpretation of what he calls "la moralité quotidienne" is closely similar to Heidegger's. Everyday moral experience is, he says, "exclusive de l'angoisse éthique" and the latter, which is described as "un phénomène postérieur et médiatisé," arises only "lorsque je me considère dans mon rapport originel aux valeurs." (*L'Être et le néant,* p. 75.) "L'angoisse" is opposed to "l'esprit de sérieux (qui) a pour double charactéristique, en effet, de considérer les valeurs comme des données transcendantes, indépendantes de la subjectivité humaine, et de transférer le charactere 'désirable', de la structure ontologique des choses à leur simple constitution matérielle." (*Ibid.,* p. 721.) Also of interest is Sartre's description of "l'homme sérieux":

(Il) recherche l'être à l'aveuglette, en se cachant le libre projet qu' est cette recherche; il se fait tel qu'il soit *attendu* par des tâches placées sur sa route. Les objets sont des exigences muettes; et il n'est rien en soi que l'obéissance à ces exigences. *L'Être et le Néant* (p. 721) .

It is interesting to note that Sartre here uses the phrase "la structure ontologique de la chose" to designate what is clearly a structure of human subjectivity in its relationship to things.

111

quality of an action is, on this view, the result of a failure or inability to treat a prior evaluative judgment by someone else simply as a fact that leaves open the question, "What shall *I* do?"[6] It is often argued that in such cases there is, in fact, an implicit appeal to a major premise to the effect that what some superordinate person enjoins is right without qualification and is to be done, and that this (implicit) premise is tantamount to an independent evaluative act on the part of the subordinate person. This may be the case, and indeed the existentialists would certainly hold that in one sense it is. But a person may not know what he is logically committed to; and it is this difference between the person who does treat his implicit endorsement of the abovementioned premise as an evaluative act and the one who does not that is at the heart of the existentialists' account of the objectivist illusion. When a person is not aware that such an endorsement is implicit in his attitude toward the evaluative authority in question, he will inevitably conceive his relationship to the latter in passive and cognitive terms. It does not, of course, follow that such persons will be passive and inactive in any other way; and it is well known that they have often been quite the reverse. Nevertheless, in the one relevant respect, they do think of themselves as discovering or knowing a fact that by itself supplies an answer to the question "What shall I do?"; and to the extent that they describe themselves and their evaluative judgments in these terms, their language lends support to the intellectualistic position.

To describe this attitude as a failure to raise a certain kind of question, or as a failure to understand that it can and in a sense must be raised, does not do full justice to the existentialist argument. It is of the essence of the latter that this failure is a motivated and quasi-deliberate failure.[7] If the necessity for a super-

---

[6] Heidegger points out that it is one of the characteristics of "Das Man" that the whole question of whose choices the various conventions and norms of collective life represent is left indeterminate. "Es bleibt unbestimmt, wer eigentlich wählt." *Sein und Zeit*, p. 268. (See also p. 21.)

[7] While Heidegger clearly indicates that the inauthentic mode of personal existence in which *Dasein* is understood on the model of things is a strategy that *Dasein* can itself adopt, it was left to Sartre to expand these suggestions into his theory of "bad faith." Bad faith is, in its simplest terms, lying to oneself; and according to Sartre it is involved in every attempt to impute

vening personal endorsement of the source of moral authority were fully appreciated, the resultant sense of being the sole and solely responsible mediator between the actual and the possible would—so the argument goes—arouse in us an intense feeling of anxiety. It is further assumed that all of us, in fact, have a kind of crepuscular awareness that our "real" situation is of just this nature; and the conclusion is drawn that the picture we construct of ourselves as passive in our evaluational capacity serves the purpose of a prophylactic against that anxiety. Instead of simple failure or inability to assume full evaluative sovereignty in one's own right, this amounts to a *refusal* to do so, and it is the kind of refusal that compels one to keep one's eye—covertly—on the state of affairs that one refuses to acknowledge.

There is a great deal that might be said about this account of the motives that underlie the mistaken assimilation of one kind of stability to another. Since it raises issues that are of fundamental importance to the whole ethical theory of existentialism, this discussion will be deferred until later chapters.[8] It is clear, however, that whatever the merits of the theory, there is a very real question as to the propriety of applying the same explanatory account and imputing the same motivation to all forms of intellectualism, from its most naïve and unreflective form, to its explicit defense as a philosophical thesis. If we disregard for the moment the question of motives, however, and appraise this theory simply as an account of how the moral world of common sense may have come to look as though the theses of intellectualism would correctly describe it, then its merits are considerable. What it asserts is that when we accept someone else's evaluative judgments as valid for ourselves without the intervention of any validating personal act of endorsement, we seem to ourselves to be subject to

---

some sort of fixed essence or nature to oneself by way of explaining and justifying what one does. Its aim is to conceal from others but mainly from one's self one's own complicity in the "nature" which, so far from being an unchangeable datum of the moral life, is progressively created by one's choices. For Sartre's account of bad faith, see *L'Être et le néant,* Part 1, ch. 2. His essay on *Baudelaire* (Paris: Gallimard, 1947) and *Réflexions sur la question juive* (Paris: P. Morihien, 1946) are examples of the way Sartre employs the concept of bad faith in the analysis of character.

[8] See ch. 7, pp. 153 ff.

an external discipline in the making of evaluative judgments that is easily assimilable to the discipline that goes with the fact-stating mode of discourse. *Ex hypothesi,* they are not the same, of course. But when the former type of discipline is not *thought* of as being self-imposed, the two are sufficiently alike to make it possible to describe the one limitation in terms drawn from the description of the other.

II

Fortunately, it is not difficult to identify the specific form of intellectualism against which Heidegger and Sartre direct their criticisms. Throughout *Sein und Zeit* there are many references to a conception of value as a special type of property that is independent of human volition, and is a possible object of cognitive apprehension.[9] The chief contemporary exemplar of such a theory that Heidegger had before him was Scheler's, to which reference has already been made; and there is good reason to think that the brief critical observations that Heidegger makes on theories of this type were primarily addressed to Scheler's formulation of the intellectualistic doctrine.[10] It is indeed possible to

[9] These comments can be found on pp. 63, 68, 99, 100, 150, 286, 293. The following quotation is typical of them all:

> Der Zusatz von Wertprädikaten vermag nicht im mindesten einen neuen Aufschluss zu geben über das Sein der Güter, *sondern setzt für diese die Seinsart purer Vorhandenheit nur wieder voraus.* Werte sind vorhandene Bestimmtheiten eines Dinges. Werte haben am Ende ihren ontologischen Ursprung einzig im vorgängigen Ansatz der Dingwirklichkeit als der Fundamentalschicht. Schon die vorphänomenologische Erfahrung zeigt aber an dem dinglich vermeinten Seienden etwas, was durch Dinglichkeit nicht voll verständlich wird. Also bedarf das dingliche Sein einer Ergänzung. Was besagt ontologisch das Sein der Werte oder ihre "Geltung" . . . ? Was bedeutet ontologisch dieses "Haften" der Werte an den Dingen? (p. 99)

Even more strongly critical observations on the doctrine of "values" can be found in Heidegger's essay on Nietzsche in *Holzwege* (p. 205 ff).

[10] Not only are there a number of references in *Sein und Zeit* to Scheler's *Formalismus in der Ethik und die materiale Wertethik* but there are also two discussions (pp. 47–48 and p. 210) of Scheler's failure to lay adequate ontological foundations for his philosophy of personalism. "Scheler wie Hartman verkennen . . . dass die 'Ontologie' in ihrer überlieferten Grundorientierung

interpret Heidegger's whole theory of value as growing out of his criticisms of all attempts to treat value as a quality or property. Considered in this light, his mode of argument is to show that these theories attempt to transfer to a (value) property a set of functions which *no* property is capable of discharging, and that these functions are properly assigned only to human beings. This rejection of value properties passes over virtually intact into Sartre's version of existentialism, where it is closely associated with the problem of the contingency of value which, for Sartre at least, is inseparable from its dependence on individual choice.[11] At the same time, however, his account of value is in a real sense complementary to Heidegger's since its effect is to show that the concept of a value property, which the latter criticizes, incorporates a contradiction that springs from the attempt to fuse, in the notion of a being that has its value as a necessary adjunct of its nature, the radically opposed modes of being of things and of persons. This piece of argumentation also forms part of Sartre's destructive analysis of the idea of God as a perfect being which will be examined in detail in the course of this chapter.

The fundamental premise on which the existentialist critique of the notion of a value property rests is that value concepts have an essentially practical character.[12] To describe value concepts as

---

gegenüber dem Dasein versagt, und dass gerade das im Erkennen beschlossene "Seinsverhältnis" zu ihrer grundsätzlichen Revision und nicht nur kritischen Ausbesserung zwingt." (p. 208, note) While Heidegger never explicitly associates the name of Scheler with the doctrine of "values" which he criticizes, there is an exact parallelism between that doctrine as stated by Heidegger and Scheler's own views on the subject; and that fact, together with these critical references to Scheler's failure to break out of the traditional ontological framework, make it clear that his treatment of "value" was fundamentally unacceptable to Heidegger.

[11] Sartre's most important statement on the subject of value is "Le pour-soi et l'être de la valeur," Pt. 2, ch. 1, sec. 3, in *L'Être et le néant,* but there are important comments in *L'existentialisme est un humanisme* (Paris, 1946) and in *Saint Genêt: comédien et martyr* (Paris: Gallimard, 1952) .

[12] The practical character of all evaluative judgments and indeed of human existence generally comes to clearest expression in Heidegger's analyses of the *Entwurf* and Sartre's closely parallel treatment of the *projet*. As the etymology of these words indicates, to say that human existence has the structure of the *Entwurf* or *projet* is to say that it is always "thrown"—or better, "throws itself"—toward its possibilities. Thus, when I say that something is "good" I project a line of action relative to that thing and the force of this application

115

essentially practical is to say that the use of a value concept necessarily commits its user to a judgment that some action is to be performed and, through that judgment, to the actual performance of that action in the event he finds himself in the situation to which it is declared to be appropriate. Now, if value concepts are generically practical in this sense, it follows that they designate relational attributes, i.e., the rightness or "fittingness" *of* a certain action *in* a certain situation. Accordingly, the intellectualist must hold that in apprehending the presence in some situation of a value property, we also come to know that some action is to be performed—namely, the action that constitutes the other term in the relational complex implicit in the value property itself. The heart of the existentialist counter-argument is simply the claim that this notion of *knowing* that some action is to be performed is a conceptual muddle, and that the practical, action-oriented char-

---

of the predicate "good" is that of a choice of that line of action which I am thereby committed to as the "right" action to perform. In saying that Heidegger and Sartre view evaluative judgments as fundamentally practical, I am imputing to them the view that "good" has to be defined in terms of "right," i.e., in terms of actions to be performed if such and such a thing is characterized as good. This imputation seems justified in spite of the fact that neither one of these philosophers concerns himself with this distinction in the form in which it has become familiar in analytical ethics. If "right" with the implications for action which it carries were to be explicated in terms of a value-attribute denoted by "good" that could simply be "intuited," this would fly in the face of express statements by Sartre to the effect that "jamais, en effet, le donné ne pourrait être un motif pour une action s'il n'était apprécié. . . . L'appréciation, si elle ne doit pas être gratuite, doit se faire à la lumière de quelque chose. Et ce quelque chose qui sert à apprécier le donné ne peut être que la fin. Ainsi, l'intention, d'un même surgissement unitaire pose la fin, se choisit, et apprécie le donné à partir de la fin. Dans ces conditions le donné est apprécié en fonction de quelque chose qui n'existe pas encore." (*L'Être et le néant*, p. 557.) If we keep in mind that a value property would have to be a "donné" and that the "fin" which "n'existe pas encore" is, or involves, a possible action, then the passage clearly implies that nothing can be designated as "good" without thereby accepting (as "right") some more or less specific implications for action. For an example of an analysis of a value judgment along these lines, see *Ibid.*, p. 508. Sartre's theory of the *projet* is stated most clearly in Pt. 4, ch. 1, of *L'Être et le néant*, especially pp. 555–60. Heidegger's discussion of the *Entwurf* can be found in *Sein und Zeit*, p. 145 ff. and in *Vom Wesen des Grundes*, pp. 39 ff. This last work contains the explicit statement that "die Transzendenz (stösst) nicht auf das Umwillen als auf etwas wie einen an sich vorhandenen Wert und Zweck, sondern Freiheit hält sich—*und zwar als Freiheit*—das Umwillen entgegen (p. 43) .

acter of value concepts is irreconcilable with the doctrine that they designate objective properties.[13]

To be sure, the view that value concepts refer to actions to be performed is not an uncontested proposition among ethicists, nor is the weaker claim that this directive function is an implicit feature of all judgments of moral value. It is difficult to see, however, how anyone could deny that value concepts must be capable of such reference to *agenda* without at the same time denying that evaluative knowledge has any relevance to the guidance of conduct.[14] Once the reference to an action to be performed is dropped out of the evaluative judgment, it becomes possible to accept such a judgment, while at the same time leaving completely open the question of what one ought to do. If an attempt is made to close this gap by asserting that it is always right to do what is good, i.e., to actualize or maintain in existence whatever bears the value-property, then the credentials of *this* principle must be independently established, and clearly they will be different in character from those that establish the presence of the value-property itself. The difficulties attendant upon such a proof will be examined later in this chapter. Here, I would merely note that even the most strenuously objectivistic theories like Husserl's and Scheler's make a place for a species of value—moral value—in which the relation to action is openly recognized;[15] and

---

[13] This point is made in a great many ways by both Heidegger and Sartre, but perhaps the most direct statement on the subject is Heidegger's.

Mit den erwarteten eindeutig verrechenbaren Maximen würde das Gewissen der Existenz nichts Geringeres versagen als—*die Möglichkeit zu handeln. Sein und Zeit,* p. 294.

Sartre's position is stated most clearly in the course of his analysis of action in *L'Être et le néant,* p. 508 ff., where every attempt to interpret actions by reference to "ces fins toutes faites et préhumaines . . . (qui) viennent de Dieu, de la nature, de ma nature, de la societé" is characterized as a denial of the liberty that is the "condition première de l'action." For explicit denials that value or the ends of action are "known," see also pp. 138 and 548.

[14] For a most interesting discussion of the whole relationship between "good" and "right," that has considerable relevance to the argument of this chapter, see W. Frankena, "Obligation and Value in the Ethics of G. E. Moore" in P. Schilpp (ed.), *The Philosophy of G. E. Moore* (2d ed.; New York: Tudor Publishing Co., 1952), pp. 93–110. Moore's reply to Frankena can be found on pp. 554–81 and pp. 592–611.

[15] Husserl's treatment of distinctively ethical or action-related values is fully presented in A. Roth (ed.). *Ethische Untersuchungen* (The Hague: Nijhoff,

117

it is apparent that if they did not, they would have erased one major distinction between ethical and aesthetic attitudes toward the world. Interestingly enough, G. E. Moore whose ethical theory resembles Scheler's at many points, has explicitly accepted this notion of a property that by itself generates an "ought" relating to some action to be performed; and in the phrase, "an ought-implying property," he has given apt expression to the very collocation of concepts that the existentialists find so anomalous.[16]

This view that ethical concepts are essentially tied to action must be explicated against the background of the existentialist treatment of possibility which was outlined in Chapter V. When we speak of acting in a certain way in a given situation, what we have in mind is a series of events which would transform that situation in certain respects and substitute for it another, presently nonexistent situation. This transformation will normally be one that is believed to be within the powers of the person or persons seeking to effect it, or at least to be the kind of thing which it is reasonable for them to attempt in the light of what they know about their capabilities, even though they do not in fact succeed in bringing it about. But the most important feature of any action, from the existentialist standpoint, is that it is always doing *this* rather than *that*, where "this" and "that" represent alternative transformations of some situation which are *both* possible.[17] Even when our action serves only to maintain in existence a situation that already obtains, the goal of that action is to realize one of the possible alternatives before us, i.e., to see to it that things remain as they are instead of changing. When we are said to act, there is thus a range of situations, any one of which might, depending upon the effort we make, follow upon the present state of affairs. These situations are possibilities, not just in the sense

1960) , pp. 123 ff. Scheler's essentially similar views are stated in *Formalismus,* pp. 153 ff. and pp. 199 ff.

[16] In his "Reply to My Critics" in Schilpp (ed.) , *The Philosophy of G. E. Moore,* p. 604.

[17] Thus Heidegger declares that "die Freiheit . . . ist nur in der Wahl der einen, das heisst im Tragen des Nichtgewählthabens und Nichtauchwählenkönnens der anderen (existenziellen Möglichkeiten) ." (*Sein und Zeit,* p. 285.)

that their occurrence is not logically excluded by our characterization of the present situation as the action of changing my dog
into Julius Caesar would presumably be, but also in the sense
that the question whether or not we will attempt to bring them
about is one that is left open by the present state of our knowledge. Finally, while it is not necessary to make any special claim
about what goes on in the mind of a person who acts to bring
about one of these alternative possibilities, it *is* necessary, if he is
to be said to act at all, that he should be able to say, or somehow
to convey in response to a question about what he is doing, his
awareness that he is doing *this* rather than *that*.

These references to the bearing of such knowledge as we possess upon our projects of action provide an occasion for noting
the general conception of knowledge and truth on which the existentialists rest their denial that value is a cognizable attribute of
actual states of affairs. This is a conception of knowledge and of
truth in which the relationship of both to the general conception
of human being is worked out; and while Heidegger denies that
he is defending the familiar thesis of the priority of practical
reason over theoretical reason, he does argue that knowledge,
generally, is simply one mode of *Dasein* or "relatedness" to things-
in-being that must be understood within the matrix of the comprehensive structures of human being.[18] Scientific inquiry thus
represents one mode of comportment within this total situation;
and the kind of truth at which it aims presupposes an opening
upon the world that can be elucidated only in terms of a reference, via action, to possible alternative states of affairs. So fundamental indeed is this orientation toward action of our whole apprehension of the world, according to the existentialists, that it
penetrates even our perception of physical objects which are in
the first instance experienced as instruments that can be made to
serve our needs. Only very gradually, are concepts of objects
formed that abstract from this primary context of human foresight and action, and that represent things as simply there—
vorhanden—and independent of any human action that may be
performed upon them, or at least of any action that has not been
assimilated to other natural forces and thus itself made the object

[18] See, for example, *Sein und Zeit,* p. 62 and p. 202.

119

of some predictive theory. When such concepts of objects are formed, the judgments in which they are used are "true" in the sense of corresponding to a state of affairs. It is this sense of truth, involving as it does a self-imposed passivity on the part of human consciousness, that the existentialist has in mind when he denies that there can be knowledge of value-properties and that value judgments can be true or false. As I will try to show, the basic reason on which this denial rests is the belief that the special passivity associated with scientific observation and theory can never be total, and that precisely in their evaluative functions, human beings break out of it in a manner which proves fatal to the intellectualist thesis when its implications are understood.

To sum up, the crucial premise of the existentialist argument is that the actions to which reference is made by value concepts are possible actions. They are actions which there is reason to think the relevant persons *could* perform if they chose; but they are also actions that are not necessary or inevitable and that those persons can also *not* perform, if they choose. To the extent that evaluative judgment involves a reference to actions, it is to actions whose mode of logical rapport with the existing situation to which they are appropriate is neither that of being excluded as incompatible with our characterization of that situation, nor that of being a necessary entailment of it. Furthermore, this setting of actual situations within a context of possibility is not just a contingent accident of the human condition, that will be eliminated *pari passu* with human ignorance, but a permanent and distinctive feature of our relationship to the world. Thus, precisely because human experience is essentially mediated by an uneliminable contrast between what actually exists and what might possibly exist, one central human function becomes the projection of a range of possible states of affairs that might be realized by corresponding human actions. "Things" by themselves are incapable of setting up their own ranges of possible alternatives and, *a fortiori*, they are incapable of designating any one of these possibilities as giving the direction in which an actual situation should evolve. Yet the concept of a value property represents both these forms of transcendent reference to possible states of affairs as rela-

120

tional attributes that are independent of human consciousness, with the result that the latter must be characterized as passively registering such relationships and reproducing them in true value judgments. In other words, it is claimed that we discover, or at least *can* discover, a special relationship of rightness or fittingness between the actual situation in which we have to act and some one of the possible actions which we project out of that situation. The fact that this relationship holds between a particular possible action and an actual situation, and that it does not hold between the latter and certain other possible actions is supposed to be what entitles us to say that that one action is the morally right one for us to perform.

As I have already indicated, it is precisely the application of the concept of truth to this peculiar hybrid of actuality and possibility that creates the difficulty. The reference to a possible state of affairs and a corresponding possible action by which it would be realized is essential if the attribution of a value quality is to have any relevance to the question, "What should I do?" Moreover, the situation in which we act must be reckoned with through an identification of some relevant feature it bears if action is to be more than a blind instinctual thrust. But in what sense could we be said to *discover* a relationship in which one term is a presently existent state of affairs and the other a merely possible human action? No doubt it is unexceptionable English usage to say of value judgments that they are "true"—in that sense of "true" which is close to "ditto" and which permits us to espouse judgments that have been made by others. There is a quite different use of "true" that is distinctive of fact-stating discourse and which requires that we be able to verify by some mode of inspection the presence or absence of the quality or relation designated by the predicate term in the judgment which is said to be "true." It is this second (and surely more fundamental) sense of "truth" of which the existentialists cannot make sense when it is associated with evaluative judgments. For in the evaluative case, *ex hypothesi*, one term in the relational complex which we are said to apprehend does not exist, and if the concept of truth is coordinate with what exists, as the existentialists assume throughout, then it cannot be extended to judgments that involve an essential reference to what does not exist at the time of judgment and, as far as the agent knows, may never exist.

A way around this difficulty might be suggested as follows. It could be argued that the fact—so strongly emphasized by the existentialists—that human consciousness is always a step ahead of the situation of fact by which it is confronted justifies an interpretation of evaluation on the model of predictive judgments. Certainly the latter—both when they are explicitly cast in the form of an estimate of what the future holds in store and when the prediction is implicit in some dispositional predicate like "soluble"—do not confine themselves simply to saying what is the case in the sense of characterizing what now exists or has existed in the past. Moreover, it would seem that judgments that involve a reference to future eventualities offer a much more satisfactory paradigm for understanding human knowledge than do those (if there are any such at all) that limit themselves rigidly to saying what is or has been the case. Especially since the existentialists regard our apprehension of natural objects as being dispositional through and through, it could be argued that it would be much more in keeping with their general position if they were to treat properties—among them value-properties—that mediate between the present and the future as standard objects of human knowledge, rather than as incoherent mixtures of radically disparate notions.

Even if this point about the centrality of dispositional properties were granted however (as it certainly would be by both Heidegger and Sartre), a crucially important distinction between predictive and evaluative judgments would still have to be made. It is quite true that prediction as it is understood in the context of scientific inquiry involves a certain suspension of our normal practical concern for the future in the interest of finding out what will happen in a given set of circumstances which we may have helped to arrange. Within limits that are themselves dictated by a practical concern at some deeper level, we become passive spectators of the unfolding of events; and as a counterpart of this passivity, the brute presence of things-in-the-world is extended, as it were, beyond the present moment into the future we are seeking to predict. Thus, while a predictive judgment rests on premises that are drawn from past and present observations of the state of the world, it always goes beyond what these premises assert to make some further factual claim for which the locus of verification is the relevant stretch of the future. Moreover, it is a commonplace of the logic books that an inductive judgment can be valid in the sense of being made in conformity with the canons of inductive logic as applied to the body of available evidence, and yet prove false in the light of what actually happens. By contrast, while evaluative judgments are often very closely bound up with assumptions of fact about a given situation and about the likely effect of acting in a certain way in that situation, it is distinctive of such judgments that all these elements of information about what is (or will be) the case receive the status of premises from which the evaluative inference then moves forward. No distinction between the validity of such an inference and the truth of its conclusion can be made, as in the case of the predictive judgment; for while the unfolding of events may often lead us to conclude that our evaluation was based on faulty premises and was therefore inappropriate to the actual situation, these events do not provide any test of the truth of the conclusion as distinct from that of the premises of an evaluative reference.[19] Predictive and evaluative judgments share, to be sure, the characteristics of being inferences, i.e., moves forward from a set of premises; and they also share the characteristic of involving a reference to the future. But the predictive judgment by virtue of its built-in susceptibility for further verification "touches down" in a future from which intervention through human action has been provisionally excluded. By contrast, the evaluative judgment, having absorbed all assumptions of present and future fact into its premises and referring as it does beyond the latter to a future that is open precisely in the sense of not being isolated from human intervention, has the character, as the existentialists are fond of saying, of a "leap" or "pro-ject" just because there is no state of affairs, present or future, to which it can be true or false.

---

[19] A similar point about the relationship of "truth" to "validity" in evaluative inference is made by C. L. Stevenson in his *Ethics and Language* (New Haven, Conn.: Yale University Press, 1944), pp. 152–73.

Why, it may be asked, does the existentialist make so much of the case in which the relational value attribute is supposed to connect an actual situation with a merely possible action, when such attributes—if they exist at all—must be capable of being apprehended equally well as relationships between situations and actions which are either both actual (having already occurred) or both hypothetical and merely possible?[20] I think the answer to this question is that the hybrid case most clearly reveals the difficulties implicit in the notion of an "ought-implying" property. As long as we talk in terms of value properties attaching to states of affairs, either real or imaginary, and do not "unpack" the reference to possible actions that is implicit in these properties, matters seem quite straightforward. Either one apprehends these properties or one doesn't. But when the reference to an action that is envisaged as merely possible is exposed, it becomes apparent that what we claim to intuit is a relational complex, one term of which is *ex hypothesi* not given, and could not therefore be apprehended in the quasi-perceptual manner postulated in most intuitionistic accounts. Once the action had been performed and the relational complex thereby completed, there would no longer be *this* obstacle in the way of claiming that the value-attribute had been discovered in a quasi-perceptual manner, although there might well be others. It would be very strange, however, if the rightness of an action could be apprehended only retrospectively and never at the moment of decision, i.e., only after I had decided without any supporting intuition that a certain course of action is right and had carried it out. The only alternative to this unwelcome conclusion seems to be to argue that what is apprehended both at the moment of decision *and* retrospectively is not a particular relational complex between *this* situation and *that* action, but a nexus of some kind between a certain type of situation and a certain type of action to which the actuality of one or the other of these terms is strictly irrelevant. In

[20] The relationship between "possibility" and the future as one dimension of temporality as well as the special importance of the latter within the structure of *Dasein* are discussed in *Sein und Zeit*, pp. 325 ff. Sartre's essentially similar treatment of the future is to be found in *L'Être et le néant*, pp. 168–74.

this way, all value intuitions are really assimilated to the case referred to above, in which both situation and action are envisaged as mere possibilities, i.e., as a purely conceptual relationship.

The view that there are synthetic a priori truths about values has not had many defenders in the twentieth century. Indeed, one of the most significant modifications of classical intellectualism introduced by both Scheler and Moore was their common insistence that the attribution of value properties must be based not on a priori proofs that situations of a certain type must have a certain value property but on intuitional apprehensions of a special kind; and both have denied that that "good" has any analyzable internal structure that could serve as the basis for such reasoning.[21] On the other hand, not only do both Scheler and Moore appear to hold that what is so apprehended may be a general evaluative truth; but it would seem, in the light of the arguments proposed above, that any intuitionistic position of this type will be forced to fall back on a doctrine of synthetic, a priori, evaluative truths. Against such a doctrine, the existentialists do not, as far as I can see, have any new arguments to offer. It would be easy for them to show however that the attempt to associate such a position with the other assumptions that Moore and Scheler make about the simplicity of value properties and the essential role of intuition can lead only to the most serious incoherencies.[22] Furthermore, they might well point to the danger that the claim that there are such synthetic a priori truths will simply coalesce for all practical purposes with an endorsement of a rule of inference sanctioning the move from a set of factual premises to a certain evaluative conclusion. If this is not to happen, and if these synthetic a priori truths are to have sufficient independence of such policies of inference and of the moral conclusions to which they lead to be able to offer them support, then it will have to be shown that they express some universal and necessary relationship; and for this undertaking the history of philosophy offers very little encouragement.

[21] See Moore, *Principia Ethica*, Preface, p. 3 and pp. 9–10; also, Scheler, *Formalismus*, pp. 37, 84, 196 ff.

[22] In the case of Moore, these difficulties have been clearly shown by W. Frankena (see n. 14, above), especially pp. 103 ff.

III

Some more general observations on the character of the existentialist argument I have been presenting may now be in order. It shows, first of all, a surprising affinity with the "open question" argument that was used by G. E. Moore against all forms of ethical naturalism.[23] Moore argued that no matter what "natural" properties a thing might have—these, presumably, were properties observable by normal scientific methods—they would leave open the question whether that thing was good or not. No "natural" fact, in other words, could by itself foreclose any evaluative possibility. Up to this point, the argument used by Moore runs parallel to the reasoning of the existentialists in spite of great differences in philosophical idiom. The difference between them is that Moore believes there is another set of properties which he calls "nonnatural" and which perform the function which the "natural" properties are incapable of discharging. These *do* settle evaluative questions, and thus put out of play what would otherwise appear to be alternative evaluative possibilities. In addition, through the conceptual connection which Moore postulates between goodness and rightness, they make certain of the actions that are possible in a given situation morally right. Unfortunately, the set of differentia that Moore offers for nonnatural qualities is so vague as to be circular. Nonnatural properties turn out to be simply the kind that does bring evaluative questioning to a stop, and natural properties are just those that cannot do so.

What the existentialists do is to press the "open question" argument not only against some subclass of properties, natural or otherwise, but against all properties as such. The reason the natural properties of an object do not provide answers to evaluative questions is not that they are *natural*, whatever that adjective may be held to signify over and above the logical deficiency just cited. The reason is that they are *properties*. Similarly, the true

[23] In this section, I have chosen to compare the existentialist position with the views of G. E. Moore rather than with those of Scheler, since the position of the former is so much better known in the English-speaking philosophical world.

126

point of the "open question" argument is not to show that the presence of one of a certain range of properties leaves questions about the presence of properties of another type unanswered. Instead, it is that *no* property that a situation might be discovered to have could possibly determine by itself the value of that situation. In order to do that, a property would have to be capable of generating a prescription relating to some action or actions which could be performed in the situation in question. This double function of denoting a property and entailing a prescription against which the existentialists have registered such serious objections is of course just the one that Moore seeks to make the predicate "good" perform. It remains to be seen, however, whether he was really able to show how the discovery that a situation or object (whether real or ideal), has a certain property can suffice to establish that it would be right to act in a certain way in relation to that situation. It is well-known that Moore believed that it was demonstrable, if not self-evident, that the morally right action in any given situation is the action which will produce the greatest amount of good of all the actions that are possible in that situation. In determining what the consequences of any action will be, we are necessarily dependent upon normal methods of prediction, although the relative values of the different sets of consequences will have to be determined by an independent intuition. Once these consequences are known and their relative values determined, the question of action is settled (according to Moore), for right action can only consist in doing that which in the light of the best available information is judged likely to produce a total state of affairs in which the nonnatural property designated by "good" is present to a greater degree than in any other such total state of affairs that we might seek to bring about.

It is not very difficult to see what is wrong with this argument, and why it fails to meet the difficulty about the reference to an action to be performed that looms so large in the opposing existentialist case. Confronted by the logical independence of any characterization of a situation in terms of "natural" properties from judgments of the value or "goodness" of that situation, Moore saves what would otherwise be an unjustifiable inference from the former to the latter by postulating a method for verifying the conclusion of that inference through an intuition of a special nonnatural property, i.e., good. But the duality he seeks to overcome in this way breaks out in a new quarter. For even if we are disposed to accept Moore's view that "good" and "right" are logically related in such a way that the statement, "It is right to do that action which produces most good," is necessarily true, this does not suffice to tie "right" and the imperative for action that it carries to any property that the predicate "good" may be used to designate. It makes no difference that such properties are supposed by Moore to be simple and unanalyzable, for "good-implying-right" obviously *is* analyzable, and neither the fact that a property is simple nor the fact that the predicate "good" has been used to designate it suffices to show by what right we also characterize that property as "good-implying-right." Here, it is of no avail to fall back on the conceptual linkage between "good" and "right," since the flavor of self-evidence that is associated with this hook-up disappears the moment it turns out to be not just definitionally true, but an association of a practical implication with a specific property or set of properties that a situation may be discovered to have. Indeed, it would appear that the indefinability of "good" within Moore's system indirectly serves to conceal the illegitimacy of this assumed equivalence of "good" *simpliciter* with "good-implying-right." For if that simple property *could* be characterized by any other (and perhaps more familiar) predicates, the logical discreetness of the attribution of the property and the implication for action would become obvious and the open question would be open again.

It is hard to resist the conclusion that apart from this illegitimate function of seeming to link indissolubly what are in fact logically distinct characterizations of a situation, the illustrious simple—"good"—plays no essential role in the open question argument properly understood. If it is to be logically tied to "right," it cannot designate a property that we could simply "discover" without our having decided thereby what it would in fact be right to do. From the moral standpoint, the crucial move will always be the one from the fact that a situation has such and such features and that a certain action in that situation can be expected to have such and such effects, to the conclusion that that action should or should not be performed. A statement to the effect that the consequences to be expected from a certain action are good would normally function as a preliminary endorsement of that action as the one to be performed. If with Moore we seek to interpret "good" in such contexts, as standing for another discoverable feature of the situation over and above those already noted, we either cancel the implication for action, or we place ourselves in the incongruous position of claiming not just that we intuit a certain property of the situation, but also that in apprehending the presence of this property we *see* the validity of an inference from the fact that the situation has this property to the conclusion that a certain action having certain expectable consequences would be right. The existentialists cannot make sense of this kind of "seeing"; and since Moore's arguments cast no light on this question of how the apprehension of a property could by itself guarantee the validity of an inference, I conclude that the intelligibility of the intellectualistic position on this crucial point has yet to be shown.

What emerges from this critique and reconstruction of the antinaturalistic argument developed by Moore and by Scheler is a radically new conception of the "openness," from the standpoint of evaluation, of all judgments of fact, whether "natural" or otherwise. As it now appears, the "openness" of the open question is due not to the logical independence of value properties from other "natural" properties, but to the perspective of possible human action in which any situation, however characterized, can be set. At this point, however, an objection may be raised. The existentialist may be asked why he denies at the level of value-properties what is so plainly effected at the level of value concepts. If we say that a man is "cruel," for example, we are both describing his behavior and suggesting attitudes toward this behavior that would normally express themselves in certain kinds of action. Indeed, a strong case can be made for the view that this kind of dual function is typical of our moral language. Nevertheless, just this analysis of the dual function of such concepts can be made to serve the existentialist's argument. By distinguishing between the descriptive and practical components within a moral concept, the way is opened to a question as to the relationship between these two elements and the sense in which this relationship can be said to be known. If this distinction can be made at all, then surely it must be possible to distinguish between the properties corresponding to the descriptive component in the concept and the relation in which these stand to some action to be performed. But this really amounts to a segmentation of the original value property, and to an abandonment of the claim that to apprehend the one is unavoidably to apprehend the other as well. This in turn is to surrender the idea that some property of an actual situation can somehow transcend itself and reach out to select, from among the courses of action that are possible in a given situation, the one that is to be performed.

This point is of considerable importance, since a number of contemporary philosophers have proposed that intellectualism be disassociated from special epistemological and metaphysical claims, and that the contrast between the objective and the subjective in ethics—between the morally justified and the arbitrary —be reinterpreted by assigning a *prima facie* authority to the various conjugations of normative and descriptive components within the moral concepts that are placed at our disposal by the language of the society to which we belong.[24] On this view, the use of evaluative and moral predicates presupposes a background of collectively accepted evaluative standards; and the authority of evaluative judgments is essentially dependent on the fact that they are only incidentally made by this or that individual, and reflect instead an impersonal and "public" assessment of the moral requirements of a given situation. Typically, the sign that such a moral consensus exists is the incorporation of these jointly accepted principles into the language of the community in question. Concepts are constructed for the purpose of describing var-

---

[24] I have in mind here a number of British and American philosophers, among them S. Toulmin and K. Baier, but perhaps the best statements of the position I describe are to be found in P. Foot, "Moral Arguments," *Mind*, Vol. 67 (1958), pp. 502–13 and J. Searle, "How to Derive 'Ought' From 'Is'," *Philosophical Review*, Vol. 73 (1964), pp. 43–58. Also of considerable interest in this connection is Mrs. Foot's paper in the Symposium on "Goodness and Choice," *Proceedings of the Aristotelian Society*, Suppl. Vol. 35 (1961), pp. 45–60.

ious actions and situations, and they are constructed in such a way that certain evaluative implications are implicit in them. The result is that users of the language cannot deny the appropriateness of certain modes of action in certain situations without an appearance of logical incongruity. Thus the "fact" that a man has made a promise implies that he ought to keep it, and the "fact" that a man owes money to another implies that he ought to repay him. The premises of these inferences can be verified, and yet they also have directly evaluative implications. This tying together of a state of affairs with an action to be performed is just what the existentialists say no value-property can be conceived of as doing. According to the variety of intellectualism under consideration, this nexus is effected at the level of concepts, and not at that of alleged value-properties; and these "amphibious" concepts are a social property which no individual can simply appropriate for his own purposes, and which imposes a common logical discipline on all who use it.

In a later chapter, I will argue that with certain very important additions this account of the basis of the objectivity of evaluative judgments could be rendered consistent with the existentialist doctrine of the primacy of individual choice.[25] In the form in which I have just stated this view, however, there can be no doubt of its unacceptability from the existentialist standpoint, or of the reasons that make it unacceptable. For the individual moral agent, the only inference that can be drawn from the fact that certain evaluative implications are built into the language he uses is that someone else has associated certain evaluative conclusions with certain descriptive premises, and through the impersonal agency of language, is exerting a subtle form of pressure on him to do likewise. In other words, the existentialist is saying that behind the "rules of moral language" there stand other human beings, living and dead, and that insofar as these rules "represent" anything, it is the actions and choices of those persons.[26] There are a number of important qualifications that have to be added in order to meet obvious objections to this view, but

[25] See ch. 8, p. 208 ff.
[26] For a fuller discussion of the whole question of moral principles and rules, see ch. 7, p. 174 ff.

only after the next (and decisive) step in the existentialist argument has been supplied. This is the assertion that the fact that other human beings have evaluated certain situations in certain ways, and have succeeded in building these evaluations into the language available for describing those situations, has no automatic normative implications. If the "existence" of a rule involves no more than a standing disposition on the part of the members of the community (or some influential subgroup thereof) to encourage behavior of a certain kind and the incorporation of these directives for conduct into our language, we can surely be said to *know* that these rules exist, even though their verbal formulations may turn out to be rather imperfect indices of what the community is effectively prepared to insist on. But knowledge of the existence of a rule in this sense would, according to the existentialists, leave open the question of the action to be taken by the individual who has this knowledge until he himself has made an evaluative appreciation of the fact that other members of his society have acted in a certain way in a situation like the one in which he finds himself, or are disposed in favor of such action. In short, the opinions and actions of others are simply additional elements in the action-situation, and are no more capable of announcing their own evaluative significance than are the other elements in that situation.

IV

Against the background of the preceding discussion, it should now be possible to offer an intelligible interpretation of the arguments by which Sartre attempts to show, in a well-known section of *Being and Nothingness,* that the very concept of a value-property involves a subtle contradiction and that this same contradiction—so far from being an (in principle) avoidable error into which human beings simply happen to have fallen—constitutes a permanent structural feature of human existence.[27] It is

[27] This discussion occurs in the sections of *L'Être et le neant* on "Le pour-soi et l'être de la valeur," and "Le pour-soi et l'être des possibles," pp. 127–47, of which the account I give here is a free paraphrase.

particularly important to disentangle these difficult passages, both because of their intrinsic interest and because Sartre here associates with his thesis that value-properties involve an internal contradiction the quite different claim that human beings are necessarily incapable of happiness. The latter is of course central to what I have called the existentialist ethos as distinct from the ethical theory which I am examining, and Sartre's assumption that these two theses stand in a relationship of implication to one another raises the general issue of the relationship between these two aspects of existentialism in an especially acute form.

At first glance, Sartre's account of the "being of value" contains statements which might seem to commit him to a theory of value very different from that of Heidegger. Thus, he insists that "unless we deal in purely verbal meanings," we must recognize that value in some way possesses being—that it *is;* and he goes so far as to speak of value as a "normative entity."[28] On closer inspection, however, it becomes evident that Sartre is denying quite as emphatically as Heidegger that values are realities, or qualities of existing things. He also holds that if they were, the resultant contingency of their being would "kill value." The being of value must therefore be ideal, as Scheler argues; but—and this is the crux of Sartre's argument—it is a special kind of ideal which human being necessarily generates, and which Sartre describes as "consubstantial" with human being. It is the idea of a value which is absolute or unconditional in the sense of being independent of (and antecedent to) choice, and toward which all acts of choice are oriented. It is in fact the self considered as absolutely founded in its being, and yet aware of itself as such. It is also, in one form, the idea of God. At the same time, this same idea of a value that is raised above contingency and choice, and that is in some sense coeval with human being, is declared by Sartre to be self-contradictory and in principle incapable of exemplification.

In explaining why it is impossible (in Sartre's view) that value should ever be realized, it will be helpful to take note of the close parallelism he postulates between the search for necessary first principles of morality and the wider metaphysical aspiration to

[28] *Ibid.*, p. 136.

overcome the contingency of finite existence by deriving the latter from a being that exists necessarily.[29] In both of these cases, we observe an effort by human beings to provide an answer to—or somehow to shut off—a question which they are in some sense compelled to ask, and which may even be said to be posed by the very relationship in which human beings stand to the "world." Thus, it is human beings who first introduce the contrast between actuality and possibility, as well as the idea of the world as that which contingently exists; and it is human beings who are afflicted with a peculiar feeling of anxiety when they think of the world as "just" existing, i.e., as gratuitously emerging from a circumambient non-being. This sense of cosmic anxiety has in turn inspired a whole series of attempts to tinker with our concepts of actuality and possibility in such a way as to make the actual world emerge as the only one that could have existed, or to represent it as the effect of a cause that exists necessarily. A necessary being would contain within itself all of the conditions of its own existence, and therefore would not be apprehended against a backdrop of alternative possibilities in the manner of contingent beings. In some sense, it would have put these alternate possibilities out of commission in such a way as to make itself ontologically complete, and to provide by itself an answer to the question "Why does it exist?" But if such a being is assumed to be endowed with consciousness and self-awareness as of course the God of Western theology is, then it is once more subtly detached from its own self-constituted being, and the old contrast between what it is and what it might possibly be resumes all its original force. No matter how hard either God or man tries to incorporate himself into a closed system that, in Kant's terminology, provides the "Therefore" to every "Wherefore," his very awareness of being so incorporated thrusts him beyond it. It is for this reason that the positing of such a totality by the very beings who inveterately reinstate the distinction of the actual and the possible involves a latent self-contradiction.

Now in a way that is very similar to the ontological incompleteness that we attribute to contingent beings, the subjects of our evaluative judgments are felt to be incomplete. Actual situa-

[29] *Ibid.,* pp. 140 ff.

tions are apprehended as deficient in some respect that has to be made good by action. Just as an ascending series of natural causes gives no relief against the anxiety about the world's contingent existence, so the parallel evaluative question, "But is it good?" proves to be self-perpetuating. Even when the answer is "Yes," it is always revocable in principle, and the prospect of a never-ending series of inconclusive evaluations arouses a feeling of anxiety not very different from the existential anxiety noted above. Once again, the idea of a being that sets a terminus to this kind of questioning is envisaged—a being that would have no deficiencies which action could supply. This is the idea of a perfect being or of the self as it ought to be, which, as the preordained goal of all my choices, anticipates them all without being itself transcended or put in question by any of them. Just as God was conceived as a self-sustaining being, so this projected self is conceived as a self-evaluating being, opaque to evaluative questioning in the sense that alternative answers are in its case not logically possible. Just as the being that exists necessarily is itself the ground of its own being, so the perfect self does not stand in need of any complementation through action; and any evaluative endorsements that human beings may confer upon it are redundant. In both cases, the subject of the evaluative as of the existential judgments is constructed in such a way as to subvert the normal relationship between actuality and possibility, and to make attribution of value and of existence follow necessarily from judgments of what is possible.

The case of necessary evaluative truths is less obviously one in which a question-stopping concept is constructed by sheer fiat, if only because many of our concepts, as has been pointed out, have in fact both descriptive and evaluative components. Nevertheless, the claim that there are necessary evaluative truths asserts more than that some concepts combine these functions; it requires that the evaluation be a logical implicate of the description. If such a nexus could be affected *in re,* then human beings would indeed confront a value to which their own endorsements would be irrelevant, and the very idea of alternative evaluative attitudes radically inappropriate. But if such a connection cannot be discovered, the declaration that it exists can amount to no more than an attempt to stop oneself from thinking in terms of contrasting evaluative attitudes toward that which the descriptive element in the concept describes, on the grounds that one of these attitudes *must* be incompatible with the latter. At the same time, in order to make clear what distinction is inapplicable, we first have to introduce the distinction between the nature of a thing and possible evaluative judgments on such a thing. Then, after we have been taught to use that distinction, we are simply told that in at least one case it must not be applied. The contradiction here is not one produced by making an assertion and then denying it. It is rather in the nature of an unresolved ambivalence in our treatment of the concept of possibility. We are at once irrevocably committed to its use and strongly moved to set limits to its range of application. If as between these two conflicting tendencies it is the attempt to circumscribe that breaks down (as the existentialists believe), that is because it is the concept of possibility that is, as it were, the going concern—the fundamental human way of looking at the world—and against this commitment to it, attempts to declare it inoperative by sheer fiat must be unavailing.

In spite of the tortuousity of his exposition, there can be no denying the power of Sartre's vision of man as the being who continually—one might almost say helplessly—opens up a gap between himself and his "world," and between himself as he is and as he might be, which his most ingenious efforts are powerless to close. Nor can there be any real doubt of the general harmony of his views on the "objectivity" of values with those of Heidegger.[30] Nevertheless, at least two points in his treatment of the whole topic of value raise serious questions about the conclusions that

[30] This seems clearly true in spite of Heidegger's denial that Sartre's position is in any way derived—except by misunderstanding—from his own. Of Sartre's "humanism" he says that in it "die Humanitas des homo humanus (wird bestimmt) aus dem Hinblick auf eine feststehende Auslegung der Natur, der Geschichte, der Welt des Weltgrundes, das heisst des Seienden im Ganzen." (*Über den Humanismus* Frankfurt: V. Klostermann, 1949), p. 11. This view which, if correct, would place Sartre in an intellectualistic and naturalistic tradition, appears to be based mainly, if not exclusively, on Sartre's *L'existentialisme est un humanisme* (Paris: Nagel, 1946); but it manifestly distorts the purport of that work, not to speak of *L'Être et le néant*.

are justified by this rejection of all value-property theories. Allusion has already been made to one of these points—Sartre's assertion that because value can never be a real property human beings are necessarily doomed to unhappiness.[31] This view has a surface plausibility, since it does follow from Sartre's conception of human beings that they will always be confronted by unfinished business. This fact in turn suggests a kind of restlessness and incapacity for final satisfaction which we may well be disposed to recognize as a form of unhappiness. What such a shaky chain of inferences obscures, of course, is the fact that there are very many different ways of having "unfinished business," and the myth of Sisyphus just is not an acceptable paradigm case for all of them. There is, after all, a distinction between lives that are crowned by achievement and those that issue in frustration and failure, and this is a distinction that is surely relevant to the business of making out—however difficult that may be—whether a man is happy or not. Or, to put the same point another way, if it can be laid down a priori that all men are necessarily unhappy because their moral being is not somehow prefabricated for them but must be fashioned and sustained by a continuing effort on the part of each of them, one can only conclude that this common unhappiness must be a very diluted, and probably by itself quite innocuous, affair. In any case, it should not be confused with the unhappiness that entails suffering and failure; and any convention of usage which (like Sartre's) fosters this confusion must be regarded as expressing the bias of an individual sensibility, and not as the inescapable consequence of an analysis of moral experience.

The second point which I wish to raise in connection with Sartre's position concerns his assumption that human being necessarily projects an "objectively valid" norm of what the self ought to be. In the account which I have given above, I have avoided this feature of Sartre's doctrine, and I have spoken instead of the postulation of such a norm as an (unsuccessful) strategy adopted by the self in an effort to suppress the anxiety that is inspired by an awareness of its own freedom. To be sure, the temptation to adopt this strategy may well be a permanent accompaniment of

[31] *Ibid.*, p. 134.

137

the human situation, and it is important to recognize how deep-seated our tendency to objectify value has been and continues to be. One goes well beyond such a recognition however when one says (as Sartre does) that human subjectivity can be defined *only* in terms of a lack of, and aspiration toward, an objectively valid moral ideal.[32] This is to commit oneself to the proposition that human beings always and necessarily entertain this ideal. Not only is this claim questionable simply on factual grounds but it has the further disadvantage of making it quite unclear how in these circumstances it would be possible to reject, in principle, all objectivistic conceptions of value. Such a rejection, involving as it does an insight into the impossibility of a value's ever being a cognizable object, surely requires a revised conception of the goals toward which human choices orient themselves. In this revision, an explicit recognition of the continuing duality of moral consciousness would replace the hopeless aspiration for absolute coalescence with one's terminal state of being. This point will assume special importance later in the course of the discussion of whether autonomy can itself become a goal. Here it is enough to observe that Sartre, by building a reference to an admittedly impossible ideal into the definition of moral consciousness, has seriously prejudged in an adverse sense that whole important question.

V

The upshot of this whole discussion is that the notion of knowing a thing to have a quality involving an essential relationship to an action which (as far as we know) may never take place, is intolerably confused and must be given up. To treat such a hybrid property as an object of knowledge is like saying that John is a father because he may some day have children; and surely this would be regarded as a very queer bit of knowledge. But if this reference from an actual state of affairs to an action to be performed is never something that is in the first instance *known*, it remains to ask whether, as the existentialists claim, it must be

[32] *Ibid.,* pp. 133 ff.

something that is *done*—a move that is made, and that can be known only reflexively and then as a first-personal act of the knower? What precise significance are we to attach to the assertion that moral judgments themselves, and not just our performance or nonperformance of what they require, have an act character? In the next chapter, in connection with my discussion of the concept of choice, I shall try to show that it is a mistake to interpret the "acts" of moral decision of which the existentialists speak as psychological events. Here, I am concerned only to show in what sense moral judgments themselves can be regarded as symbolic actions.

There are, as I have already suggested, great obstacles in the way of a recognition of the act character of moral judgments. Especially when established evaluative attitudes have been enshrined in the very language we use for talking about different kinds of situations, it becomes very difficult not to think of our own evaluative judgments as reports of a kind of phantom transcendence, carried out as it were in the third person, and the trajectory of which is simply to be retraced by the action itself. Nevertheless, even within the intellectualistic theory itself, which builds on this sense of the subordination of our particular evaluative judgments to prior standards over which we exercise no control, some indirect recognition of this act-character can be found. Surely, when such theories speak (as they often do) of value-properties as supervening properties, this participle suggests, in addition to a relationship of dependence of value properties on other nonvalue properties, an element of activity in this relationship.[33] Of course, it is the "properties" themselves that are said to supervene, and evaluative activity is thus conceived of once more as going on rather mysteriously in full independence of the human spectator. It may be suggested, however, that this talk of the "supervening" of the value property amounts to a tacit recognition of a kind of activity on the part of the moral agent who moves from the fact that X has certain other properties to the conclusion that he should act in a specific way. In any case, there

[33] In his essay, "The Concept of Intrinsic Value," *Philosophical Studies* (London: Routledge and Kegan Paul, 1922), G. E. Moore appears to be defending such a view of value properties although he does not speak of them as "supervening."

is a very obvious drift away from the conception of value properties as directly observed, toward a view that makes something beyond the mere content of present intuition necessary in the making of a value judgment. But, consistently with the underlying intellectualistic bias, the inferential movement beyond the presently-given must be represented as one that orients itself upon independent standards of validity (i.e., the universal truths that serve as the major premises of evaluative inference).

Even in its most strictly orthodox form, however, intellectualism after its own fashion treats moral judgment as an *act* which the individual moral agent performs. To be sure, it is an act of discovery, not of decision, and while I may be responsible for certain circumstances that can cause this act of judgment to deviate from its true object, I am not responsible for the fact that the moral truths which I discover are what they are. More relevantly for our purposes, there is implied in this notion of an act of moral judgment an element of explicit and deliberate focusing upon certain priorities of action that is quite different from any merely habitual and imperfectly objectified compliance with the established mores of a community. Moreover, there is associated with this personal responsibility that we assume in making a moral judgment, a measure of freedom from a whole range of pressures and coercions which have to be discounted or removed if our apprehension of the moral facts is not to be distorted. Together, these features of the act of moral judgment yield a distinctly intellectualistic conception of autonomy as the assumption of personal responsibility for the ascertaining of what is objectively right and wrong. This conception can be of assistance in understanding the still more radical interpretation of the act-character of moral judgments that is proposed by the existentialists. What I am suggesting is that the existentialist view of moral judgment as itself an act evolves out of the conception of an element of activity involved even in the apprehension of objective moral relationships, and that this evolution occurs precisely when (and because) the status as objects of knowledge of such relationships has been challenged and finally rejected.[34] A moral judg-

[34] This does not, of course, preclude the applicability of the more radical conception of act to the judgments and actions of persons who have not seen

ment is thus a decisional act, just in the sense that it is conceived as a determination which an individual human being makes for himself and as one for which there is no counterpart *in re*.

It is sometimes suggested that simply because I come to regard objective moral relationships as a kind of illusion, it does not follow that all moral judgments must be decisional in character, and that there are other alternatives beyond those given by the "knowledge or choice" disjunction. In a sense this is true, for I can, under certain circumstances, adopt a point of view external to the situation of the moral agent who has to make moral judgments, and simply register the incidence of certain expressions of approval and disapproval within the discourse of other persons without ever concerning myself about the degree to which these attitudes reflect an explicit and reflective assumption of a moral position by the individual involved. From this point of view, value judgments would be just so much grist for the behavioral scientist's prediction mill, and it would make little difference whether they had been "internalized" or not. They would simply occur, and the fact that they do not represent any kind of discovery would not, by itself, justify me in assuming that they are (in any meaningful sense) the issue of some conscious legislative activity on the part of those who are said to make them. The point to be made on behalf of the existentialists here is that this externalization of moral judgment can be only provisional, and that the paradigm case for analyses of moral judgment must be that of the person who recognizes that he himself must make his own judgments of what is good and right. If that is so, then it becomes much less obvious that there are other possible answers to the question about what one is doing in so judging; and while it can not be *proved* that the "knowledge–choice" disjunction is in fact exhaustive, the burden of proof is surely on those who deny that it is. If I cannot avoid thinking of myself as having to resolve one way or another certain questions of action, and if I am convinced that whatever form this resolution takes it cannot properly be represented as an apprehension of objective moral relationships,

---

through the objectivist "illusion," although the sense and degree of this applicability do pose some questions which are discussed in ch. 7.

then the possibility of a kind of somnambulistic carrying out of this function of moral judgment is eliminated. *Ex hypothesi* I know that I am *making* a judgment, and that this judgment cannot be reduced to a species of cognition. In these circumstances in which the question of what I am doing *has* been raised, I can only think of myself as establishing for myself the priorities which are not there to be discovered.

Something must be said here about the relationship of this conception of moral judgments as decisional acts to various theses about the linguistic vehicles that properly express them. There is a long tradition which holds that if moral judgments are not fact-stating in character, they must be viewed as concealed imperatives, and ideally should be cast in the imperative mood, which is supposed to be the appropriate means for expressing acts of volition just as the declarative mood is for acts of intellection. This conclusion (which seems to follow so naturally) has been widely accepted by partisans of the emotive theory, although it is in fact, open to many objections. While moral judgments are addressed to the person who makes them as well as to others, the notion of a command addressed to oneself is too unfamiliar, and in certain respects, too perplexing to serve as a useful model for understanding this function of moral judgments. Even in those cases in which moral judgments are primarily addressed to others, the notion of a command still raises difficulties, since in its standard use it presupposes a definite social relationship by virtue of which the person who commands does so rightfully, as in the case of a parent or a military officer. Such hierarchical relationships are not presupposed by moral judgments, however, and it would therefore appear that the effect of treating all moral judgments as commands would be both restrictive and in a special way tendentious.

There are a few passages in which Sartre appears to endorse an imperatival interpretation of moral judgments, but he has never developed this view at any length, so it may be doubted whether this endorsement has any special significance.[35] Certainly there is no reason to think that Sartre is committed to the view that one grammatical mood is uniquely appropriate as a vehicle for moral

[35] See *L'Être et le néant,* p. 720.

judgments. In so far as he may be said to have an explicit theory of the form of moral judgments at all, it would appear to be one that stresses not the grammatical type of such judgments, but rather their status as acts effected within a linguistic medium. Perhaps the clearest indication of this act-character of moral judgments is to be found in the sense of responsibility that attaches to them. In genuine (as distinct from hypothetical) deliberation on moral issues, the enunciation of a judgment to the effect that a certain action would be right or wrong commits the person making it in much the same way as the action itself would. Attitudes of praise and blame directed to the action quite naturally extend to those who endorse or recommend it, and the making of a moral judgment thus comes to be treated as a kind of action itself, a symbolic analogue of the decision that the person to whom the judgment is addressed is called upon to make.[36] This conception of the act–character of moral judgment remains undeveloped in Sartre's writings, perhaps because he rarely considers the kind of situation in which a moral judgment is not accompanied by action (e.g., situations in which judgments are offered to others as counsel or guidance).

One final point. The intent of this chapter has been to show that a certain view of evaluative predicates cannot be maintained in the face of the difficulties raised by the existentialist analysis of action; and that any satisfactory analysis of such predicates must be consistent with the volitional or decisional character which they have been shown to have. It should be made clear, however, that this conclusion does not provide by itself any complete interpretation of "good" or "right," and it most certainly does not establish that these words are somehow meaningless. Perhaps the cardinal error of intellectualism is its tendency to assume that if a predicate is meaningful, it must have a descriptive, property-denoting function. It would simply be another version of this error if a denial that value-predicates function in that way were to lead to the conclusion that they are a mere *flatus vocis*. For the

[36] Sartre's whole conception of "une littérature engagée" and of the moral responsibility which attaches to what one writes and says, whether one recognizes it or not, is his most extensively developed application of this theory of language as symbolic action.

moment, however, the mainly negative conclusions of this chapter must be allowed to stand until I undertake in Chapter VIII a positive interpretation of the notion of "right" and "obligation" that will be consistent with the anti-intellectualist conclusions reached in this chapter.

CHAPTER VII

FREEDOM AND CHOICE

In an earlier chapter, in the course of a discussion of Kant's ethical theory, a distinction was made between two quite different senses that the term "freedom" may bear in ethical contexts. One of these was the freedom of causal indeterminacy, and the other was the freedom of autonomous moral legislation. When the existentialists say that man is free, they mean that he is free in both of these senses, and they hold that both kinds of freedom can be seen to follow from the general account they have given of human being. In this chapter, I propose to examine the views of Heidegger and Sartre with respect to both kinds of freedom. This review should then make it possible to gain a better understanding of the central existentialist thesis that *man makes himself,* as well as of the equally well known definitions of human being as "care" and as a "project." This in turn will lead to an inquiry into what Heidegger and Sartre mean by choice, and to a consideration of the much-vexed topic of the relation of choice to moral rules and principles. Here again I will argue that the doctrine of the existentialists has been largely misunderstood, and that their position is not correctly described as an extreme individualism that makes no place for general rules within the structure of the moral life. Instead, it is a view of the status of general rules in their relationship to particular acts of choice; and while this view breaks sharply with the Aristotelian interpretation of the relation of choice to rules, it should not be interpreted as denying the need for consistent policies in the conduct of the moral life.

I

When the existentialists discuss causal determinism, they usually treat it as a set of methodological assumptions distinctive

145

of the scientific study of the natural world.[1] Their main argument is that this mode of treatment of natural phenomena not only develops out of the quite different conceptual system of common sense, but also remains dependent upon that prior mode of construing the relationship of human being to "things," and cannot be used to suppress or eliminate the latter. The familiar prescientific understanding that we have of our relationship to the world implicitly recognizes the uneliminability of alternative possibilities of action. Its characterization of human beings is organized around the notions of responsibility and choice that presuppose the reality of such alternatives. Scientific determinism, by contrast, following in the path of Spinoza, undercuts this whole set of concepts by treating the belief in alternative possibilities as a product of our ignorance of the true mechanism of nature—human nature included—and it projects a reflexive application to human beings of causal and deterministic assumptions that were originally developed for the purpose of controlling physical nature. The existentialists' counterargument, in essence, is that this mode of self-objectification is one that human beings cannot really carry out in a thoroughgoing and consistent way, and that even when the attempt is made, the more primitive nondeterministic set of concepts reasserts itself. The profound sense of their defense of human freedom is accordingly that of the Kantian argument that human beings are so constituted as to be unable to think of themselves as being causally determined; and they go on to add (as Kant did) that to be unable to think of yourself except as free is in effect to *be* free.[2]

While this assertion may sound strange to many ears, it does not proclaim any occult metaphysical doctrine. Indeed, it would be much more accurate to regard the existentialist defense of human freedom as antimetaphysical in intent than the reverse. It

[1] See, for example, Heidegger's essay, "Die Zeit des Weltbildes," *Holzwege*, especially pp. 73–74. While the existentialists have been mainly concerned to deny the applicability of deterministic modes of thought to human action they are not always prepared to concede them more than a provisional validity even in their application to nature. See Sartre's rather surprising statement on this subject in *Critique de la raison dialectique*, p. 129.

[2] *Grundlegung einer Metaphysik de Sitten*, ed. E. Cassirer (Berlin: B. Cassirer, 1913), Vol. 4, p. 307.

is antimetaphysical just in the sense that it refuses to undercut or devaluate our profound tendency to read the world in terms of alternative possibilities of action in the interest of some preconception of what the real must be. It undertakes to show that no scientific account of human action and behavior can ever, by itself, lay down the attitudes and perspectives of action that may supervene upon it, and it goes on to point out that a determinism that attempts this task must remain, as it were, a God's-eye-view which leaves human beings to resolve exactly the same indeterminacies as before.[3] As such, determinism is perhaps irrefutable but also gratuitous, since the assumption it makes is by no means necessary to the consistent carrying-on of scientific inquiry. While it may satisfy some deep metaphysical craving, it has the positive disadvantage of treating as a mere appearance what is in fact central to our understanding of the relation between action and knowledge. There is a kind of paradox involved in the notion that we are indissolubly committed to a concept—that of alternative possibilities—which we believe to be really inapplicable to anything. The course taken by the existentialists is that of refusing to abandon the concept of alternatives, and of interpreting scientific inquiry in such a way that it presupposes a relationship to the world in which alternatives have a place, instead of trying to fit human action into a conceptual world from which both alternatives and choice have been excised.

This way of arguing for the reality of human freedom has certain obvious sources as well as some perhaps not-so-obvious affinities with forms of argumentation that are current in the English-speaking philosophical world.[4] Its primary inspiration is clearly the transcendental point of view of Husserlian phenomenology; and from this point of view, as Merleau-Ponty has re-

[3] See Sartre's comments on Marxist determinism in "Matérialisme et Révolution," *Les Temps Modernes,* Vol. 2 (1946) , pp. 1–32, especially pp. 14 f.

[4] I have in mind here recent works like S. Hampshire, *Thought and Action* (London: Chatto and Windus, 1959) , and D. Pears (ed.) , *Freedom and the Will* (New York: St. Martin's Press, 1963) , as well as a number of articles like P. Herbst, "Freedom and Prediction," *Mind,* Vol. 66 (1957) , pp. 1–27, and K. Popper, "Indeterminism in Classical and Quantum Physics," *British Journal of the Philosophy of Science,* Vol. 1 (1950) , pp. 117–33 and pp. 173–95.

marked, the only way an object can be said to influence human consciousness is by serving as a point of departure for a new configuration of meaning.[5] Causal understanding of the world is only one such possible configuration of meaning; it cannot by itself give an account of the activity of conceptualization itself, or invalidate any competing set of concepts that may have presuppositions which conflict with its own. At the same time, it must be understood that in denying the reflexive applicability of deterministic modes of thought to human beings, the existentialists are not saying that the human organism and human behavior cannot be studied causally, but rather that there are other modes of concepualizing the latter and that whatever its value in its own sphere, causal explanation cannot, without becoming explicitly and inadmissably metaphysical, claim to override or to absorb all other modes of conceptualizing our experience—in particular, the evaluative mode. Their primary interest—like that of many analytic philosophers of the "ordinary language" persuasion—is in maintaining the integrity of distinctions that are operative at the phenomenological level, rather than in establishing—as classical metaphysics undertook to do—either that freedom is a mysterious power resident in the noumenal self, or that there are real possibilities in the world quite apart from its relationship to human subjectivity. What the existentialist line of argument establishes, if it is successful, is not that from some external and absolute "God's-eye-point-of-view" man is free, but rather that within the human situation the notions of predictability and freedom are complementary and interdependent.

The way in which the existentialist argument against determinism proceeds is not difficult to grasp; it is essentially similar to forms of argumentation that have been used for the same pur-

---

[5] *Phénoménologie de la perception,* pp. 496 ff. This chapter, "La liberté," contains Merleau-Ponty's most important statement on the subject of freedom and it takes the form of a sustained critique and revision of Sartre's theory of freedom in *L'Être et le néant.* At the end of the chapter, however, Merleau-Ponty reaffirms his original assertions that "rien ne me détermine du dehors" adding only that this is not because I choose myself "à partir de rien," because "je puis à chaque moment interrompre mes projets . . (et) commencer autre chose . . . il n'y a pas de cas où je suis entièrement pris." (pp. 515–16)

pose by nonexistentialists.[6] The paradigm of all such arguments is given by the case of a prediction of the way the stock market will behave. If this prediction becomes known, speculators may well act differently from the way they would have acted if it had not; and the prediction may be falsified as a result of becoming known. If the example is changed so that the prediction not only concerns the action that some human being will take in certain circumstances but also is made in accordance with some scientific theory about human behavior, it becomes possible to make the existentialist point against determinism quite concisely. If I am informed of this prediction of my behavior, this knowledge will open up alternative possibilities of action in the situation in which it is predicted that I will act in a certain way. In existentialist parlance, the prediction as well as the theory from which it derives and the sequence of events which that theory projects, become elements in my situation to which I can react in a number of different ways that are not determined by the theory itself. But, if coming to know a predictive theory of some kind by itself modifies the situation in question in a way that is relevant to the possibilities of action in it, then the deterministic case can be saved only by expanding the original theory to take account of these modifications. There would, therefore, have to be a second

[6] What follows represents an attempt to state in non-technical language the central ideas implicit in Heidegger's account of human existence as *Sich-vorweg-sein*. This is the notion of human existence as being constitutionally "out ahead of itself" and as anticipating the outcomes of sequences of events that are in progress with a view to making choices among them; and as such it is intimately associated with the concept of *Sorge*. It involves both a reference from the present to a projected future state of affairs and a reference backwards from that future to my present action. This is what Heidegger calls "das in der Zukunft gründende Sichentwerfen auf das 'Umwillen seiner selbst.'" (*Sein und Zeit*, p. 327). This *Sich-vorweg-sein* is also the basis of the indefeasible incompleteness of human existence and of the fact that "im Dasein immer noch etwas *aussteht*, was als Seinkönnen seiner selbst noch nicht 'wirklich' geworden ist." (p. 236) Furthermore, precisely because every attempt at an exhaustive characterization of human existence leaves a residue of possibilities of action, any deterministic theory of human nature will necessarily—and not just by virtue of some remediable error—become an element within a system of human praxis, i.e., of the projection and realization of possibilities of action, which it does not itself comprehend. Sartre's theory of freedom is in its essentials very similar to Heidegger's and is fully stated in *L'Être et le néant*, pp. 508 ff.

law-based prediction in which my reaction to the circumstances specified in the first law, as well as to the prediction itself, would be taken into account. But the same issue arises with respect to this second law: does it predict what I will do in these circumstances if I also know of *this* new prediction? It appears that as long as I know what it is predicted I will do, a series of possibilities opens up that cannot be foreclosed by that prediction. Even if I went ahead and did what it was predicted I would do, knowing that it was so predicted, the case would be the same. Because this action that I thus perform is now only one among a number of alternative modes of reaction to my knowledge of the prediction, I will have to think of myself as having done this *rather than* something else; and this is to say that I would have chosen to do it.[7] Thus, when the prediction is known, even the course of action that confirms it does so in a way that offers no support to determinism. For I can not be sure that I will not use my knowledge of the law cited in the prediction for the purpose of intervening to forestall the predicted outcome. As a result, my predictive certainty must always remain at one remove from the point at which the question of action arises. Only after making a choice *without* any theory-based assurance of what that choice must be does it become possible to assess the "influence" of that knowledge upon the choices I make. And even if I succeed in expanding my original theory so that it incorporates that influence, the same kind of uncertainty as before will have reproduced itself at a higher level.[8]

[7] I may, of course, in a quasi-deliberate way, *avoid* thinking of what happens as my action and think of myself instead as passively awaiting an outcome. Heidegger calls this strategy of the inauthentic self *"Erwarten,"* or *"Gewärtigen,"* and it amounts to a concealment of the *Sichvorwegsein* discussed in n. 6:

Das Dasein kommt nicht primär in seinem eigensten, unbezüglichen Seinkönnen auf sich zu, sondern es ist besorgend *seiner gewärtig aus dem, was das Besorgte ergibt oder versagt. (Sein und Zeit,* p. 337.) Vom Wirklichen aus und auf es zu wird das Mögliche in das Wirkliche erwartungsmässig hereingezogen *(ibid.,* p. 262) .

[8] The existentialist argument is intended to show that it is impossible for me to predict what I will do. For a defense of the same thesis by an analytical philosopher, see C. Ginet, "Can The Will Be Caused?" *Philosophical Review,* Vol. 71 (1962) , pp. 49–55.

It would be easy to imagine predictions made in circumstances that clearly exclude the possibility of any course of action alternative to the one predicted. Thus, if a man is falling from a building and I shout to him, "You are going to be killed," it is hardly plausible to suggest that his awareness of this prediction conjures up a range of possible courses of action by which the prediction will be falsified; nor would it be sensible to say that by continuing to fall he shows that he has chosen to do so. But to treat an example like this as fatal to the existentialist argument would be to assume—erroneously—that the latter claims some sort of effective omnipotence for human beings.[9] *Ex hypothesi,* there is in this case no possible *action* that will keep the falling man from being killed. All the existentialist needs to claim, however, is that in every situation there is some respect in which a spread of alternatives is open, and that it is impossible for a human being to build himself and his conscious life into a predictive scientific theory in such a way as to close down all but one possibility of action. The possibilities that *are* effectively open may be insignificant ones as in the case of the falling man, or momentous ones that will affect the whole subsequent course of our lives. In any case, as long as the slightest penumbra of possibility surrounds what is unchangeable in our experience, there is no limit that can be set to the eventual difference that may be made by the actions we institute, and nothing can remain wholly immune to the contingency that is introduced into the world by the possibility of action.[10]

It has often been pointed out, even by philosophers who would

[9] If proof is needed that no such omnipotence is being claimed, there are many passages in *L'Être et le néant* which make this very clear. See especially pp. 562, 568, 576.

[10] In this connection, the tendency of the existentialists to speak of a "choice" of the world, or, as in Heidegger's case, of an *Weltentwurf,* can be misleading unless two qualifications are understood. One has been stated explicitly by Sartre: "Nous choisissons le monde—non dans sa contexture en-soi, mais dans sa signification." (*L'Être et le néant,* p. 541.) The other is that, like some idealists who thought that the absolute was the final subject of all predications, the existentialists tend to say that the object of all choices is a certain state of the world even though it is only some relatively minor feature of the world that can actually be affected by our choosing one way or another. In other words, we "choose" that the world remain as it is in those respects in which we are not seeking to change it.

accept much of the existentialist case as presented so far, that it leaves open the possibility of a study of all human activities on deterministic principles, provided the inquiry and the predictions it produces are somehow kept isolated from the system of events that forms its subject matter.[11] Since this condition is in fact often satisfied, at least for all practical purposes, and since even when it is not, the motive of refuting a prediction in order to demonstrate the indeterminacy of voluntary human action is in most cases either weak or nonexistent, it can be argued that the inability of human beings to think of themselves as determined does not really constitute a serious obstacle to the "objective" scientific study of voluntary action. This may well be true, but it should be noted that in one important case—that of the scientific inquirer himself—the scientific theory cannot be kept isolated from the actions it is supposed to predict; and here, at least, it will open up possibilities of action that do not themselves come within the purview of the theory.[12] From the point of view of the scientist who formulates a theory, the behavior of all persons to whom that theory applies but who are themselves ignorant of the latter and therefore cannot make it a premise of any of their practical deliberations, will no doubt seem "determined." At the same time, to the extent that they are conceded to be capable of comprehending the theory in question in the way that its formulator already does, their relation to it is potentially the same as his currently is; and if they *were* to stand in this relationship to the theory, the same indeterminacy would prevail with regard to the possibilities of action it suggests to them. From the existentialists' point of view, it is a kind of accident that human beings are located at different levels of the knowledge pyramid and the only proper characterization of their relation to what they *know* about themselves is given by what we might call "the view from the top." This kind of presentation of the human situation is cer-

[11] A very interesting discussion of the requirement that knowledge of a prediction be kept from the person whose behavior is being predicted can be found in D. Mackay, "The Logical Indeterminacy of Free Choice," *Mind*, Vol. 69 (1960), pp. 31–40.

[12] For a discussion of the pervasive tendency to overlook this fact, see M. Mandelbaum, "Some Instances of the Self-Excepting Fallacy," *Psychologische Beiträge*, Vol. 6 (1962), pp. 383–86.

tainly misleading to the degree that it suggests that we all stand in the same relationship of total "presence" to the whole sum of what is known about us, but it has the merit of not committing the self-excepting fallacy by which the special relationship of the scientist to his theory is virtually suppressed and allowed no place in our general characterization of the *praxis* of human beings.[13]

II

The nature of autonomy—the second kind of freedom distinguished earlier—can be understood by analogy with the causal freedom that I have just been describing as well as by inference from the conclusions reached in the last chapter.[14] This kind of

[13] Sartre's theory of human *praxis* has been extensively developed in *Critique de la raison dialectique*.

[14] Incomparably the most important statement of the positive existentialist theory of autonomy is contained in Pt. 4 of *L'Être et le néant*, especially ch. 1, "Être et Faire: la liberté." While the foundation for that theory was laid by Heidegger, there is no detailed analysis of action as such, or of practical deliberation to be found in his works, except as can be extracted from his discussions of *Entwurf* and *Sichvorwegsein* and *Sorge*. The latter, of course, provide the basis for Sartre's whole analysis of action, but the advantage of that analysis lies just in the fact that it effects a partial translation of the above notions into the language traditionally used for talking about practical deliberation. It is a misfortune that this section of *L'Être et le néant* has not been read with more care by the various exponents and critics of existentialism, since such a reading would dispel most of the misapprehensions of Sartre's philosophical intentions by which so much critical discussion of his work has been marred.

The central assertion of Sartre's theory of autonomy is that "la liberté n'a pas d'essence. Elle n'est soumise à aucune nécessité logique . . . Elle se fait acte et nous l'atteignons ordinairement à travers l'acte qu'elle organise avec les motifs, les mobiles et les fins qu'il implique." (*L'Être et le néant*, p. 513.) Freedom is also said to be "l'unique fondement des valeurs"; and since these values "se révèlent par essence à une liberté," they cannot be apprehended "sans être mises en question puisque la possibilité de renverser l'échelle des valeurs apparaît complémentairement comme *ma* possibilité." (*Ibid.*, p. 76.) On the other hand, the "world" of everyday experience which my free acts help shape *does* have an evaluative structure and we are often misled into supposing that an antecedently established structure confronts our liberty itself. When Sartre describes freedom as "un échappement au donné, au fait," he is signalizing precisely this independence of any such logical compulsion, as well as the constitutive role of our freedom in relation to the structures of reasons and ends that emerge from practical deliberation. Thus, "le donné

freedom has to do with the analysis of the situation in which action is to be undertaken and not with the possibility of alternative courses of action as the first did. The function of such analysis is to select those features of a situation by virtue of which a certain line of action becomes appropriate, and on the basis of this determination, to characterize the situation in such a way that it "points" to that action as its appropriate fulfillment. When I organize a situation for purposes of action in this way, I may be said to transcend the features of it upon which I light by incorporating them into a temporal *Gestalt* of which the other pole is some outcome or resolution that has yet to take place, and the occurrence of which is at least partly dependent upon my action. Once this analysis has been carried out and the situation has been conceptually oriented toward action in the manner described, I can speak of the "fact" that the situation has the features in question as my "reason" for acting in the way I propose to act, and of this state of affairs itself as calling for a certain kind of action on my part.

The freedom human beings enjoy in structuring such situations with reference to action—the freedom of autonomy—consists negatively in the fact that a situation does not indicate by itself which of its features are criterial for what kind of action. This is no more than to restate the conclusion of Chapter VI according to which it makes sense to say that it is true that X is a feature of situation Y, but no sense at all to say that it is true that feature X of situation Y is reason for acting in a certain way. Positively, this notion of autonomy is intended to signify that the transformation of a situation of fact into one that is oriented toward action is itself an act that individuals perform, and for which they alone are ultimately responsibile.[15] This is an act of

---

n'est ni *cause* de la liberté (puisque il ne peut produire que du donné), ni *raison* (puisque toute 'raison' vient au monde par la liberté." (p. 567) Another term that Sartre often uses to convey the relationship of a free agent to the states of affairs, the "facts" upon which his action supervenes is "recul néantisant," and by that "pulling back" Sartre says "la liberté fait qu'un système de relations s'établisse du point de vue de la fin entre 'les' en-soi, c'est à dire entre le *plenum* d'être qui se révèle alors comme *monde* et l'être qu'elle a à être . . . au milieu de ce *plenum*." (p. 567)

[15] See *L'Être et le néant*, pp. 522 ff. Sartre speaks of "la conscience qui découpe le motif dans l'ensemble du monde . . (et) s'est donné ses fins" and

conceptualization through which a particular situation is characterized by reference to selected features which are thus made to
function as the springboard for action of a certain sort. Thus, to
characterize another person's conduct as "disrespectful" or as
"cruel" is to place it in a particular perspective of action, at the
same time that it states a fact about that person. The autonomous
character of this act naturally requires that it should have been
possible for me to conceptualize the same situation differently,
but this requirement which is closely connected with my *causal*
freedom is not the whole story. The more important feature of
autonomy is what I have called our logical freedom in evaluation, which results from the absence of any standard of truth to
which such acts of evaluative conceptualization should somehow
correspond or by reference to which they might be justified.

The relationship between causal freedom and logical freedom
or autonomy can now be stated. If human beings were not causally free in the sense that there always remain unreduced alternative courses of action in some sphere of their lives, there would
clearly be no point in speaking of them as enjoying evaluative autonomy, since the notion of action would have lost its application. But the existentialists also contend that if human beings
were causally free but not autonomous (i.e., not logically free),
the concept of action would have been effectively subverted
again.[16] This is a more difficult thesis to accept because it is by no
means clear that the concept of action, as ordinarily understood,
by itself excludes the availability of objective moral truths. But
while we may hesitate to make this logical freedom an element in
the concept of action, the arguments of Chapter VI appear to
show that in the full sense appropriate to human beings, action
requires both a range of possible alternatives and an autonomous
structuring of the action situation through which the latter is
oriented toward some possible course of action as its appropriate

---

he argues that "cette organisation interne que la conscience s'est donnée
. . . est rigoureusement corrélative du découpage des motifs dans le monde."
(p. 525)

[16] Thus, Sartre explicitly declares that "angoisse," considered as an awareness, however indistinct, of the absence of extrinsic justification for one's
action, is a condition of action itself and "fait partie de l'action même."
(*L'Existentialisme est un humanisme,* p. 33.)

resolution. What this comes to, in practice, is that all established and "impersonal" ways of tieing situations of fact to projects of action (however natural and rationally compelling they may seem), are in principle decomposable into the elements of fact and evaluation. Stated in this way, the existentialist doctrine would take the form of a claim that it is always possible in principle to dismantle the whole structure of established evaluative concepts, and thereby to reach a kind of ground-zero of the moral life which will serve as a base-point for our understanding of the latter. It is to say that there is no association of an evaluative attitude with a type of situation that is so inveterate or so inevitable as to be able to resist permanently such analytic isolation and recombination of its elements. Of course it may be that no exact translation of an implicitly evaluative concept into factual and evaluative components will be possible because of the indefinitely large range of implications for action that such a concept may suggest, depending on the circumstances, but at least the general lines on which such a translation would proceed can be made clear. If human beings are, in principle, capable of carrying out this kind of analysis of what seem at first to be seamless unities of description and evaluation, they must also be capable of experiencing for themselves both the absence of logical controls over the way in which these unities are constituted and the act-character of the evaluative judgment by which factual premises are associated with conclusions that direct to action.

The preceding remarks suggest that we need to think of autonomy in two rather different ways.[17] First, there is the logical freedom which consists simply in the absence of any independent standard of truth or validity governing the way in which evaluative premises are associated with factual premises. Still, a negative logical freedom of this kind might conceivably obtain without a person's ever recognizing it for what it is or finding any positive equivalent for it in his own moral experience. This possibility makes it necessary to consider autonomy as an attribute or capa-

[17] The distinction between negative and positive aspect of autonomy is reflected in Sartre's statement that "l'injustifiabilité (du choix) n'est pas seulement la reconnaissance subjective de la contingence absolue de notre être, mais encore celle de l'intériorisation et de la reprise à notre compte de cette contingence." (*L'Être et le néant*, p. 542.)

bility of persons, rather than just as a feature of the language used for the formulation of moral judgments. Even if we accept the "decomposability-in-principle" of all concepts in which factual and evaluative claims are associated with one another, we may well wonder whether there are not people who are unable to make sense of this notion and who do not in fact experience any logical gap between the set of factual premises describing their situation and the course of action which they consider to be right. In what sense could such persons be said to possess a freedom that they are unable to recognize in their actual moral experience? It might be argued, too, that such an inability is not exceptional but typical of the familiar moral situation in which most of us find ourselves. This situation is one in which we more or less unthinkingly accept and employ a wide range of implicitly evaluative concepts for the purpose of identifying and describing persons, situations, objects, institutions, etc. To the extent that we do this—and all of us of course do—we live in a preevaluated world; and the more habitual our acceptance of an established way of tieing situations of fact to certain specified modalities of action, the less sense we are likely to have of either the first-personal act-character of evaluation, or of the absence of logical limitations on the form that evaluation takes. Indeed, to the moral consciousness that is firmly rooted in some operating moral consensus of this kind, the claim that human beings are autonomous in either of these senses will seem not just problematic but directly contrary to the plain testimony of common sense. Here, then, is a situation in which the 'vulgar moral consciousness' appears to deny the applicability to it of the very conclusions with respect to autonomy which we have felt compelled to accept. We are therefore forced to ask what features of ordinary moral consciousness justify us in applying to it the very characterization which it rejects; and also, to what extent this rejection itself might have the effect of limiting the relevance of the enriched existentialist concept of action to that ordinary moral consciousness.

This issue of how the concept of moral autonomy is to be meaningfully applied to persons who do not in fact recognize themselves as autonomous has been the occasion of a rather serious disagreement among the existentialists themselves.[18] Briefly, this disagreement has turned on the question whether freedom or autonomy can be said to be capable of degrees, or whether it is necessarily absolute and total wherever it exists. In the existentialist idiom, this becomes the question whether the consciousness that confers the evaluative indeterminacy on natural events by virtue of which we are enabled to set them in alternative perspectives of action is a special reflective development of ordinary consciousness, or whether this function is attributable to *all* states of consciousness. Sartre has defended the latter view, and Merleau-Ponty and others have argued for a conception of freedom as susceptible of degrees of realization. They have argued that it is possible simply to *be,* e.g., a worker or a bourgeois, without having the special form of self-consciousness that at once detaches us from our condition and communicates to it the volitional character of which I have spoken. This amounts to saying that it is not only possible but normal for human beings to remain almost entirely within a single mode of evaluative conceptualization which they share with others, and which they tend to treat as an unanalyzed whole without ever feeling a need to resolve it into its factual and evaluative components, and consequently without having any sense of autonomous activity on their own part in connection with the use of such concepts. As Merleau-Ponty puts it, these "public" evaluative concepts constitute a kind of *intermonde* between the evaluative indeterminacy of things and the self-conscious evaluative activity of the individual.[19]

Sartre, by contrast, has argued that there is, in addition to the explicit reflective form of self-consciousness which he concedes is by no means universally shared, a "nonthetic" form of self-consciousness which *is* a necessary structural feature of all conscious experience, and through which we all are aware of our

---

[18] See M. Merleau-Ponty, *Phénoménologie de la perception*, p. 496. These criticisms of Sartre's conception of the *pour-soi* are developed further in Merleau-Ponty's posthumously published *Le visible et l'invisible*, pp. 75–130. For a defense of Sartre against Merleau-Ponty's criticisms, see F. Jeanson, *Le problème morale et la pensée de Sartre*, pp. 302–11.

[19] For a more detailed explanation of this notion of an *intermonde* see Merleau-Ponty, *Phénoménologie de la perception*, pp. 409, 410.

own moral freedom.[20] It may be that this prejudgmental form of self-consciousness amounts to no more than the capability in principle of all human beings for the kind of explicit objectification of their situation that breaks down established fact-value unities.[21] If such an analysis were permissible, then to say that a man is absolutely free would mean that there is no feature of his condition that could not be made a theme for self-conscious reflection and, thereby, the object of a range of possible attitudes and the point of departure for different courses of action. But it often seems that Sartre's categorical attribution of freedom to human beings goes well beyond any purely dispositional interpretation; and to the extent that it does, it has the disadvantage of making it sound as though the task of organizing our experience around foci of self-conscious reflection were accomplished *ab initio*.[22] By thus introducing the sophistication of more highly developed levels of self-consciousness into all states of mind, the illusion is created that *all* choices are made from the vantage point of an absolute self-consciousness that has surrounded its entire natural condition with the halo of evaluative indeterminacy that frees for action. Considered as a description of the state of mind

[20] See Sartre's account of this "pre-reflexive" or "non-thetic" consciousness of self, *L'Être et le néant*, pp. 66–23. Applying this doctrine to freedom, he says that since "rien n'existe dans la conscience si non comme conscience non-thétique d'exister . . . je dois nécessairement posséder une certaine compréhension de la liberté." (*Ibid.*, p. 514.) A similar distinction between ontological and pre-ontological understanding of being is made by Heidegger, *Sein und Zeit*, p. 12.

[21] This is suggested by Sartre's conception of human existence as a *pouvoir-être* which seems to imply that freedom while very different from our ordinary powers and capacities, has in some sense a dispositional character and does not therefore have to be constantly in exercise. Thus, Sartre can say that "nous sommes tels, par le choix même de notre liberté, que nous pouvons toujours faire apparaître l'instant comme rupture de notre unité ek-statique." *L'Être et le néant*, p. 544.

[22] This seems to be suggested by the following passage:

(Le choix) ne fait qu'un avec la conscience que nous avons de nous-même. Cette conscience . . . ne saurait être que non-positionnelle: elle est con-science-nous puisqu' elle ne se distingue pas de notre être. Et comme notre être est precisément notre choix originel, la conscience (de) choix est identique à la conscience que nous avons (de) nous. (*L'Être et le néant*, p. 539.)

that accompanies action in the great majority of cases, this account is, of course, simply false. Since a categorical attribution of total freedom will always tend to be understood in this way, it seems much wiser to guard against such a misrepresentation of ordinary consciousness by adopting the progressive and dispositional form of the theory of autonomy that is favored by Merleau-Ponty.

The advantages of this version of the theory are considerable and obvious. If freedom were always total and not susceptible of degrees, then everyone would be equally free; the slave who fought to free himself would enjoy no greater freedom than the slave who passively accepted his chains. In Merleau-Ponty's words, there would be no "natural analogue" to ontological freedom, since the latter would be equally compatible with all conditions of life. In order to account for actual progress from a condition of slavery to one of freedom, we would obviously have to assign much greater importance within our theory of freedom to those acts of reflective moral consciousness by which a gap is opened up between our situation and a range of possible alternatives. We would also have to de-emphasize correspondingly the role attributed by Sartre to nonthetic consciousness, on the ground that the freedom associated with the latter proves almost impossible to distinguish from the simple absence of logical restraints discussed above.

At the same time, in avoiding Sartre's error, we must be careful not to fall into its opposite. If it is a mistake to talk about human beings in such a way as to suggest that their relationship to their situation and themselves is wholly in the volitional mode and that they are always subtly detached from whatever positive characteristics they possess by the logical freedom with which they are endowed, it would be equally erroneous to conclude that the *only* sense of autonomy that is applicable to most human beings is the first one distinguished above, i.e., autonomy conceived as the mere absence of any logical obstacle to the dissolution of the specious unities of fact and value which are the common currency of the moral life. This would amount to saying that in most cases the application of the second sense of autonomy, which requires at least a measure of personal realization of this freedom, must remain entirely hypothetical. Now there certainly is an important hypothetical aspect to the existentialist attribution of autonomy to human beings, since its characterization of our condition takes the form of a number of implications which we would have to accept if we were to follow through to the end of a certain path of reflection on our moral experience. It may be freely conceded that most of us have not gone very far along that route, and as I have already remarked in connection with Sartre, one legitimate criticism of the existentialist doctrine of autonomy is that it seems to imply that we have moved much farther toward a condition of self-conscious moral freedom than many of us in fact have. At the same time, all of us in at least some area of our lives do think of ourselves as devising and choosing our own policies of action within a measure of logical freedom.[23] This freedom may be thought of as operating only in the less important areas of our lives, and as limited in its range by objective norms over the validity of which we exercise no control. After all, autonomy does not have to be all-pervasive in order to be genuine. Just as causal freedom requires not that we be omnipotent but only that in some area of our lives there remain some unreduced alternative courses of action, so an attribution of autonomy should not be taken to imply that we have actually carried out an analysis into factual and evaluative components of all the action-directing concepts we employ, or even that we have recognized the possibility in principle of such analyses. It would imply merely that somewhere in our actual moral practice we reveal our ability to carry out this kind of analysis, and are aware of a hiatus between our situation and our projects of action. I do not think it is outra-

[23] This point is clearly made by Sartre in *L'Existentialisme est un humanisme* when he declares that the "angoisse" which he elsewhere explains as "l'absence totale de justification en même temps que la responsibilité à l'égard de tous," is not some exotic experience unknown to the great mass of humanity.

Il s'agit d'une angoisse simple, que tous ceux qui ont eu des responsabilités connaissent. Lorsque, par exemple, un chef militaire prend la responsabilité d'une attaque et envoie un certain nombre d'hommes à la mort, il choisit de le faire, et au fond il choisit seul. Sans doute il y a des ordres qui viennent d'en haut, mais ils sont trop larges et une interprétation s'impose, qui vient de lui . . . Il ne peut pas ne pas avoir, dans la décision qu'il prend, une certaine angoisse." (p. 32)

geously audacious to suggest that any human being who is capable of moral judgment at all is very likely to be capable of some form of such analysis. If so, the existentialist attribution of autonomy to such an individual would signify not just that there is no logical obstacle in the way of extending such an analysis to all fact-value concepts, but also that there is a positive presumption that he can raise the kinds of question that lead into such analyses of an indefinitely large class of these concepts. No doubt he may break off at some point, either because he no longer really knows how to perform the analysis at the level of generality that has been reached, or because he resists the demand for such analyses on philosophical grounds of his own. Even so, if we hold that such philosophical objections must fail, then the "decomposability-in-principle" of all such concepts signifies simply our justified presumption that human beings are in fact capable of pressing that analysis at least some distance, and in any case cannot *justify* their refusal to press it further. As in the case of causal freedom, where even the most exiguous residue of alternative possiblities of action suffices to bring an element of uncertainty into the whole structure of our predictive knowledge, so a very small amount of effectively realized autonomy sets us on a track of moral interrogation on which there can be no turning back.

III

Very little has been said up to this point about choice, and yet the concept of choice is of fundamental importance to the ethical theory of existentialism, as the writings of Jean-Paul Sartre in particular make clear.[24] It is time now to turn our attention to

[24] Although the whole of Pt. 4, ch. 1 of *L'Être et le néant* has a direct bearing on the topic of choice, Sartre's detailed discussion of it begins on p. 539. Of particular importance in this section are the identification of choice as "l'acte fondamental de la liberté" (p. 539) and the equating of choice and action. "Notre déscription de la liberté ne distinguant pas entre le choisir et le faire, nous oblige à renoncer du coup à distinction entre l'intention et l'acte." (p. 564) It should also be noted that, while Sartre sometimes speaks as though the fact that a thing has been chosen were the *reason* why it has value, his true view of the relationship of goodness and choice seems to be rather that to assign a value to a thing *is* to choose it.

this concept, and to attempt to dispel some of the persistent confusions and misinterpretations that have been characteristic of
much critical discussion of its place and function within existentialist philosophy. These clarifications will in the first instance
bear upon the nature of choice itself, and are intended to show
that the choice of which the existentialists make so much is not,
as many critics have supposed, a kind of psychological event. The
positive account of choice which I will propose is one that follows
quite directly and obviously from my earlier discussions of logical
freedom in evaluation, once these misunderstandings are set
aside, and after outlining it briefly, I will show how it can be
made to yield acceptable interpretations of such characteristically
existentialist uses of the concept of choice as "choice of oneself"
and "total choice."

If the assumption that choice must be a psychological event is
the most serious obstacle to an understanding of the existentialist
position, another potential source of misunderstanding has already been dealt with in the discussions of this chapter and the
preceding one. I have in mind the very widespread tendency to
suppose that choice is not only an inner act of self-determination,
but also that it can properly supervene only *after* the action-
situation has been analytically laid out in such a way that its ac-
tion-relevant features are made evident. This is indeed the classical, Aristotelian account of choice, and as I have already shown,
it rests on the further assumption that there are independently
valid moral principles by which the identification of these fea-

---

Thus, in *L'Être et le néant,* p. 541, he can say that "la valeur des choses. . .
ne [fait] rien d'autre qu'esquisser mon image, c'est à dire mon choix." Finally,
Sartre's clarification of the sense in which choice can and cannot be properly
described as "absurd" is of importance:

Ce choix n'est pas absurde au sens où, dans un univers rationnel, un
phénomène surgirait qui ne serait pas relié aux autres par des *raisons:* il est
absurde en ce sens qu'il est ce par quoi tous les fondements et toutes les
raisons viennent à l'être, ce par quoi la notion même d'absurde reçoit un
sens. (p. 559)

Once again, there is no discussion of choice as such in Heidegger's writings,
but there are numerous passages in which he uses the terms *"Wahl"* and
"Wählen" in a way closely similar to Sartre. See, for example, *Sein und Zeit,*
pp. 42, 268, 283, 287.

tures of the situation is controlled. By contrast, the existentialist concept of choice is one that embraces this initial characterization of the action-situation itself.[25] What this means is that the choices we think of ourselves as making on the basis of a certain analysis of the morally relevant features of a situation are only the visible tip of a much more radical choice which includes that analysis itself. It also means that no feature of any state of affairs can confer on itself the status of being what is called a "good-making consideration" or reason, and that it acquires this status only within the context of the very system of evaluative preferences for which it is supposed to provide some measure of independent support. The force of the existentialist thesis that to treat some feature of an existing situation as a reason is—implicitly at least—to choose or decide that it should be one, is to remind us that once we understand the underivability of our eval-

[25] "Les motifs, les mobiles et les fins, comme aussi bien la manière de saisir les motifs, les mobiles et les fins sont organisés unitairement dans les cadres de cette liberté et doivent se comprendre à partir d'elle." (*L'Être et le néant*, p. 529.) This triad—"motifs, mobiles, fins"—represents the structure of action and of choice according to Sartre and a correct understanding of its meaning is of great importance. First, a "motif" is "la *raison* d'un acte. . . l'ensemble des considérations rationnelles qui le justifient." (*Ibid.*, p. 522.) It is also "objective" since it designates "l'état de choses contemporain, tel qu'il se dévoile à une conscience" (p. 524) or some portion thereof. It would presumably include also any purely predictive judgments of the effect of acting in one way or another. The "motif" is thus something very like a factual premise in a practical syllogism; and with respect to it Sartre has three main points to make. It is, he argues, identical with the "mobile" or motive considered as a subjective disposition like ambition or jealousy, since to be, e.g., ambitious in the sense that is relevant to the understanding of action is precisely to take some state of affairs as a reason—"motif"—for acting in a certain way. (See p. 525.) Sartre's second point, which has already been made clear, is that the ends or "fins" to which action is directed are posited or chosen and chosen from among the possible outcomes which can be influenced by something it is in my power to do. (*L'existentialisme est un humanisme*, p. 50.) Finally, and most important, Sartre asserts that no "donné," no apprehension of a state of affairs can yield a "motif" except "dans et par le projet d'une action" i.e., no "fact" becomes a "reason" except by virtue of an evaluation which is at bottom the same choice as the choice of the end. "Il n'y a pas de signes dans le monde" (*ibid.*, p. 50) , and all justification however elaborate it may become takes place within a system of choices which imply "un recul par rapport au donné . . . une rupture de continuité." (*L'Être et le néant*, p. 557) ; and this holds true whether the "continuity" is, as Sartre says, "purement logique (*raison*) ou logico-chronologique (cause, déterminisme) ." (*Ibid.*, p. 548.)

uative judgments from anything that could be called a truth (whether necessary or contingent) , we have no alternative but to espouse them as our own choices.

Nevertheless, this very clarification of the scope of the existentialist concept of choice reinforces the difficulties associated with the interpretation (referred to at the outset) of choice as an episode in the mental life. If the determination of what are the morally relevant features of any given situation is to be thought of as having been accomplished in the course of such episodes, then simply at the factual level the claim that the existentialists appear to be making will strike many people as obviously and even grotesquely false. Very likely they will have no recollection of any such episodes in their own past, and the notion that they have been making such radical choices all along without being aware of it will strike them as highly implausible as indeed it would be if this were an accurate statement of the existentialist view.[26] From earlier discussions in this chapter and the last, it should be clear that the existentialists are not making a claim of this sort. They are not saying that some event occurred in our past of which we nevertheless have no present recollection; but rather, that there is no valid alternative mode of description of what did occur in the relevant portions of our past that does not make use of the concept of choice. This leaves open the possibility that at the time we did not think of what we were doing as making a choice or at least not a choice of fundamental moral principles. But even if we did not, perhaps because we believed that those principles were truths of some sort, the existentialist tells us that we must now retrospectively revise our description of what we did and that from now on, we must think of ourselves as choosing in a great many contexts which we may previously have thought of as beyond the range of choice.[27]

[26] Heidegger does speak of a "forgetting" (*Vergessen*) that is characteristic of the inauthentic self, but what is forgotten ("suppressed" would be a better word) is not choice-episodes in our past but the radical choice-character of our life as a whole. (See *Sein und Zeit,* p. 339.)

[27] This seems to me to be what Heidegger has in mind when he speaks of "das Sichzurückholen aus dem Man," i.e., the assumption of authentic and responsible selfhood, as being accomplished through a "Nachholen einer Wahl" which he explains also as the choice of a choice. The "choice" that is

In seeking to dispel some of the confusion that surrounds these existentialist views on the subject of choice, it will be useful to appeal to a distinction that is widely recognized in analytical ethics. This is the distinction between two uses of the verb "to choose." One of these leaves open the question whether the person who is said to choose or to have chosen in fact *did* whatever it was that he chose to do. The other use of "choose" carries the implication that that person either did (or tried to do) what he is said to have chosen. Thus we can say that X chose to take a chemistry course instead of physics, but changed his mind before the term began and took physics. Alternately, we can say that Cato of Utica *chose* death in preference to dishonor, and thereby convey the fact that he actually killed himself. In the first case, the choice reported by a statement is not unnaturally interpreted as expressing a perhaps private resolution or decision—an episode in our conscious lives that may be of primary importance in leading us to behave in one way rather than in another but which can (logically) occur without our actually going on to behave in that way. By contrast, to say in the second sense that X chose to do Y is really equivalent to saying that X *did* do Y. Whatever preliminary resolutions may have preceded that action, these are not what the verb reports; and it is really quite indifferent whether they took place or not. To choose (in this sense) is simply to act in a voluntary and intentional manner, and the action need not have anything private or mental about it.

For reasons that are not entirely clear, most critics of existentialism appear to assume that as between these two uses of the verb "to choose," the existentialists have unambiguously opted in favor of the first (or psychological) use. Not only is there no basis in the relevant texts for such an assumption; there is also a great deal of evidence that this interpretation of their views is quite alien to the existentialists themselves. Against it, there are explicit statements by existentialists that any theory of choice as a kind of datable episode is misconceived; and there is also their general rejection of the whole doctrine of intramental events that

chosen is presumably one that was not clearly understood *as a choice* when it was made. (See *Sein und Zeit,* p. 268.)

is presupposed by this account.[28] A choice is not one event to which the action itself is then superadded as a second event. Instead, a choice is a certain kind of *doing,* and working out what the existentialists mean by choice consists in showing what the special features of this kind of doing are. In this connection, it will be convenient as well as in accord with the normal linguistic practice of moral philosophers to reserve the term "action" for the designation of this special kind of doing that is tantamount to choice.

A primary condition that must be met if a given stretch of behavior is to qualify as an action is that the person in question must have envisaged his situation in terms of alternatives of some kind. He must have believed that there were at least two things that he could do in the situation; and he must think of himself as having done one of these rather than the other. This much has been made clear by earlier discussions of the concept of action, and need not be discussed further here. Of equal importance is the fact that every action has an intentional *structure.*[29] According to Sartre, a situation must be apprehended in such a way that certain of its features become "reasons" for trying to bring about a new state of affairs with which the actual situation is implicitly contrasted. In other words, the situation in which we are to act must be analyzed, in such a way that its structure reproduces that of a practical syllogism in which the factual premises at once describe the actual state of affairs and justify the "inference" to the conclusion which declares that some alternative state of affairs is to be realized. Thus, the fact that my friend is in financial need is a reason for my lending him money in order to restore his solvency. In summary, an intentional action is a change I make in a situation that has been implicitly conceptualized in such a way as to make it call for that change by reason of some feature that it bears.

It is perfectly possible for an action of mine to have this kind

[28] Sartre's rejection of the "episode" or "occurrent" theory of choice is most forcefully stated in *L'Être et le néant,* pp. 543–45. The non-identity of "choice" with "deliberate choice" which involves "une conscience analytique et différenciée" is shown in *ibid.,* pp. 539–48; and the special character of deliberate choice is discussed on p. 527.

[29] See *L'Être et le néant,* pp. 512 ff.

of intentional structure without my ever coming to a full stop, as it were, and going through an explicit verbal recital of the morally relevant features of a situation, the relationships of precedence among them, etc. As the discussion of concepts in Chapter V indicated, there are a great many different ways in which the posssession of a concept can express itself; and inner discourse is only one of them. But if the "structuring" of action situation need not be thought of as concentrated in a single self-declaring verbal performance, whether private or public, then the professed inability of many persons to recall any such acts loses any importance it may have seemed to have for critics of existentialism. The error of such critics lies in their assumption that the existentialists must be talking about some single act in which a situation is explicitly parsed for purposes of action. It is doubtful whether any such episodes need occur even when the choice under consideration is of the more restricted and familiar kind that presupposes a certain analysis of the situation; it is quite certain that they are highly exceptional, although not for that reason unimportant, in the case of underlying moral principles. Presumably even the most chronically forgetful or extroverted among the critics of existentialism will concede that they often speak or behave in ways that normally count as treating a feature of a situation as a good- or right-making characteristic; and while it is readily understandable that many people do not think of these activities of moral classification and description as choice-like in character, this fact, so far from having any damaging implications from the existentialist standpoint, makes clear why these critics have difficulty applying the existentialist view to their own case. They are prepared to regard as a choice only what they themselves thought of as a choice at the time of making it, whereas the existentialist position is that we often choose without clearly recognizing that we are doing so.[30] As I have already argued, the existentialist must assume that human beings are capable of understanding the more radical conception of choice

[30] That it is possible to fail to recognize one's own choices for what they are without *necessarily* thereby falling into "bad faith" is stated by S. de Beauvoir, *Pour une morale de l'ambiguité*, p. 68. "Dans l'univers du sérieux certains adultes peuvent vivre avec bonne foi: ceux à qui est refusé toute instrument d'évasion, ceux qu'on asservit ou qu'on mystifie."

which he seeks to introduce, and that they give evidence of this understanding in at least some area of their lives; but he emphatically does not have to assume that they have identified everything as a choice that should be so identified. When the existentialist says that on some occasion a person who does not think of himself as having made a choice has nevertheless done so, he is saying simply that the objector must accept what may indeed be for him a novel view of the matter in question, and that he must do so because he cannot show any relevant distinction between this case and other cases in which he does recognize an element of choice. It is certainly legitimate to distinguish, as Merleau-Ponty does, between a retrospective attribution of a choice-character to a segment of the past of a person who did not at the time think of himself as making a choice and the essentially prospective claim that we must henceforth treat as choice-like much that we have not previously so regarded.[31] We may also wish to lay greater emphasis on the former and, instead of insisting on the sense in which the existentialist thesis has always been true, we may present it rather as effecting a special kind of change in the character of our moral experience. In either case, however, the net effect of an acceptance of the existentialist position is to force a person to view as choice-like something that he had not previously so viewed.

Turning now to the characteristic existentialist employment of the concept of "choice" in such phrases as "choice of oneself" and "total choice," I must once again begin by turning aside a mistaken conception of what the existentialists intend to convey by these locutions. They are absolutely not to be understood as denials of the patent fact of initial and continuing human passivity in the face of multiple features of our situation which we do not choose.[32] Neither Heidegger nor Sartre has any stake in explain-

---

[31] "Il ne faut pas dire que je me choisis continuellement, sous prétexte que je *pourrais* continuellement refuser ce que je suis. Ne pas refuser n'est pas choisir. Nous ne pourrions identifier laisser faire et faire qu'en ôtant à l'implicite toute valeur phénoménale et en déployant à chaque instant le monde devant nous dans une transparence parfaite." (*Phénoménologie de la perception*, p. 516.)

[32] For evidence of this recognition of human limitation, see Sartre's discussion of the several aspects of "situation," *L'Être et le néant*, pp. 561–638,

ing away the brute fact of the innumerable natural limitations that confront every human-being. Some of these are physical, such as the different degrees of strength and skill or of resistance to disease that are the lot of different individuals. Some of them are psychological, although the existentialists are not often willing to recognize the "given" aspect of such personal traits as cowardice or cheerfulness since they so strongly emphasize how often we make ourselves the accomplices of our "natural" dispositions and disingenuously seek to represent ourselves as their helpless victim. Still others are historical and cultural—our having been born into a certain kind of society at a certain place and time. All of these features of our situation produce different "coefficients of difficulty" for the various projects in which an individual in a given set of circumstances engages himself in order to realize a certain goal. Not only do the existentialists not deny or minimize the significance for human action of the historical and natural environment in which it takes its rise: they emphasize repeatedly the brute contingent givenness—the facticity—of the situation in which we find ourselves, and the necessity for every human comprehension of the world to be rooted in a specific place and a specific time. Similarly, the slave makes himself what he is by his relationship to the fact of being a slave, by his way of setting up a range of possible meanings that this condition may have, and by the selection he makes among these possibilities. It is not necessary that such a person be able to describe what he is doing as "making or choosing himself," nor is it even necessary, if we adopt the dispositional interpretation of autonomy suggested above, for a person to detach himself completely from some predefined system of self-characterization (e.g., I am a peasant, a noble, a worker). Nor should this notion of a "choice of oneself" be taken to mean that the object of choice is always an image of the self in some narrow psychological sense that would eliminate

---

especially the section devoted to what Sartre calls the "coefficients d'adversité" connected with a project of action. Of interest, too, is Sartre's declaration that it may be impossible to distinguish, within any given situation, the obstacles posed by the "existants bruts" it contains from those created by our own previous choices (p. 558). Merleau-Ponty makes much the same point, *Phénoménologie de la perception,* p. 517.

relationships to other human beings and the social and institutional framework within which the self develops. In fact, the existentialists believe that it is quite impossible to isolate a self that is independent of other selves, and in saying that the object of choice is always the self, they are not in any way restricting the sphere of choice. What they mean is that our moral personalities are constituted by the choices we make, and that no one can make these choices for us. To act in a certain way in a certain situation contributes to making us persons of a certain sort; and there is nothing else that can do so. It might be objected to this view that it is a truism that follows from the existentialists' definition of moral personality, but it certainly does not imply that all choice is dominated by a narcissistic image of what the (psychological) self is to be.

This point is closely connected with the question of whether there is anything that can be called a "total" or "original" choice of oneself. It is Sartre's view that there is, and he has often spoken of this total choice of oneself as though it were implicit in all the particular choices we make.[33] But just as Sartre's attempt to think of freedom as a categorical and degree-less attribute of human beings generates the difficulties I have already noted, so this attempt to think of total choice as a kind of super-choice that in some measure controls subordinate choices is extremely difficult to reconcile with our sense of psychological reality. In fact, however, such a view is by no means essential to existentialism and has not been adopted by Merleau-Ponty, for example.[34] In his

[33] Sartre's conception of total choice of self is stated in *L'Être et le néant*, pp. 539–55 and pp. 643–63. Notice his statement, on p. 542, of the "modificabilité perpétuelle de notre projet initial" which may, however, require "une conversion radicale de mon être-dans-le-monde," if I reverse the trend of my previous choices. This is virtually a recognition by Sartre of what Merleau-Ponty speaks of as "une sorte de sédimentation de notre vie: une attitude envers le monde (qui) lorsqu'elle a été souvent confirmée, est pour nous privilegiée." (*Phénoménologie de la perception*, p. 504.) Sartre does not, however, recognize the "intentions non-décisoires" which according to Merleau-Ponty, our fully explicit and conscious decisions presuppose (*ibid.*, p. 502). Heidegger's discussion of choice of self by *Dasein* are mainly to be found in the sections of *Sein und Zeit* devoted to the authentic recognition and incorporation of death into life as its ultimate "possibility." See, for example, pp. 287–88.
[34] See *Phénoménologie de la perception,* pp. 499 ff.

view, "total choice" can only mean a kind of resultant of all the particular choices we make. Each of these may, of course, have implications that extend beyond the particular case, but no one of them dominates the whole of the moral life, nor can their meaning be made clear even to the actor himself except in the light of their ulterior development. To the degree that these choices acquire a measure of systematic unity, we can speak of a life as being a kind of unitary choice; but this notion is an essentially retrospective one and entirely avoids the bizarre questions that immediately confront a theory like Sartre's that represents this choice as somehow operating from the wings throughout the course of our lives.

Underlying all these conceptions of self-choice is the profound Heideggerian conception of man as the being that founds his own being.[35] This is the notion that at least in some sphere of their lives, human beings must take alternative possibilities of action seriously in such a way that even if, as we say, they fail to act, they must think of themselves as having acted. In this sphere, what they are—the identity they bear—is sustained solely by the spectrum of possibilities they effectively entertain and by what they do or try to do, so that it is proper to say, as Heidegger and Sartre do, that human beings have to *be* (or act out), what they are. The same idea is at the root of Heidegger's overall characterization of human being as care.[36] The human function *par excellence* is not just to set up a gratuitous interplay of actual states of affairs with alternative possibilities, but to be concerned about the future in the sense of feeling unavoidably responsible for what happens whether by reason of action or "inaction." The force of this characterization lies in the claim that if there were no area of human life in which the notion of alternative possibilities was allowed to retain its full value together with the allied notion of responsibility for what happens, the difference this made would be so great as to make it problematic whether we would want to call such beings "human" at all.

There is a sense in which this notion of "founding" one's being carries over even to those aspects of one's situation that are sim-

---

[35] See *Sein und Zeit*, pp. 284–85 and *Vom Wesen des Grundes*, pp. 43–54.
[36] See *Sein und Zeit*, pp. 180 ff.

ply given and in no way the outcome of purposive action.[37] This is the sense in which, in order to act at all, one must take certain relevant features of one's situation as the premises of one's action. A slave, for example, who proposes to change his condition must first *assume* it, and there is a subtle but important difference between simply being a slave and objectifying one's situation as a slave as a prelude to some action affecting that status. The latter is an active assumption or taking over of what had previously been one's "state," and the existentialists argue that only by this acceptance of an identification with one's situation is one able to act in it. Action thus involves two different and opposed movements: one by which we detach ourselves from a situation through a contrast with possible alternatives, and another by which we assume that condition in order to act upon it.

The most dramatic example of this assumption of features of one's condition, by which they are lifted into the sphere of action, is the case of death.[38] From one point of view, it is just a fact that human beings die, although it is, as Heidegger points out, a very peculiar sort of "fact" that is quite unlike the empirical "endings" to which we all tend to assimilate it. In any case, whatever its peculiarities as a special kind of fact, it is certainly independent of our will and confronts us as a final negation of human effort and purpose. Nevertheless, most human beings spend their lives avoiding the fact of death, usually by treating it as a "natural" or observable event, i.e., something that happens to other people. According to Heidegger, this motivated avoidance of death in its authentic first-personal form is itself one way of making death a theme or a premise of one's life; but there is another way of "building death into life" by explicit recognition and acceptance of oneself as a finite being—a being that dies. What is meant by *"Sein zum Tode"* is simply living with the understanding that one will die and doing what one does *as* a being who will

[37] For discussions of this extended sense of responsibility, see *Sein und Zeit*, pp. 280 ff. and *L'Être et le néant*, pp. 638–42.

[38] See Heidegger's discussion of "das Sein zum Tode," *Sein und Zeit*, pp. 235–67. Sartre has criticized Heidegger's treatment of death as a "possibility" which I can freely espouse and he proposes instead that death should be regarded as an element of my "facticity," i.e., of my situation. See *L'Être et le néant*, pp. 615–33.

die. To the extent that one's actions may be said to differ, not just by virtue of what is done, but also by virtue of the considerations on which they are based, a life that by internalizing death adds a premise to all its practical deliberations constitutes a new activity, even when in another sense what is done remains the same. It is hard not to see in this transformation of death into a distinctive modality of human being a final crowning of the voluntaristic effort to introduce an element of volition and of freedom into our relationship to what has always been regarded as the most unassimilable fact of human life.

IV

While reference has been made to the structure of the practical syllogism, I have said nothing about the major premise of such a syllogism which traditionally expresses a universal moral principle of some sort. This omission has been deliberate since earlier discussions have eliminated the possibility that any "moral truths" might be allowed to figure among the premises of practical deliberation as the existentialists envisage the latter. It has also become clear that if a moral rule does not express a truth of any kind, it can have no other status than that of a choice. In other words, if such a rule directs that in a situation of a certain kind, a certain type of action be undertaken and if this association of a type of action with a type of situation can rest neither on a factual nor on a logical nexus between the two, then all one can say is that the two are *put* together, and the only agent that can do that is an individual human being. Even if through general acceptance such a rule becomes an integral element in a culture, and is handed down from generation to generation, laden with the prestige of history and backed by the discipline of a whole society, its only "reality" lies in being accepted; and that acceptance, too, must be the act of individual human beings. Once the question of the "truth" of moral principles has been abandoned as unprofitable, however, its place is taken by a question about what this acceptance involves, and what kind of commitment for future choices it can constitute. If, as seems obvious, the distinctive feature of moral principles is that they are choices not just for a single situation but for all situations of a given type, then we must ask whether it is in fact possible to choose not just for one situation at a time but for a whole class of situations and, if so, in what sense such a choice can be binding for later individual choices in situations that come under the general rule.[39]

[39] The belief that existentialism involves a repudiation of all general principles of action is widely accepted, even among philosophers who appear generally sympathetic to its main theses. (See for example the defense of existentialism, interpreted as rejecting the requirement of universalizability, by A. MacIntyre, "What Morality Is Not," *Philosophy*, Vol. 32 (1957), pp. 325–35.) To my knowledge, however, such interpretations are rarely backed up by any actual citation of texts; and most frequently betray a confusion of the authentically existentialist doctrine of the ultimate choice-character of all moral principles with the claim that our particular acts of choice are necessarily capricious and arbitrary, although the non-equivalence of these views has been specifically pointed out by Sartre. (See *L'existentialisme est un humanisme*, pp. 73–79.) In the case of Sartre, to whom this antinomianism is most often imputed, the charge is most obviously without foundation. In the essay just referred to there are many passages in which particular choices are declared to have a general or exemplary significance. Thus, "il n'est pas un de nos actes qui, en créant l'homme que nous voulons être, ne crée en même temps une image de l'homme tel que nous estimons qu'il doit être." (p. 25) I have already pointed out that these formulations still leave unanswered certain questions about the precise sense in which, as Sartre says, what is good for us is good for all; but there can be no mistaking Sartre's recognition of the role of universality in morals when he says such things as "je construis l'universel en me choisissant" (p. 70) and "on doit toujours se demander: qu'arriverait-il si tout le monde en faisait autant." (pp. 28–29)

In *L'Être et le néant* there is an important discussion of the relationship of rules to particular choices in the course of which a parallel between rules of grammar and rules of conduct is developed. After explaining his view that "c'est en parlant que je fais la grammaire" Sartre goes on to argue that language, considered as "l'exemple d'une technique sociale et universelle," suggests a solution to the problem of the relationship of the individual to the species which he states as follows (p. 601–02):

Sans espèce humaine . . . il ne demeurerait qu'un pullulement irrationnel et contingent de choix individuels, auxquels nulle loi ne saurait être assignée. Si quelque chose comme une vérité existe, c'est l'espèce humaine qui peut nous la fournir. Mais si l'espèce est la vérité d'un individu, elle ne saurait être un *donné* dans l'individu sans contradiction profonde. . . . Le pour-soi ne se constitue pas comme soi-même à partir d'une essence d'homme donnée a *priori*; mais, tout au contraire, . . . les liaisons nécessaires qui suivent les elements de l'essence d'homme ne paraissent que sur le fondement d'un libre choix; en ce sens, chaque pour-soi est responsable dans son etre de l'existence d'un espece humaine.

In the case of Heidegger, if there is no repudiation of general principles of action as distinct from the inauthentic routines of Das Man, there is also no

In its broad outline, the existentialist view of the relationship of particular choices to general rules is quite clear. It is that an individual can accept a moral rule or policy only by acting in accordance with it, and that the particular choices or actions by which such rules are effectively accepted are themselves logically prior to, and independent of, the rule itself. No verbal declaration or inner resolve, however impressive, can by itself, amount to an acceptance of a moral principle unless it is backed up by action that conforms to the rule. But if it is an action that constitutes acceptance of a moral principle, then no action can do so any more than any other; or, if it does, it is only in the sense that some actions have more extensive and more significant repercussions than others do, and therefore commit us more deeply to a certain line of action. Apart from the increasing difficulty of disengaging oneself from a policy that one has pursued over a period of time, the earlier choices we make in accordance with a moral principle do not commit us to it any more finally than do later choices. The point here is that the whole question of the acceptance of any moral principle is always "reopenable" and each choice that we make in accordance with that principle can become the occasion of a new appraisal of all the considerations bearing upon our acceptance of it. Even if we make these choices more or less mechanically, and without any re-appraisal of their ultimate bases, we are implicitly endorsing the principle. This amounts to saying that there can be no such thing as making particular choices in advance by adopting a rule that will control the

discussion of the place that such principles might occupy in an authentic moral life. That Heidegger recognizes that they may have such a place, however, seems to be clearly suggested by a passage in his *Kant und das Problem der Metaphysik* (Frankfurt: Klostermann, 1951), p. 145, in which he paraphrases with apparent approval Kant's doctrine of the free subjection of the moral self to its own law in the language of his own account of *Dasein:*

In der Achtung vor dem Gesetz unterwerfe ich mir selbst. In diesem Mich-mir-unterwerfen bin ich als ich selbst . . . erhebe ich mich zu mir selbst als dem sich selbst bestimmenden freien Wesen. Dieses eigentümliche unterwerfende Sich-erheben seiner zu sich selbst offenbart das Ich in seiner 'Würde' . . . Die Achtung ist demnach die Weise des Selbst-seins des Ich auf Grund deren es 'den Helden' in seiner Seele nicht weg-wirft. Die Achtung ist die Weise des Verantwortlich-seins des Selbst sich selbst gegenüber, das eigentliche Selbstsein.

decision we make in cases that have yet to arise. When the time comes, the whole matter can be re-opened if only because it cannot be shut off; if we then act in accordance with the rule laid down on a previous occasion, that decision stands on its own legs and makes exactly the same contribution to our acceptance of the principle as does the earlier choice even though the latter may have represented itself as legislating in advance for future cases.

It can be illuminating to interpret the relation between general moral rules and particular choices as interpreted by the existentialists, by analogy with the relationship of judicial decisions to statute law, and to argue that individual choices should be regarded as further specifications of the general rules under which they are made. Thus, to take a familiar example, a judicial decision to the effect that it is indeed illegal to drive a baby-carriage on an airport runway further specifies the statute forbidding the use of vehicles on runways. In one important respect, of course, this parallel proves misleading since in the legal case, the judge is placed by the nature of his office in a subordinate relationship to a body of statute law that is created by independent legislative action. In the general moral case, of course, this kind of pre-established relationship to a body of rules is lacking and there is no distinction comparable to that in the legal case between legislative and judicial authorities. We must accordingly think of the whole corpus of moral rules as the precipitate of particular choices, i.e., as a body of "law" built up wholly by particular judicial determinations that have taken on a measure of systematic unity and internal consistency. Since these modifications of the normal judicial model really amount to an abandonment of it, it may in fact be better, if we seek analogies, to compare the relationship of choice to moral rules to that of the sovereign power to the body of statute law which it has created but by which it can never be finally restrained.[40]

There is another feature of existentialist ethical theory that is of great importance in understanding the treatment accorded to

[40] It is interesting to note that many of the puzzles about "dispositional" and "categorical" attributions of autonomy and the relation of the latter to rules also arise in connection with the sovereign power that is attributed to political society. For a discussion of some of these, see H. L. A. Hart, *The Concept of Law* (Oxford: Clarendon Press, 1961), ch. 4 *et passim*.

177

general moral rules. This is the view that such rules can be justified only on the ground that they are the most effective policies
for achieving some end that has been judged desirable.[41] The existentialists appear in fact, with certain significant exceptions to
be discussed later, to be committed to what has been called the
"summary" view of the relationship of moral rules to individual
cases, i.e., the view that moral rules are generalizations summarizing the choices made in particular cases by the person who is said
to accept the rule, and that they are thus logically posterior to
these particular choices.[42] Admittedly, this view does violence to
the sense most of us have of coming into new situations requiring
moral choice with a prior set of accepted policies which we assume will be controlling for this situation as it has been for others in the past. It also runs afoul of the difficulty—encountered
in rule-governed activities such as games—which stems from the
fact that quite often one cannot even *describe* the alternative
courses of action between which one has to choose without implicitly recognizing a certain rule (e.g., the rule of promise keeping) as applicable to that case. On the other hand, when one considers less straightforward cases in which we do not have this
sense of a choice-situation's being uniquely classifiable under
some single moral rubric, and are torn instead between two conflicting rules both of which seem to have some claim to control
our decision in this case, the point of the existentialist argument
becomes both clearer and more plausible. In such cases, a question arises about our relationship to the moral rules that are in
conflict, and this is not a question that can be satisfactorily dealt
with by an appeal to rules of precedence stipulating which rule is

[41] In this respect, at least, the existentialists share the views of the utilitar-
ians of whom they are otherwise extremely critical. In S. de Beauvoir, *Pour
une morale de l'ambiguïté* (Paris: Gallimard, 1947), this teleological aspect of
existentialist ethical theory is strongly emphasized. While "utility" is declared
to have no absolute meaning (p. 179) and is quite clearly to be a function of
choice, the necessity for reckoning the consequences of acting in a certain way
in a given situation is asserted and blind reliance on moral "recipes" is
condemned. For a very clear analysis of the role of choice in judgments of
utility generally, see I. M. D. Little, *A Critique of Welfare Economics*
(Oxford: Clarendon Press, 1957), chs. 2 and 3.

[42] I borrow the term "summary view" from J. Rawls who contrasts it with
the "practice" view of rules in "Two Concepts of Rules," *Philosophical
Review*, Vol. 64 (1955), pp. 3–32.

to be followed in what kinds of conflicts among rules. For what is the status of these superordinate rules and what is involved in a person's adoption of one of them? If a conflict of rules arises for the first time in a person's entire moral experience, is he to deduce the proper line of action from a general rule of precedence? This would presuppose that he already accepts the rule of precedence before he has ever acted on it. He may of course have been taught this principle and have given sincere verbal allegiance to it, but in this case as in the case of primary moral rules the criterion of action is the only satisfactory index of what one really accepts in the way of moral principles. It follows that by acting in accordance with a rule of precedence we in effect *choose* the policy reflected in that rule, and the existentialists are saying simply that that choice must be dictated by the end we are seeking to realize.

For purposes of illustration, let us take a person who subscribes to the moral principle that forbids lying, and also the principle that directs us to avoid actions that cause unnecessary suffering to others. Let us suppose further that he is successively confronted with a number of different situations in which telling the truth would require that he cause significant suffering to others. It may well be that in all these cases he will choose to tell the truth in spite of the fact that he is strongly disinclined to hurt other individuals in the way he sees to be inevitable if he does so. How are we to describe the relationship to the general rule against lying, of these choices each one of which involves the necessity of a choice between lying and causing suffering? Is the conclusion: "Tell the truth" simply deduced from the general rule by subsuming the particular case under it and drawing the consequences? This would require that the rule contain a rider to the effect that when circumstances of the kind in question are present in a case when the duty of truth-telling is applicable, they are to be ignored in favor of that duty. But surely this would be merely an ingenious *post factum* rationalization and if the rule has this content, then it is conferred upon it by the individual choice itself which does override the other considerations in favor of the duty of truth-telling. A general moral rule may serve as a formula that reminds us of what our response is to be in situations considered simply as situations in which we have either to lie or tell the truth, but they cannot, by themselves, tell us what to do in any individual case. For that, a decision has to be made that this principle is to take precedence over other considerations that might lead us to act otherwise; and this decision is logically prior to, and independent of, the rule itself.[43]

The point of the existentialist polemic against the domination of our understanding of morality by rules can now be stated. As has already been stated, what is at issue is not the desirability or the possibility of establishing consistent, long-range moral policies. In so far as the existentialists address themselves to this issue, their contribution is simply to point out that it is extremely difficult, and often practically impossible to enunciate, in advance, principles of conduct that do not have to be successively modified and qualified by the particular choices we make.[44] They are also concerned to make evident the dangers implicit in the sort of reliance on rules that really consists in a systematic refusal to look at the features of particular choice-situations that might lead to a modification or suspension of the rule. Perhaps the best way to

[43] Sartre's well-known discussion in *L'Existentialisme est un humanisme* (p. 39–47) of the young man who had to decide whether to join the Free French forces abroad or remain with his widowed mother is the most obvious example of the use of cases of conflict of duty as paradigms for moral deliberation generally. Unfortunately, this discussion is sometimes interpreted as showing merely that the young man had to choose arbitrarily between two opposed moral principles. Of course he had to do that, but Sartre is also saying that even within a single moral position the necessity to amplify the principles one accepts by further individual choices can not be avoided and that these amplifications have the character of "inventions." In his analysis of another example (pp. 86–88) Sartre seems to assert that even when moral freedom is the guiding principle of action, contradictory alternatives may arise which can only be resolved by choice.

[44] The refusal to recognize and to deal with this difficulty typically involves the pretense that the issue at stake has been irreversibly closed, whether by a previous decision or by the "nature" of the case itself; and as such it offers a paradigm case of "bad-faith." This does not mean that we have an obligation constantly to re-open every matter that has been decided. What it does imply is that we must ourselves recognize and not try to conceal from others that our refusal to re-open is itself a decision. See, for example, Heidegger's statement that the "resoluteness" of a decision does not mean that the authentic self must "sich auf die Situation *versteifen* . . . (sie) muss verstehen dass der Entschluss seinem eigenen Erschliessungssinn nach frei und *offen gehalten* werden muss für die jeweilige faktische Möglichkeit." (*Sein und Zeit*, p. 307.)

characterize the existentialist attitude toward moral rules is to say that it sees them as emerging from a progressive resolution of individual cases, and as gradually increasing in stability and reliability, but also as never wholly immune from review and revision.

In a sense, however, this statement of the existentialist view of the dependence of all general moral policies on particular choices may prove misleading. It fails to bring out the degree to which every particular choice is itself general in character.[45] I have already tried to show that every action and every choice must involve an appreciation of the relevant features of the agent's situation and that these features will normally be repeatable traits that can be designated by means of universal predicates. Similarly, the other element in choice—the projected transformation of the existing situation—can only be described as the bringing about of a certain type of situation. To use an example, I may say that I helped a neighboring family *because* everyone ought to help those who are in distress. To say this is to identify the feature of the situation by reference to which my action has to be characterized, and it may be possible to justify this criterion by showing that it is derivable from yet more general criteria of action. When I cite general rules in this way as the reasons for my action, I really only re-describe *what* I have done by laying bare

[45] I do not, of course, wish to be understood as claiming that Sartre defends the doctrine of the universalizability of moral judgments in the extreme form in which it requires that all proper names occurring in such judgments be replaced by general terms. (See E. Gellner, "Ethics and Logic," *Proceedings of the Aristotelian Society* (1955), Vol. 55. pp. 158–78.) While he quite clearly does not hold the view that an action may be right in one situation and not in another without there being some relevant difference between the situations, I suspect that he would lay great emphasis on the difficulty in practice of enunciating the general principle which is implicit in one's action and to which one is prepared to commit oneself as controlling all cases of the same type. We often feel a great deal surer that we have done the right thing on a particular occasion than we are that everyone ought to do the same thing on all "like" occasions, if indeed we are clear as to what those would be. No doubt, we must seek to reduce this kind of uncertainty by reflecting on our principles of action but it is doubtful that it can ever be eliminated. When this feature of moral choice is overlooked, as it often is by contemporary analytical philosophers, a very peculiar picture of the moral life results in which an action must announce its own fully universal principle on pain of not being "moral." For a statement of such a view as well as a caricature of the "existentialist" position, see R. M. Hare, "Universalizability," *Proceedings of the Aristotelean Society* (1955), Vol. 55, pp. 295–312.

the deeper intentional structure of that action. Whatever level of generality this description of my action attains, the principle so exposed can be accepted only by the action that falls under it; and each such action, logically, commits me to the principle quite as much as any other. What is meant by saying that the individual choice is logically prior to the principle it instantiates is that when I have described an action by reference to the most general criteria that apply to it, I still have to decide whether by performing that action I shall accept the principle implicit in it or not; and this decision cannot itself be derived from that principle. By acting in one way, I accept the principle and by acting in another I reject it. However automatic that policy may become with time, my acceptance of it remains contingent upon my actions in particular cases, each of which can, in principle, be made to raise all the issues of the moral life. Nothing commits one to a moral principle except an individual action, and no individual action can do so for once and for all. Like Descartes' world which has to be sustained in existence from moment to moment by the omnipotence of God, so the acceptance of moral principles is effectuated by the very actions which are subsumed under them, and remains conditional upon such future actions.

There are several important objections that can be raised to the position which I have been presenting in this section. One of these is addressed to the view that a person's actions are the only satisfactory index of his moral convictions and it consists in arguing that this forces too rigid a standard of consistency on the shifting amalgam of professed beliefs, unwilling compliances and partial defaults that mark even the most firmly defined characters.[46] This criticism has considerable merit since there is a danger that the use of action as a criterion of conviction may be misinterpreted as a new version of the kind of moral rigorism which

---

[46] For a good statement of these and other objections to using action as the sole criterion of moral conviction, see P. Gardiner, "On Assenting to a Moral Principle," *Proceedings of the Aristotelian Society* (1954/55) Vol. 55, pp. 23–44. In this connection it should be noted that Sartre's statement that "le choix étant identique au faire, suppose pour le distinguer du rêve et du souhait, un commencement de réalisation" (*L'Être et le néant,* p. 563) amounts to an express endorsement of action in some form as a criterion of moral attitudes.

refuses to allow any weight to special circumstances and treats imperfect or irregular compliance with a professed moral principle as equivalent to a repudiation of it. In fact, few of us are capable of perfect conformity to any principle even in the most favorable circumstances; and when we waver and act in violation of principles which we profess, this may reflect a real lack of *any* stable conviction rather than a rejection of the principle in question. There are, moreover, cases in which, by reason of obstacles that may be either external or internal in nature, compliance presents special difficulties which justify us in saying that a man really believes that one ought to act in a certain way, even if he did not do so himself on a given occasion. In such cases, it is often proper to seek assurances that an effort to comply was made in good faith, and that the individual in question is not just using the difficulty as an excuse for non-performance. Nevertheless, when all allowances have been made and a realistic standard of conformity has been defined, the core of the existentialist position remains intact. In so far as we have even semi-definite moral convictions, the proof that we have them is provided by the way we act. While we often give people credit for the convictions they profess and may not have the opportunity to express in action, that attribution to them of a moral belief always remains conditional upon and revocable in the light of their relevant actions, should occasions for the latter arise.

There is another kind of objection to the existentialist treatment of moral rules, however, which is inspired by the feeling that the existentialist just cannot, with the means at his disposal, give a strong enough sense to the notion of being bound by a rule.[47] If no action or set of actions can by itself constitute such conclusive acceptance of a moral principle that further actions of the same type become no more than applications of a rule that is no longer subject to further "ratification by action," to what ef-

---

[47] Sartre's reply to this objection that "les valeurs ne sont pas sérieuses puisque vous les choisissez" is characteristically pungent. "À cela je réponds que je suis bien fâché qu 'il en soit ainsi; mais si j'ai supprimé Dieu le père, il faut bien quelqu'un pour inventer les valeurs. Il faut prendre les choses comme elles sont. Et par ailleurs, dire que nous inventons les valeurs ne signifie autre chose que ceci: la vie n'a pas de sens, à priori (*L'Existentialisme est un humanisme*, p. 89).

fective restrictions will the moral agent be subject? Without the acceptance of rules, so the argument runs, there would be no such thing as morality; and if a rule is accepted, one must act in accordance with it in cases subsumable under it. People must, in other words, be prepared to act on principle, contrary to inclination; and to the objector it is just not clear how the existentialist with his doctrine of the permanent re-openability of all moral questions can do justice to this feature of morality. The charge implicit in this objection is that existentialism cannot make sense of moral obligation; and while this charge will be fully considered in the next chapter, some preliminary clarifications of the existentialist position can be offered here.

In this connection, the existentialists' doctrine of our relation to past events generally and to our own past choices and actions in particular has peculiar relevance since from the perspective of any present situation in which we have to act all previous occasions of a similar kind in which we have followed a certain principle lie in the past.[48] Now to say with the existentialists that past decisions are *just* events, and that it is just a "fact" that we resolved these earlier situations in a certain way is equivalent to saying that they do not have any automatic and indefeasible normative significance for the person who is presently faced by a similar situation. Even if the practical and social necessity for uniformity and consistency is kept in mind as one reviews such past choices under a rule, these considerations, too, form part of a comprehensive set of data which must be structured for action once more by a new moral choice. Certainly a situation that falls into a class of situations in which we have acted in the past carries with it implicit suggestions as to what its decisively important features are, and these are suggestions that we may accept by acting once again in the same way. But in any important sense the problem we confront now is the same one we confronted when we first had to bring such a situation under some general policy, and it is complicated only by the addition of considerations concerning the likely effects of changing our policy now.

[48] See Sartre's discussion of *my* past as an element in *my* situation, *L'Être et le néant,* pp. 577–585.

Furthermore, this set of considerations does not evaluate itself now anymore than it did then; and even if we follow the established rule "blindly," this too is a new choice—a choice not to re-appraise the elements in an action-situation—and this choice not to choose contributes in a special way to the acceptance of a certain policy. What is often called, with somewhat pejorative connotations, "existentialist individualism," is in fact just this doctrine that the individual moral consciousness is the permanent forum before which *all* considerations that may be relevant to action, including our own and others' past choices, appear, and in which precedents are decisive only because they are made so.[49]

Against this background, it may be possible to isolate within our hypothetical objector's rejection *en bloc* of the existentialist position, a more restricted point which the existentialist can surely accept. This is that without a certain level of correspondence between our verbal acceptances of moral principles and our effective acceptances of them through action, human society would be reduced to chaos. Consistency and principled behavior, for social purposes, are largely a matter of correspondence between what we say publicly and what we do; and it can be conceded that as a person (or for that matter, a society) gradually succeeds in bringing a wider and wider range of cases under stable policies, our *sense* of the logical freedom of choice in each individual case may progressively give way to a view of ourselves as proceeding under orders. It does not follow that in the sense stipulated by the existentialists these individual decisions are no longer logically free nor that the descending order of practical deliberation that starts from a verbally accepted moral principle enjoys a logical priority, in the determination of what is to be done, over the ascending order that proceeds from a certain action in a situation characterized in a certain way to an acceptance of a general rule. All it means is that from a practical point of view, our logi-

---

[49] For a discussion of the senses in which existentialism is and is not "individualiste," see S. de Beauvoir, *Pour une morale de l'ambiguïté*, pp. 218 ff., *et passim*. Also, J.-P. Sartre, *L'Existentialisme est un humanisme*, pp. 90 ff.

cal freedom may in certain circumstances become a less important feature of our choices than the coherency and predictability of the system of practice which they collectively compose; and a recognition of this fact is in no way incompatible with a strong emphasis on this residual logical freedom of the individual, even after an impressive degree of order has been achieved—if only for the purpose of reminding us that no system is proof against shocks and accidents that may force us to rebuild it from the ground up.

There is, then, a sense in which we may be said to choose independently of rules even in those situations which are most naturally subsumed under such rules, and in which we seem to ourselves to be simply applying a familiar and accepted rule without any hesitation or deliberation. It has already been pointed out that this independence of individual choice that plays such an important role in existentialist ethical theory is to be interpreted not in a psychological or descriptive sense as denoting a hitherto unnoticed episode in our inner lives, but rather in a logical sense that makes it a function of the absence of logical restrictions on the criteria we use in evaluation. There are not, therefore, two choices whenever we act—one under the rules and one outside the rules. Instead, every choice made under the rules is in principle capable of being transformed by successive re-description into a choice that is outside the rules because it is a choice *of* the rules and of the criteria of evaluation they incorporate. Sometimes, in exceptional situations for which no governing principle readily suggests itself, we are made aware that we are in fact choosing those features of the situation that are to be the indices for whatever action we may take. Most of the time, however, we live within the pre-evaluated and anonymous world that our language presents us with, and here the criteria of choice are so firmly established that a great effort is required to conceive alternatives to them—much less think of these systems of moral classification as calling for a choice by us. It is a fact that existentialist critics habitually construe the whole of our moral experience on the model of the cases in which we are either forced, or force ourselves, to become aware of the whole set of moral procedures that we apply, and in effect incorporate these into a description

186

of what we are doing. But, whatever its bias in favor of such cases, existentialism is not just an ethical theory for crisis situations; and the most banal choices "under rules" are also choices outside the rules because they are made in a logical freedom that can become an explicit theme of reflection.

CHAPTER VIII

AUTHENTICITY AND OBLIGATION

Thus far, my discussion of the ethical theory of existentialism has concentrated almost exclusively on the evaluative judgments of individual human beings, and has attempted to define the nature of the freedom in which those evaluations are made. Nothing has been said about the moral relations in which such autonomous individuals stand to one another, nor about the compatibility of a general ethical theory of the type outlined in earlier chapters with a recognition of some kind of moral obligation toward other human beings. This lack of attention to the social aspect of morality, it must be admitted, reflects a corresponding neglect on the part of most of the existentialist writers; and this neglect has led many critics to conclude that the concepts used by the existentialists in the analysis of evaluation are radically incapable of dealing with the phenomenon of moral community and the complex moral relationships to other human beings which such community comports. This charge has at least a *prima facie* plausibility about it which makes it all the more necessary to explore in detail the implications of the views developed so far for the whole topic of moral relationships among human beings. In this chapter, I will attempt to show that, while the existentialists do not have a fully developed theory of obligation, they have presented in embryo at least a conception of what the basis of moral relations between human beings should be.

This apparent lack of interest on the part of the existentialists in the social dimension of morality is in striking contrast to the current orientation of much moral philosophy in the English-

speaking world.[1] On the whole, the latter may be said to assume
the existence of a more or less stable and harmonious society with
a developed moral code and a highly articulated set of concepts
defining the different role-relationships in which human beings
may stand to one another, as well as the rights and duties associated with these roles. Under these circumstances, the job of
moral philosophy is typically conceived to be the making explicit
of the principles and rules with which, in such a state as this, we
are assumed to be familiar, even if we may be unable to state
them very clearly. Usually the acceptance of such rules is taken
for granted and is not itself the subject of inquiry, but when a
justification of the whole corpus of moral principles is called for,
it is characteristically provided by arguments showing that an acceptance of these principles is in some sense definitive of human
nature.[2] Since the human nature such writers have in mind is, in
fact, the fully moralized human nature of a stable and relatively
harmonious society, there is a sense in which in spite of its circularity this argument can claim a certain rough truth. In any case,
one main result of approaching the subject matter of morality
from this angle is that purely individual decisions (i.e., decisions
for which a determinate moral context is lacking), are treated either as external to the whole province of morality, or are assigned
to the interstices of the moral life in which the moral rules we do
accept leave us free either to act or not to act in a certain way.

If we consider the examples used by the existentialists from
this point of view, sharply different presuppositions immediately
become evident. These examples almost uniformly concern individuals who are forced to act under circumstances in which the
support given by established moral institutions is for one reason
or another unavailable. Even when the background of choice *is* a
functioning society to which the moral agent belongs, it is usually
described in such a way as to undermine any assumption that a

---

[1] For a somewhat different characterization of the contrasting approaches to
ethical questions of existentialists and most English-speaking philosophers, see
I. Murdoch's contribution to the symposium on "Vision and Choice in
Morality," *Proceedings of the Aristotelian Society,* Sup. Vol. 30 (1956), pp.
32–58.
[2] See, for example, R. S. Peters, "Nature and Convention in Morality,"
Proceedings of the Aristotelian Society, Vol. 51 (1950–51), pp. 223–53.

moral consensus or any genuine moral reciprocity exists. The paradigm situation from which a general characterization of morality is to be derived is thus one in which the individual moral agent is compelled to choose and to act in isolation from, or in the absence of, any collectively accepted and reciprocally applied body of moral rules. Correspondingly, the "normal" situation in which such guidance and support are available receives relatively little attention from the existentialists. Since action in such circumstances is, as we shall see, permanently threatened with "inauthenticity," it qualifies at best as a borderline example of the "moral." The latter is thus made coextensive with the whole province of human action, and no special importance is attached to the distinction between broader questions of individual self-determination and the kinds of question that are usually thought of as being answered by reference not to an individual ideal but to a rule that is common to at least some group of human beings. Instead of excluding the former—as often happens—from the moral sphere because they do not clearly involve the application of shared rules, the existentialists tend to feel that rule-governed situations can be included within it only to the extent that they can be shown to involve individual choice. Or, to put the same point another way, morality as a whole is the province of individual self-determination, and the social dimension of morality and relationships with others come in simply as one element in the design of an individual life.

It would be unprofitable here to debate the advantages and disadvantages of a conception of morality that takes individual choice in its purest form as its paradigm case, and sees in shared moral rules only a special case of individual self-determination.[3] The more important issue is to determine just how adequate an account of the moral relationships among human beings can be given by a theory that sets out from these root assumptions. As I have already indicated this inquiry carries one well beyond the limits of any moral theory that has so far been provided by the leading figures in the existentialist movement. In fact, it assumes

[3] An interesting discussion of the place of "rules" and "ideals" within morality as a whole can be found in P. Strawson, "Social Morality and Individual Ideals," *Philosophy*, Vol. 36 (1961), pp. 1–17.

the character of an effort to expand the few hints and suggestions that have been thrown out into a positive account of moral obligation. The possibility of such an extension of existentialist ethical theory is precisely what I want to establish in this chapter. Before undertaking this task, it will be useful to examine a little more closely some of the reasons that have made the existentialists so reluctant to develop any account of obligation at all.

I

It is not difficult to locate the sources of the antipathy which the concept of obligation typically evokes in existentialist philosophers. The root notion in that concept is one of being bound in the sense of being subject to an effective restriction on the permissible range of human choice. Traditionally, this restriction itself has been thought of as independent of, and unremovable by, human volition. Indeed, many moralists have argued that it *must* be independent of choice if we are to be able to talk—as we all do—of what we ought to do even when we do not do it.[4] If morality were, at bottom, a matter of will and choice as the existentialists believe, then all obligations would be self-imposed. An obligation I have created, however, is one from which I can release myself; and the latter, so the argument goes, is no obligation at all. Particularly in cases in which our practice is at variance with our declared principles, the decision to act in a way that violates a recognized obligation might appear to be tantamount to such a release; and the sense in which, barring special circumstances, one could still be said to believe sincerely that acting otherwise would really have been right becomes very unclear. Moreover, beyond this special difficulty, there is the general problem of how the will can bind itself at all if it is not confronted with objective

[4] The view that moral obligation must be independent of human volition should not be confused—although it often is—with the quite different requirement that it be of such a nature that there *can* be conflicts between what we *want* to do and what it is our obligation to do. Sartre, as his theory of obligation shows, is certainly prepared to recognize that conflicts of the latter type occur but at the same time he holds that obligation as such is constituted by joint acts of choice.

192

moral relationships *in re,* and as Hume said, "has no object to which it could tend but must return to itself *in infinitum.*"[5] A will-created obligation would thus turn out to be simply an indefinitely prolonged series of acts of will which could never produce an uncancellable change in the "relation of objects" by which it would then be bound. By contrast, a truly binding obligation must have its basis outside the will, and would impose a restriction upon the will in much the same way as the antecedent determinacy of fact is supposed to define the goal of theoretical inquiry. Once the meta-ethical stamp of intellectualism is thus set upon the concept of obligation at the very outset, it becomes automatically unincorporable into any ethical theory based on the idea of moral autonomy; and it is to this fact that the existentialists' avoidance of the concept of obligation can most obviously be traced.[6]

There are, however, other sources of this negative attitude toward the concept of obligation that are internal to the existentialist analysis of human being itself. For the existentialist, and for Sartre in particular, the primordial relationship in which every human being stands to every other tends to be one of conflict.[7] This is not to deny that agreement and cooperation among

---

[5] See his *Treatise of Human Nature,* ed. Selby-Bigge (Oxford: Clarendon Press, 1888), Bk. 3, Pt. 2, sec. 5 "On the Obligation of Promises," especially the footnote on pp. 517–18.

[6] Thus, I would interpret Sartre's very strong denial that anything can oblige me to adopt any course of action (*L'Être et le néant,* p. 69) not as a denial of the possibility of obligation as such but rather of there being obligations which simply confront the moral agent without his having in any way helped create them. It should be noted, also, that Sartre speaks of the unavoidability of choice as "une obligation perpetuelle," but this use of the term is so different both from traditional conceptions of obligation and from Sartre's own conception of self-created obligations that I have not given it any special attention.

[7] "Le conflit est le sens originel de l'être-pour-autrui" (*L'Être et le néant,* p. 431). In Pt. 3, ch. 3, of *L'Être et le néant,* Sartre seeks to establish this thesis by detailed analyses of "les relations concrètes avec autrui," among them love, hate, and sexual desire; and in each case he argues that we are caught between the alternatives of sadism and masochism, of treating the other as an object for one's self, or oneself as an object for the other. While neither of these strategies can succeed in suppressing our awareness of subjectivity and freedom—whether our own or the other's—Sartre insists that the disjunction they form is exhaustive. "C'est . . . en vain que la réalité–humaine cherche-

human beings ever occur, nor is it to attribute a disposition to hostile and aggressive behavior to all human beings. Like Hegel in his famous analysis of the dialectic of the master and the slave, Sartre has in mind a type of conflict that is rooted in the very structure of the reciprocal relationship in which two human consciousnesses stand to one another.[8] The basis of this conflict is moral, and it lies in the fact that there can be no guarantee that the choices made by the "other" as an autonomous moral being will coincide with, or even be compatible with, my own. The appearance of another being enjoying the same moral freedom as I do is thus a challenge to, and a potential disruption of, "my" moral world which the other may well perceive simply as a set of facts or objects cut off from the context of possibility and first-personal choice with which I endow them. Since another human being cannot *be* the effort of transcendence that I am, and within which I experience and give meaning to my world, he can only *know* me and my world in the objective mode and this knowing collapses the properly evaluative dimension of our acts and leaves them stranded as so many natural events awaiting another evaluative interpretation which may or may not coincide with mine. Because this "collapsing-cognitive" apprehension of my values as "mere facts" is conceived by Sartre to be primary and inescapable in my relationship to other human beings, the advent of the "other" is a harbinger of conflict and not of concord. Even if the other moral consciousness proved to be in harmony with my own evaluations, there could be no guarantee of the indefinite contin-

---

rait à sortir de ce dilemme: transcender l'autre ou se laisser transcender par lui. L'essence des rapports entre consciences n'est pas le *Mitsein*, c'est le conflit." (p. 502) Although this inevitable conflict is said to be the origin of the "guilt" of each human being in relation to every other, this guilt can evidently not be expiated and even if I were to act in accordance with Kant's categorical imperative and make the moral freedom of the other my end, "cette liberté deviendrait transcendance-transcendée du seul fait que j'en fais mon but." (p. 479) It seems quite clear that this denial of the possibility of mutuality among human beings is in conflict with Sartre's later views as expressed not just in *Critique de la raison dialectique,* but in *L'existentialisme est un humanisme,* and was in fact abandoned by him.

[8] Sartre's most powerful description of this antagonistic relationship of human consciousnesses to one another can be found in the section entitled "Le regard," Pt. 3, ch. 1, of *L'Être et le néant.* Sartre's play, *Huis Clos,* has the same theme.

uation of that harmony in which the possibility of conflict is therefore always latent. Thus, either by anticipation or in actual fact, the presence of another autonomous moral being like myself imposes upon me the ordeal of having my actions "devaluated" in the medium of another consciousness. In its most radical form, this devaluation may extend not just to the evaluative ordering of my world which I effect through my actions and choices, but to my very status as a moral personality. That is to say, another moral consciousness can do more than simply evaluate a situation differently from the way I do and thereby reduce my evaluations to the status of "facts." It can also deny me the status of a moral agent altogether and treat me merely as an instrument to—or an obstacle in the way of—the realization of its own values. It can, in short, treat me as a thing rather than as a person, and repudiate or never recognize at all those principles of reciprocity that hold between human persons who mutually recognize one another as such. The appearance of an alien moral consciousness involves not just the threat of a conflict with my "values," but the threat of my being absorbed into the moral world of the other through being denied recognition as an autonomous moral being.

When views such as these of other human beings as primarily sources of ultimate moral conflict dominate a theory of human relationships, it is not surprising that there should be little place within the latter for a doctrine of moral obligation. Sartre has, in fact, sometimes written as though there were no possibility of any genuine mutuality among human beings—only the alternatives of an aggressive imposition of one's own moral perspective upon others, or a kind of masochistic submission to their aggression.[9] But this is not the whole story. Sartre is at least as emphatic in his assertion that the refusal of recognition to alien moral personalities, like the refusal to recognize one's own autonomy, can "succeed" only through what he calls "bad faith." That is, in order to seal off my world from the intrusions of an independent moral consciousness, I must first locate and identify the latter, much in the way in which the hypnotic subject must "know" where a given object is in order *not* to be able to find it. Sartre's point is that there is an internal contradiction in such denials of moral

9 *L'Être et le néant*, p. 502.

195

personality to which there corresponds a very special duplicity or dishonesty in our relation to ourselves. More generally, in spite of his very sharp distinction between the evaluative sense that my actions have for me and the moral appreciation that may be made of them by others, Sartre recognizes that we cannot simply dismiss or disallow the image others form of us. In one dimension of our being—the public and the social dimension—we *are*, so he says, what we are for others; we cannot invoke our own conflicting sense of ourselves to invalidate that public assessment of what we are.[10] Sartre does not, it is true, develop this doctrine of publicity and of the authority of an external view of our actions as the basis for a theory of obligation; and he sometimes seems to be saying merely that we must accept the fact that we are for others something quite different from what we are for ourselves. But elsewhere in his writings he does appear to be defending—and even pressing to the limits of paradox—the view that it is the public signification of my actions that is controlling in moral contexts, and that to the degree that the moral consciousness issues into the world and creates or accepts definite relationships to others, it cannot by itself control, in the sense of modifying by its own individual fiat, its situation vis-à-vis those persons.[11] In this sense at least, "being bound" is an inescapable feature of any moral experience that is more than a private reverie.

As I have already noted, it is in the work of Maurice Merleau-Ponty that a recognition of the central importance of this element of publicity receives a specifically moral interpretation, and some suggestive hints are given as to the way in which a theory of moral community might be developed in a manner compatible

[10] For Sartre, the experience of shame is "une *reconnaissance* de ce que je *suis* bien cet objet qu'autrui regarde et juge." (*L'Être et le néant*, p. 319.) As one would expect, Merleau-Ponty's conception of the relationship among human consciousnesses differs significantly from Sartre's. For Merleau-Ponty, the consciousness of the other as an object is exceptional and marks a withdrawal from a shared understanding that human beings have of themselves and of others as active, purposive beings. See *Phénoménologie de la perception*, pp. 412 ff.

[11] It does not, of course, follow that we are the prisoners of the other in the sense of having to accept our identity for the other as our own sense of ourselves. As Sartre says, "je m'échappe d'autrui en lui laissant mon Moi aliéné entre les mains." (*L'Être et le néant*, p. 345.)

with the fundamental existentialist doctrine that all morality rests ultimately on choice. Where Sartre is willing to recognize only the self-defining activity of human consciousness, set over against the moral opacity of the *en-soi,* Merleau-Ponty introduces a third, intermediate level—that of collective, funded meanings—which constitutes precisely the impersonal moral milieu in which most of our experience is situated. Not to reject the evaluations that are proposed to us by the community in which we live, is not *ipso facto* to *choose* them unless, Merleau-Ponty argues, we are prepared to suppress the distinction between our ordinary mode of consciousness and the specially cultivated mode in which all choice situations are antecedently marked out as such.[12] Merleau-Ponty is even willing to go so far as to say that, if negation is the basic attribute of subjectivity, it is possible only by virtue of the tissue of collective meanings upon which it supervenes.[13] No one of these has for Merleau-Ponty, any more than for Sartre, a compulsory hold upon the individual moral agent; but if he can opt out of any one of them, he can do so only in favor of another publicly defined mode of construing a certain type of situation, which may be recognized already, or which may have yet to establish its credentials.

Merleau-Ponty is here emphasizing, against Sartre and Heidegger, the essential place of the *"On"* or *"Das Man"* in any adequate account of the moral life. These writers condemn the anonymity of all "values" that are not, in the first instance, one's own first-personal choices, and see in any reliance upon collectively held standards of evaluation and action the antithesis of the fully self-conscious autonomy which they call authenticity. By contrast,

---

[12] *Phénoménologie de la perception,* p. 516. The central difference between Sartre and Merleau-Ponty on this point is not that the latter recognizes the *"sollicitation"* of the social milieu—Sartre recognizes that just as clearly—but rather that Merleau-Ponty attributes a "privileged" status to long-established policies and does not feel that *"la généralité du rôle"* must be consciously assumed in a purely individual choice as Sartre appears to do. (See *L'Être et le néant,* pp. 602–03.)

[13] "Si c'est par la subjectivité que le néant apparait dans le monde, on peut dire aussi que c'est par le monde que le néant vient à l'être. Je suis un refus général d'être quoi que ce soit accompagnée en sous-main d'une acceptation continuelle de telle forme d'être qualifiée (*Phénoménologie de la perception,* p. 516) .

Merleau-Ponty views the mediating function of public "meanings" as an indispensable element in the dialectic between the individual and the moral community to which he belongs. It would be a great mistake, however, to suppose that he assigns to these impersonal significations any kind of objectivity in the sense of ultimate independence of choice that is denied them by Sartre or Heidegger.[14] His point is simply that individual choice exercises itself, not in the first instance upon all the logically possible options associated with a given situation, but rather upon the standing, socially established ways of interpreting those situations. He is also recognizing the fact that these evaluations present themselves with a certain impersonality, and that when we simply "go along" with them as most of us do most of the time, we are doing something that is subtly different from what we do when we explicitly adopt or reject them. The dialectic of moral self-definition is thus a confrontation of individual choice and established moral codes; and not, except in extreme cases, one between individual choice and an *en-soi* that has been stripped of all the accretions that an established moral tradition in a historically continuous society imposes upon it.

It has been widely recognized among existentialists that the true locus of these collective evaluations is the language we use. This is true of the writers who like Heidegger and Sartre are most insistently hostile to all supra-individual tendencies in morality, and also of those who like Merleau-Ponty recognize the interdependence of individual choice and cumulative or "funded" evaluations.[15] In Merleau-Ponty's own words, the function of language is to make us see ourselves as another "other," that is, to es-

---

[14] See for example his *Phénoménologie de la perception,* pp. 518–19.

[15] Thus Sartre can say that " (la totalité du langage) ne peut rien être si ce n'est la *praxis* elle-même en tant qu'elle se manifeste directement à autrui, le langage est *praxis* comme relation pratique d'un homme à un autre et la *praxis* est toujours langage par ce qu'elle ne peut se faire sans signifier. . . . En fait les 'relations humaines' sont des structures interindividuelles dont le langage est le lieu commun." (*Critique de la raison dialectique,* p. 180.) In spite of the Marxist overtones of this passage, its meaning is not really very different from Heidegger's characterization of speech as "das 'bedeutende' Gliedern der Verständlichdeit des In-der-Welt-seins, dem das Mitsein zugehört, und das sich je in einer bestimmten Weise des besorgenden Miteinanderseins hält." (*Sein und Zeit,* p. 161.)

198

tablish an intersubjective milieu within which the privileged position of the self is suppressed in favor of a standpointless and neutral mode of reference to all selves.[16] Similarly, when our choices receive expression in language, they are cast into a medium over which no individual has complete control, and which can therefore serve to express the joint evaluative attitudes of many. This is preeminently not a language in which a sharp distinction is made between our characterization of "situations" and our evaluative construals of them; when we use the words of this language to convey our own individual attitudes and choices, the latter are thereby subtly modified because the public language in which they are expressed lends them certain implications and subjects them to certain criteria of reasonableness that may run counter to the actual sense of our choice and may even cause our own judgments to appear "alien" to us. This phenomenon of the alienation of moral attitudes when they come to be expressed in a public and objective language has generated a counter-demand for the no doubt impossible elimination of all dependence upon an established moral consensus in our language and our personal moral choices. The real point of the existentialist argument on this issue, as it emerges from Merleau-Ponty's critique of Sartre, is not that we are, or should ideally be, entirely free of all dependence upon an *inter-monde* of public moral meanings; but rather that, whatever our degree of commitment to the latter, we can never be finally locked into any set of evaluations by the logic of our language. Certainly the very impersonality of the moral concepts we use, coming down to us as they do from a nameless past, conceals their origins in choice. When this happens, the rationality and order that are the achievement of a progressive systematization of individual choices come to be regarded as transcriptions of a rationality that is somehow implicit in the very situations with which our moral codes and concepts are designed to deal. In these circumstances, the inhibitions against revisionary individual choices are no longer just the practical difficulties that are inevitable whenever a system of commitments is called into question, but the kind of logical and metaphysical difficulty that

[16] See his "Sur la phénoménologie du langage," *Signes* (Paris: 1960) pp. 105–122, especially p. 121.

prevents an individual from even thinking of himself as a potential critic of the code he has inherited. What the existentialists have done is precisely to resist the sorcery of language by which the objectivity of an established social consensus as reflected in the articulation of our moral concepts becomes confused with another kind of objectivity that choice is powerless to modify.

Nevertheless, important as all these observations on the role of publicity in the moral life undoubtedly are, they remain undeveloped in the writings of the existentialists. Their most serious attempt to provide a constructive theory of moral relationships among human beings is to be sought instead in their elaboration of the notion of authenticity, and in their effort to show that the very autonomy which as we have seen defines the moral condition of man, can also yield a principle of reciprocity on which a human community can be founded. I turn now to an examination of this doctrine of authenticity with a view to determining whether or not the existentialists are right in thinking that a positive ethic can be founded on the concept of moral autonomy.[17]

[17] While both Heidegger and Sartre disclaim any intention of drawing directly normative conclusions from their "ontologies" of human existence, and deny indeed that any such can be drawn, there can be no doubt that both of them in fact make a normative use of the concept of autonomy. In Heidegger's case, it is quite clear that the denial of normative intentions has to do with the possibility of using his theory of *Dasein* to generate answers to specific questions about what is right and wrong. (See *Sein und Zeit,* pp. 294, 298, 312). Heidegger himself states that "der durchgeführten ontologischen Interpretation der Existenz des Daseins liegt . . . . eine bestimmte ontische Auffassung von eigentlicher Existenz, sein faktisches Ideal des Daseins zugrunde." (p. 310). He goes on to say that while "existentiale" or, as one might say, "second-level" analysis can never authoritatively settle "existentielle" or "first-level" questions about possible courses of action and obligations, it nevertheless has a certain "first-level" content.

"Wenn das Sein des Daseins wesenhaft Seinkönnen ist und Freisein für seine eigensten Möglichkeiten, und wenn es je nur in der Freiheit bzw. Unfreiheit gegen sie existiert, vermag dann die ontologische Interpretation Anderes als ontische Möglichkeiten (Weisen des Seinkönnens) zugrundezulegen und diese auf ihre ontologische Möglichkeit zu entwerfen? Wenn die Analytik als existent iell eigentliches Seinkönnen die vorlaufende Entschlossenheit zugrundelegt, ist diese Möglichkeit dann eine beliebige?" (*Sein und Zeit,* pp. 312–13.)

To this last question Heidegger's answer is plainly "No"; and he develops a theory of conscience according to which *Dasein* constantly calls itself back

II

Up to this point, moral autonomy has been described simply as a state in which human beings find themselves. Unavoidably, they see their situation in terms of possible alternatives among which they must choose; but they do not choose to see the world in this way.[18] So conceived, moral autonomy is not itself the source of any directives for human conduct; it is, instead, the relationship to ourselves and to the world that is presupposed by any such search for specific principles of action. Quite obviously it would be pointless to urge human beings to achieve moral autonomy when it is their inescapable state of being. On the other

---

from its absorption in the world to a recognition and acceptance of itself as a free and responsible being. In spite of the metaphorical character of this treatment of conscience as a "call," Heidegger makes it quite clear that it has no mystical implications and that to hear the "call" is simply "sich in das faktische Handeln zu bringen," i.e., to *act* in the full sense of that term. Once again, conscience does not tell us for what we are responsible or what we ought to do. "Die Antwort vermag nur der Entschluss selbst zu geben . . . ihrer selbst sicher ist die Entschlossenheit nur als Entschluss," (*Ibid.*, p. 298) . Very significantly, a "public conscience" that does gives answers to questions about conduct is identified as the voice of *Das Man* (p. 278) ; and "morality" is described as emerging from a conscience that is wholly individual (p. 286) . For Heidegger's discussion of conscience and guilt, see *Sein und Zeit*, pp. 267–301.

Sartre's denial that ontology has normative implications can be found in *L'Être et le néant*, p. 720. Especially in *L'Existentialisme est un humanisme* he defends a view that is very similar to Heidegger's with respect to the use of autonomy as a goal, namely that it can yield a certain style of moral existence that excludes conduct based on "bad faith" but does not give answers to specific moral questions. Like Heidegger, Sartre's rests his case for a normative use of autonomy on the fact that "l'homme est un être libre qui ne peut, dans les circonstances diverses, que vouloir sa liberté"; but he does not develop a theory of conscience and appears to hold simply that freedom, as the "nature" of man, implies a "volonté de liberté" without showing any concern about possible charges of circularity against which Heidegger defends himself at length. (*Sein und Zeit*, pp. 314–16.) At the same time as he shares this general position with Heidegger, however, Sartre also associates the Kantian notion of reciprocity with this "volonté de liberté," as Heidegger does not, and argues that while the content of morality is variable, its form is universal and this "form" includes not just the individual autonomy on which Heidegger insists but a respect for the autonomy of others. See *L'Existentialisme est un humanisme*, pp. 84–86.

[18] See *Sein und Zeit*, pp. 284–85 and *L'Être et le néant*, pp. 558–59.

hand, if the existentialists wish to say (as they clearly do) that we can, and also that we should, choose to be free and autonomous beings, and that the achievement of this autonomy is the proper objective of a truly human life, the autonomy that is thus to be achieved cannot be the same as the autonomy that is a datum of human life.

As I have already suggested, a way out of this difficulty is provided by Merleau-Ponty's "dispositional" interpretation of moral freedom. If the latter is conceived as a capacity for envisaging one's situation in terms of alternative possibilities of action, then it is certainly possible to distinguish between having such a capacity and activating it, and also between exercising it only within a very restricted area of one's life and seeking to extend it to all aspects of life. Whether one has such a capacity at all is presumably very much like the question whether a given type of being has the capacity for learning a language. One either has it or one has not—it is not chosen or achieved. But if autonomy is understood not just as a latent capacity but as the progressive development and exercise of that capacity, then it is, at the very least, not senseless to make this development itself a goal of moral effort. Interpreted now as identifying an object of choice and purposeful effort, the concept of autonomy would generate a directive to realize in ourselves an intensified moral self-consciousness, and to subject wider and wider tracts of our experience to analysis in terms of alternatives of voluntary action. It would presumably also direct that in relation to others one should do whatever one can to encourage and facilitate the development by them of a similarly heightened moral self-awareness. It is of course not at all easy to say just what steps would be required to this end but it seems highly probable that they would involve far-reaching and radical changes in our method of moral education.[19] In any case, the mode of life in which this distinction between choice and non-choice is rigorously enforced, and in which every choice is in-

[19] The relationship between moral education and an ethical theory based on the concept of autonomy is discussed in A. Montefiore "Moral Philosophy and the Teaching of Morality," *Harvard Educational Review*, Vol. 35 (1965), pp. 435–449. Of fundamental importance for any consideration of this question is J. Piaget, *The Moral Judgment of the Child*, trans. M. Gabain (New York: Free Press of Glencoe. 1932).

dividual in character, is what the existentialists mean by an authentic human existence. Authenticity (or *Entschlossenheit*) may indeed be regarded as the prime existentialist virtue; it consists in the avoidance of that false relation to oneself and to others that is set up when choices are represented as something other than what they are—something for which the individual is not responsible. Inauthenticity, by contrast, is the arch-principle of mystification in the relationship between human beings and in the relationship of an individual human being to himself. As Sartre's writings make very clear, it is the main obstacle in the way of any truly human relationship based on a reciprocal recognition of one another as fully responsible moral agents. The authentic human being is one who has so thoroughly defined his relationship to the moral attitudes characteristic of the community to which he belongs—either by assimilating or by modifying or by wholly rejecting them—that he is able to make moral judgments in his own name and not just in the ventriloquistic and impersonal manner of a communal morality.

It still remains to ask whether the progressive development of this way of looking at the world—this profound moralization of the self—is a good thing and also, more importantly, whether the recognition of oneself as an autonomous moral being can provide a logically sufficient and necessary condition upon which moral relationships among human beings could be founded. It is this latter claim that is unmistakably suggested in the writings of the existentialists—particularly Sartre—but which has never been *argued* by any of them.[20] Some critics who have noted both this claim and the failure to support it by argument, have treated it as simply a hasty borrowing from Kant of a principle that does not emerge from the existentialist analysis of human nature at all but that is needed if the latter is not to issue in an unacceptable

---

[20] Sartre does give at least a sketch of such an argument in *L'Existentialisme est un humanisme*, pp. 81–82, when he tries to show that "la mauvaise foi est . . . un mensonge" and that "l'attitude de stricte cohérence est l'attitude de bonne foi." What he is getting at here is the fact that the person who claims to be confronted by moral "données" cannot present what are really his claims and preferences in a form that makes a reciprocal understanding with others possible. The latter must either take or leave his "intuitions" of moral truth, and in any case there is no basis for true mutuality.

moral solipsism.[21] This way of treating the existentialists as simply inconsistent plagiarists in their constructive ethics, in its own way begs the same question to which Sartre and others have yet to give a reasoned answer: is the recognition of oneself as an autonomous moral being uniquely fitted to provide a principle of respect for and cooperation with other like beings? At this point, the interpreter of existentialism must make the effort alluded to at the beginning of this chapter, the effort to determine whether or not a constructive argument in support of the existentialists' affirmative answer to this question—the argument that the existentialists have failed to provide—can in fact be found.

It is always tempting to seek to justify the designation of some goal of human effort as a universally valid moral ideal by claiming that the human capability by which this goal is achieved represents the essence of man. Thus, we might be led to argue that a capacity for autonomous choice is the quintessentially human function and not simply one capacity among many, whose relationship to and priority (if any) over other traits and powers of human beings has yet to be determined. It may indeed be the case, as the existentialists seem often to assume, that there is a certain progression in our ways of conceiving our own natures, and that this progression converges upon a definition in terms of capacity for autonomous choice.[22] Thus, we begin with the "natural" attitude in which we virtually coalesce with "what we are," i.e., with the attributes of physique, race, nationality, and culture that distinguish us from other human beings. At this stage, the capacity for self-objectification and self-choice may play virtually no part at all in our image of ourselves. This is also the stage at

[21] See for example, O. Bollnow, "Existentialismus und Ethik," pp. 995 f.

[22] Such a development seems to be postulated by S. de Beauvoir, *Pour une morale de l'ambiguité,* p. 51 ff. where she speaks of adolescence as the period in which "l'individu doit enfin assumer sa subjectivité."A similar progression toward a stage of moral autonomy is described in detail in Piaget, *The Moral Judgment of the Child,* especially ch. 4. Piaget describes autonomy in a way that is strikingly similar to the conception of reciprocity outlined in this chapter. "The morality of autonomous conscience does not tend to subject each personality to rules that have a common content: it simply obliges individuals to place themselves in a reciprocal relationship with each other without letting the laws of perspective resultant upon that reciprocity destroy their individual points of view." (p. 397)

204

which the cleavages between the various natural communities into which human beings organize themselves are most absolute and unbridgeable. But when these characteristics that separate one human group from another lose their importance and their criterial status, as they tend to do with increasing communication and cooperation among these groups, the capacity for autonomous self-determination very likely will assume a prominence it did not previously have, although even then (as Sartre's analysis of bourgeois personality shows) an ostensibly disinterested and "objective" attitude may in fact conceal highly restrictive criteria of equality.[23] Even if it could be shown, however, that our various and partial conceptions of human nature converge on one in which the capacity for self-objectification and self-determination is separated out from all the irrelevancies of race and nationality and economic class, the properly normative question would still remain unanswered. What claim after all has *this* special capacity to be treated as the cornerstone of morality, whatever its place in some hypothetical schedule of human development may be? Unless the existentialist can show persuasively that the human capacity for interpreting experience *sub specie possibilitatis* generates distinctively moral relationships to other beings sharing this capacity, how can he defend himself against the charge—often made by critics—that he is simply proposing another form of moral essentialism and that what he puts forward as the essence of human nature reflects no more than his own arbitrary preference for one human capacity over others? I am assuming here that however large a place a writer like Sartre wishes to make for autonomous choice *within* his account of moral personality, he is not prepared to present that account itself as no more than his own choice.[24] I am also assuming that the only satisfactory answer to this challenge would be a moral one, i.e., a demonstration that autonomy provides the basis for moral community as other "essences" do not, and that "ontological" assumptions about what

[23] See, for example, Sartre's acrid reflections on "bourgeois universalism" in its relation to colonial populations in his Preface to Frantz Fanon, *Les damnés de la terre* (Paris: F. Maspero, 1961).

[24] This seems clear from Sartre's statement that "le choix est fondement de l'être-choisi mais non pas fondement du choisir." (*L'Être et le néant,* p. 561.)

really constitutes human nature merely conceal the need for this kind of supporting moral argument.

While an argument must be made along these lines in behalf of the existentialist position, it is important not to pitch one's expectations too high. Even if it proves to be possible to show that the achievement of authenticity has a special relevance to some conception of obligation that is consistent with other stands taken by the existentialists on issues of ethical theory, it would by no means follow that this is the only goal to which our actions and choices must ultimately be directed. At times, some of the existentialists seem to espouse this latter view and have gone so far as to suggest that from the ultimate goal of moral freedom all other subordinate goals can somehow be extracted.[25] Clearly, however, such an extreme downgrading of "empirical" desires and goals to the status of mere symbolizations of an ultimate and exclusive goal of freedom would prove as implausible as Hegel's quite similar treatment of finite conation, and would seriously underestimate the independence and—in another sense of the term—the "autonomy" of the quite ordinary needs and desires that we all share. It may well be, as I will suggest later on, that authenticity is not just one more goal with no particular relationship to any others we may have; and that instead, it interpenetrates the whole corpus of our antecedently established aspirations in a peculiarly intimate way. But even if this proves to be the case, there can be no justification for simply assuming that this relationship is of the means-ends type or that all goals other than self-conscious moral freedom have a purely derivative and instrumental function.

There is a still more important *caveat* to be entered at this point. It is one thing to argue, as I propose to do, that certain distinctively human capabilities have a special importance in connection with the establishment of relationships among human beings that can effectively bind them to the performance of cer-

[25] See, for example, S. de Beauvoir, *Pour une morale d'ambiguïté*, p. 34, where freedom is described as "la source d'où surgissent toutes les significations et toutes les valeurs." While Mme. de Beauvoir also speaks of freedom as "la condition originelle de toute justification de l'existence," she too often speaks of freedom as though it stood in a end-means relationship to other subordinate goals.

tain actions. It is quite another matter to argue that the possession of these capabilities by itself constitutes a sufficient condition for its being true that we have a moral obligation to respect the moral freedom of other human beings. If certain existentialists, like Simone de Beauvoir, hold, as they appear to, that the fact that we are autonomous beings provides a sufficient condition of our being under such an obligation to all human beings, I can only say that I think this is a mistake.[26] There are a number of familiar difficulties in the way of any effort to prove that man ought to be a moral being at all, i.e., that he has a duty to constitute communities with other beings like himself—whatever trait or capability is taken to provide the basis of that likeness—within which everyone is recognized as having a right to equal consideration. Many attempts have been made in the course of the history of moral philosophy to show that there is such an unconditional duty, but it is difficult not to feel that they have succeeded only by being circular and by inserting among the fundamental attributes of moral personality the very disposition to communal life that then duly emerges in the conclusion. If we agree with Aristotle's view that a wholly non-social being would have to be a beast or a God, as I think we must, and if, as can be plausibly argued, living in the society of other human beings necessarily involves an implicit assent to the validity of some general rules governing relations between members of the group, then the interesting and important question for the philosopher is to determine how and on what basis this relationship among human beings is to be constituted, and not to prove that it ought to be set up at all. If a person were really disposed to challenge this assumption that human beings must, one way or another, live together on the basis of some shared understanding, and to reject root and branch the discipline and the restrictions that such a mode of life inevitably requires, it is not clear how one could even seek to persuade him to do otherwise, although one might well predict that

[26] See her *Pour une morale de l'ambiguïté,* pp. 95–103. Sartre is more cautious and admits that "la liberté comme définition de l'homme, ne dépend pas d'autrui"; but he argues that "dès qu'il y a engagement, je suis obligé de vouloir en même temps que ma liberté la liberté des autres." *L'Existentialisme est un humanisme,* p. 83. Whether "obligé" here refers to the obligation of logical consistency or of practical necessity is not altogether clear.

he would be unable to carry out consistently his plan of living without any dependence on others. On the other hand, if as can normally be assumed to be the case, there is an initial disposition to find some basis for moral community, then it can be shown that certain capabilities which we "naturally" possess assume a special importance. By themselves, however, these capabilities, whether they be the ability to reckon consequences or to choose between alternative courses of action, do not signify that they must be used for the purpose of establishing a moral community among human beings.

III

It is time now to turn to the concept of obligation itself, and to take note of certain of its features before going on to ask what the special relationship between authenticity and obligation may be. We may begin by considering the way in which claims that human beings have certain general duties can be established in the face of possible challenge. As has already been pointed out, such challenges are often met by arguments intended to show that the mode of conduct that is being called for is somehow part and parcel of our human nature, and thus cannot rationally be rejected by us. Since all conceptions of what constitutes our nature are themselves open to challenge, many philosophers have come to feel that the nature to which appeal is made must be one that has somehow been recognized as such by the person to whom the argument seeking to establish the reality of the obligation is being made. In the history of political philosophy, this perception has led to the elaboration of contractarian theories of obligation like Rousseau's, which justify all limitations on what may permissibly be willed by reference to certain postulated acts of assent by the very persons who are thus subject to what are really self-imposed obligations. The effect of such theories is to base all obligations on the obligation to keep a promise, and while some of the proponents of this view have associated it with excessively literalistic conceptions of the form assumed by these contractual undertakings to which they appeal, the notion of promises as the basis of obligation generally can be separated from these irrelevancies. When this distinction has been made, the conception of promises as self-engaging acts proves to have great power and suggestiveness as a model for understanding moral relationships among human beings. I will argue that, when suitably interpreted, it can provide the elements of a theory of obligation and of moral community that can be accepted by the existentialists consistently with their commitment to the doctrine of moral autonomy.[27]

Promising is, of course, merely the clearest and most dramatic example drawn from the larger class of what might be called self-created obligations. What distinguishes obligations of this kind is the fact that the obligation is explicitly assumed by a given person at a more or less definite point in time. This assumption is often, as in the case of promising, a linguistic performance of a certain kind, and involves the public use of a form of words that has the effect of placing the person who uses them under an obligation to the person to whom the promise is made. The effect of the use of the promise-formula is to license an expectation on the part of the person to whom the promise is made. What may not be so obvious but is of great importance for our purposes is that in so licensing another's expectations I must implicitly disallow in advance an appeal to any justifications for a failure to do what I have promised to do, other than those that fall within a certain more or less precisely defined range of excuses. One "reason" for non-performance that is disallowed by this formula would certainly be any such statement as "I don't want to" or "I have changed my mind." A person who tried to justify non-performance in this way would merely show that he did not understand the promise-making formula he had used. It is thus an intrinsic feature of the latter that it does effectively "change the situation" between two or more persons in a way that cannot be canceled by just any subsequent decision *not* to do what one decided to do in making the promise. The change thus made is not some magical modification of the relationships in

---

[27] In the outline I give here of a theory of obligation I have drawn at various points on the views of John Rawls as stated in "Justice as Fairness," *Philosophical Review*, Vol. 67 (1958), pp. 164–94, and in other articles.

which "objects" stand to us, but rather a linguistically effected change in the relationship between the person who makes the promise and the person to whom it is made. Given normal circumstances, once a person has put himself "on the hook" by engaging in the promise-making practice, he has bound himself in a way that carries with it all the externality and rigor that any deontologist could require.

It has sometimes been alleged that even self-created obligations require as a condition of their effectiveness that there be moral principles such as "Promises are to be kept," the truth of which is certified by an act of intellection that is logically prior to all particular acts of promise-making. In this way, the authority of special obligations is assimilated to what is assumed to be the standard case in which rational necessity is the basis of moral authority. It is perfectly possible, however, to agree with the cognitivist that "Promises are to be kept" is necessarily true; and yet, to hold at the same time that this is an analytic truth which generates an actual obligation only if we decide to engage in the promise-making activity. Thus, we come to be obliged only because we choose to use the promise formula, and if we chose never to use it, we would not be under an obligation. It would not make sense to argue that *Pacta sunt servanda* means that we *ought* to engage in promise-making practices; and therefore the obligation is one that we put ourselves under when we do so engage. It is of course true that most people do not think of themselves as deciding to take part in, or not to take part in, the promise-making activity which is a going social concern into which we are in some sense "born." The established social character of this practice does not, however, imply or require that there is any corresponding "natural" obligation with respect to promises at all; and it seems much more plausible to treat the whole logically structured activity of promise-making as a human contrivance, as Hume thought, and as one which does not have to be thought of in cognitivist terms at all.

To be sure, self-created obligations are usually held to be only one type of obligation. There are many others such as the obligation to deal justly with other human beings, or the obligation to prevent unnecessary suffering, which do not seem to lend them-

210

selves so readily to an analysis along these lines, and certainly do not involve any express acts of self-commitment as promise-making does. But the case of special obligations still provides a useful clue, because it is quite possible that even where such explicit verbal performances are absent, there may be other less obvious means by which, in effect, we authorize an interpretation of what we do or say, which becomes an implicit element in our relationship with other persons and has much the same force as an obligation. For example, it can be argued that simply by speaking a language we authorize others to assume that we are saying what we believe to be true; so that when we lie, we violate an obligation accepted implicitly through our use of language. So too, when we accept what has been determined by some principles of justice as our fair share in some distribution, the other participants are justified in assuming that we accept these principles and will abide by them in like cases even when it may be more advantageous to us not to do so. In this case, we have again and by our own action (though not by any explicit linguistic performance) accepted a rule of action—in this case, a rule of justice—and have, in effect, disallowed "I don't choose to" as a defense in the case of non-performance.

These examples suggest that the notion of a self-created obligation may be susceptible of generalization. While Hume was perhaps the first to propose a conception of rule-governed reciprocity as the basis of moral obligation generally, it is Kant's vision of the human community as a kingdom of ends that most clearly suggests the form this conception might take if pressed to the limit.[28] In place of Hume's rather skimpy list of the possible forms of reciprocity, Kant makes the principle of reciprocity the governing norm for all relationships among human beings. If I must never, as Kant says, treat any other human beings merely as a means (i.e. as a thing), then I must judge only those actions to be morally permissible which I can justify to those affected by them, by appealing to considerations which I would be prepared

[28] In his *Grundlegung einer Metaphysik der Sitten*, ed. E. Cassirer (Berlin: B. Cassirer, 1913) Vol. 4, pp. 291 ff. Kant's notion of a kingdom of ends is frequently referred to by Sartre, and while his comments are often critical, there can be no mistaking the influence of Kant's ethical theory on his treatment of moral questions.

to accept if the situation were reversed. What is important here is not so much the actual content of these jointly acceptable rules of conduct, nor Kant's claim that this content can be uniquely determined by purely logical tests, but rather the mode of human relationship within which this consensus emerges. Each human being recognizes all other human beings as being, like himself, morally free and as endowed with the capacity for understanding, accepting, and carrying-out jointly acceptable policies; and this recognition becomes a principle of respect for the moral freedom of others through each person's disallowing an appeal to mere disinclination or subjective preference as a ground for non-performance of obligations deriving from those policies. A "kingdom of ends" as Kant calls it, or a "moral community" is simply a human society in which the fundamental relationship in which all the members stand to one another is that of persons to whom a rational justification by reference to considerations they can freely accept is due for all actions that significantly affect them.

There are, to be sure, features of Kant's conception of a moral community that pose difficulties for any radically voluntaristic ethical theory that seeks to appropriate it. It has already been pointed out that Kant did not for one moment suppose that the obligations connected with this mode of human relationship were self-created in any sense that implies choice. Furthermore, while he recognized that we can and too often do *choose* not to comply with the requirements of the moral law, he did believe that all of us unavoidably recognize the controlling normative status and validity of the mode of human relationship on which the kingdom of ends rests.[29] In other words, with every *Willkür* there is associated a rational will; and the presence in each of us of the latter insures that, whatever our professions, we will all be aware at some level of the true moral quality of our actions. What these assumptions seem to support is a belief that a moral community is always and necessarily realized among rational beings, even when it remains "invisible" by virtue of their failure to act in the manner required by the principles whose validity, on this account, they nevertheless recognize. But when we consider the ac-

[29] See ch. 3, n. 6.

tual state of most, if not all, human societies, it becomes highly problematic not only whether any of them would qualify as a moral community in the sense of one that effectively realizes a rational and just ordering of human relationships, but also whether there is the kind of universal though tacit recognition of the authority of this ideal. At the very least, the evidence is ambiguous; if we sometimes seem to give a paradoxical recognition to the ideal of true mutuality by seeking to *justify* inherently unjust arrangements to the very persons who suffer most from them, there are also large and unrecognized lacunae in our moral consciousness that are hard to reconcile with the view that we always envisage and judge our own actions from the standpoint of a member of a community of rational and moral beings. In any case, doubts about the degree of acceptance that the ideal of a moral community finds at any level make it necessary to go more deeply into the questions that were taken care of for Kant by his assumptions about the rational will present in each of us.

These are questions about the institution and acceptance of moral community among human beings. They are rendered more difficult by other weaknesses in the Kantian scheme, and by the unavailability to us of a number of alternative rationales of obligation which Kant, to be sure, repudiated, but which other moral philosophers have used extensively. If passing Kant's test of the validity of moral maxims is at most a necessary condition of the rightness of an action, and not a sufficient condition as he seems to have supposed it to be, then we will still be confronted by a number of formally valid but incompatible policies of action in any given situation. It becomes evident that if such conflicts are to be resolved and jointly acceptable policies are to emerge, a detailed consideration of specific empirical claims and needs will be necessary. Moreover, if we cannot simply assume, as Kant does, that there is a natural and unconditional obligation to submit one's claims to a rational adjudication, neither can we argue that treating other human beings as ends is the only rational policy for the conduct of life when prudence and self-interest are the standard of rationality. Here again the evidence is far from clear and may even be generally favorable to this thesis. Even so, there is a notable disproportion between the strictness of the obligation to respect other human beings, as most of us would interpret it, and the incomplete, and in many respects ambiguous state of the evidence showing that to do so will always be in our interest. But if we drop, or in one way or another qualify, these assumptions which Kant associated with his conception of a moral community, the effort to realize this community will inevitably come to seem more like one possible policy, among others, which we might adopt in our relations with other human beings; and one which we must think of ourselves as choosing, and as choosing for reasons that themselves reflect certain evaluative preferences on our part.

If we were to allow this last point to stand without any further elaboration, however, we would in effect have given up all prospect of establishing *any* special connection between authenticity and obligation; and this chapter is intended to show precisely that such a connection exists. In fact, the assertion that adherence to the ideal of a moral community is an arbitrary choice needs to be qualified in two important respects. First, it needs to be pointed out that while adoption of the principle of moral reciprocity and mutual respect does involve a choice, repudiating that policy in a really consistent way would be extremely difficult. All of us are reared in societies in which the notions of reciprocity and of justification play some role, however ambiguous and precarious that role may be; and while every individual is, in principle, free to assume in his own case, or reject, the "choices" made by others that are reflected in the moral code of the society in which he is reared, there is, in practice, an obvious limit to the degree to which he can consistently reject these principles while continuing to be a member of that or any society. Since we have been formed by these practices, we cannot repudiate them *in toto* and continue to be the social beings they have made us. Even when we ostensibly reject only some portion of these rules, there is a great likelihood that we will go on tacitly appealing to and counting on the rejected principle, at least in cases in which it is advantageous to us to do so. If we do, we could hardly refuse to accept the authority of the principle in those cases in which it would require the sacrifice of some short-run interest of our own. In this sense, the authority of moral principles might be said to be just the reverse side of the practical difficulty of rejecting more than a sharply limited segment of prevailing moral practices *without* committing inconsistencies of this kind. There is no portion of that corpus of rules that is in principle immune to revision, but the abandonment of the whole would be tantamount to the dissolution of all social relationships based on reciprocity with other human beings. In this sense, principles *are* authoritative and independent of our wills; and their authority would be simply that of the standing presumption that we do wish to continue to benefit from existing forms of mutuality, as well as of the practical difficulty of consistently doing anything else. Of course, this presumption may be shown to be false in particular cases, but it could still be used to account for the general authority that is claimed for the whole range of forms of social cooperation.

In some sense, then, moral communities do exist, and in some measure all of us have been formed by them, and as a practical matter would find it very difficult to "opt out" of the obligations they entail, even if we were so minded. The further point that needs making is that if we are dissatisfied with the various "natural" communities to which we belong, and are dissatisfied not because these associations involve the acceptance of obligations to other human beings, but because these obligations seem arbitrary and irrational and irrelevant to our real needs and desires, then only a purified conception of obligation as joint self-commitment based on mutual respect for one another's status as autonomous moral agents affords much prospect of a stronger and more satisfactory mode of human relationship.[30] More specifically, if what we want is more community and not less, then only self-initiated obligations will prove to be effectively binding when the supporting assumptions on which other conceptions of obligation rest have been abandoned. To be sure, when I signify to others a desire to work out with them understandings that will then be jointly accepted as norms governing my actions and theirs, I do not thereby surrender the right to criticize or to seek to revise the

[30] This is the sense in which I would understand Merleau-Ponty's somewhat cryptic statement that "la moralité est à faire." Merleau-Ponty himself explains this statement as meaning that "apart from a pure heteronomy accepted by both sides. . . . there is no given universality; there is only a presumptive universality." (*The Primacy of Perception*, pp. 30–31.)

policies we progressively elaborate. I do, however, place myself in a position in which, barring quite exceptional circumstances, I must regard a refusal by me to do what these understandings require of me as unjustifiable, and therefore as wrong in the only sense of that term for which any common authority can be claimed. Even if I invoke my inalienable power to re-open the questions that were resolved by our joint understandings, and proceed to answer them differently and thus cancel that understanding, I cannot by the fiat of my will alter the fact that this was a shared, a public understanding, in which one crucial element was the surrender of unrestricted discretionary powers by all parties. I could consistently repudiate the publicly understood content of that understanding only by retreating into a kind of solipsism of the present moment, in which I deny that anything that I may have permitted myself to be understood as accepting at some moment in the past has any relevance to, or authority over, what I now judge to be my right. Certainly these understandings, like all policies that have a temporal stretch to them, are effectuated by a whole series of choices that we make over a period of time; but here, the initial choice has a quite special function which is both to create a locus of moral objectivity and to place it beyond our own sole control. That locus of objectivity is the "other"—the moral community that is constituted by these joint understandings; and if one major attribute of autonomous moral personality is the ability to reopen and to decompose into their elements of "fact" and "value" all policies of action that are proposed to it, then another equally important power is this ability to alter our situation vis-à-vis other human beings in a way that gives rise to a sense of right and wrong that we cannot repudiate.

Inevitably, a theory of obligation constructed on these lines will have a narrower range of application than our ordinary concept of obligation is thought to have; and to many, there will quite understandably seem to be as little continuity between the one and the other as there is, according to some critics, between our ordinary understanding of what is involved in choice and the existentialist version of that concept. The existence of these discontinuities may be freely conceded; as may the fact that there are great practical difficulties in the way of a review in the light of this sharpened concept of obligation, of what are ordinarily thought of as being our duties to one another. Nevertheless, even in the absence of such a review, we are not entirely without means of giving effect to the ideas presented above. We can, after all, ask ourselves whether a given policy or principle is one that others *could* accept consistently with what we know about their needs and aspirations. While nothing, finally, can take the place of participation by those affected in the formulation or review of such policies, raising questions in this hypothetical form may at least enable us to eliminate many alternative courses of action on the ground that others can have no rational motive for assenting to them. Thus, it may be that many of the social arrangements and practices in the design and institution of which most people have had no share whatever, can be defended at least as interim expedients on instrumental or utilitarian grounds, and thus as presumptively acceptable to those affected by them, even though *ex hypothesi* they cannot claim any degree of "obligatoriness" in the special sense now attaching to that notion. If we seek, wherever possible, to transform that presumptive consensus into a real one by the widest kind of consultation and discussion, it is hard to see what justification there could be for dismissing this revised conception of obligation simply on the ground that it involves a break with more familiar and current ideas on the subject.

IV

Now that an account has been given of both authenticity and obligation, the question of whether there is some special relationship between them must be faced. Does recognition by human beings of one another as morally autonomous beings, together with a disposition to intensify and extend wherever possible the kind of self-awareness on which this recognition rests, supply a uniquely suitable basis for a moral community characterized by binding relationships among its members?[31] There are reasons for

[31] The notion of authentic existence or *Entschlossenheit* as developed by Heidegger seems to be wholly lacking in social or other-regarding implica-

thinking that it does, assuming always that there is a disposition to communal living based on something other than force or fear. It must also be assumed that the human beings who are so disposed have needs and desires that are not so hopelessly disparate as to be incapable of joint satisfaction, and that the powers with which these persons are endowed are not so incommensurate as to cancel out any motive that the stronger party might have for cooperation with the weaker. These material conditions seem to be roughly satisfied by human beings as we know them; and so, too (although here, no very great assurance is appropriate) is the further condition that the kind of choice of which the persons entering into these relationships to one another must be capable is not just momentary preference, but long-term commitments to joint policies, with all the implications for disciplinary controls over the actions of individuals that such policies involve.[32] Even though from the existentialist point of view there can be no once-and-for-all commitment to such policies that eliminates any subsequent reconsideration of the issues they pose, no long-range commitment at all can be made by persons who are constitutionally unable to resist impulses which may run counter to a line of conduct they have adopted. Unless these conditions are met, no stable human community is likely to be founded on whatever basis. When they are, however, the special kind of self-consciousness associated with authenticity has a contribution to make which must now be described.

Let us consider first the implications that a recognition of oneself as a morally autonomous being might have for the way one presents oneself as a candidate for moral relationships to other

---

tions; and it is not even clear whether there is, in his view, an authentic mode of relationship to other human beings, although the passage from his book on Kant noted in ch. 7, n. 39, makes this seem likely. A hint of such an aspect of authenticity is contained in Heidegger's brief discussion of *Fürsorge* in *Sein und Zeit*, p. 122. In one of its forms, "die *Fürsorge*, die wesentlich die eigentliche Sorge—das heisst die Existenz des anderen betrifft, und nicht ein *Was*, das er besorgt—verhilft dem Anderen dazu, *in* seiner Sorge sich durchsichtig und *für* sie *frei* zu werden."

[32] The notion that choice has a temporal stretch to it is common to all the existentialists, but it must be conceded that until Sartre developed his theory of obligation in *Critique de la raison dialectique* there had been little emphasis on any element of discipline associated with choice.

human beings. The most salient of these implications can be very simply stated. If a man thinks of himself as a morally autonomous being, the very nature of this character that he imputes to himself is such as to absorb any other feature of his nature which he might designate as the basis for his relationships with other human beings, and on the strength of which he might demand respect and acceptance from them. Let us suppose, for example, that a man proposes to make the fact that he is a proletarian—or a white man—or a Buddhist—the primary basis of his association with other human beings. Since he is at the same time, as I am assuming, committed to the doctrine of moral autonomy, he will be forced to admit that his being a proletarian, or a white man, assumes the criterial function he assigns to it only as the result of a choice on his part. In fact, *being* a proletarian or a Buddhist or even a white man in any sense which implies the imposition of priorities by which e.g., being a white man takes precedence for purposes of action over being something else, inescapably turns out to involve an exercise of the same autonomy that presides over the whole moral life. If this is so, then to demand that one be respected in one's capacity as a white man or, as a proletarian is to demand respect as one who "chooses himself" as a proletarian, and could have "chosen himself" as something else. This, in turn, is indistinguishable from demanding recognition as a free moral agent—with this reservation, that it is not explained why respect is to be confined to those moral agents who freely choose themselves in this one way. The relevant point here, however, is that once the agent adopts the autonomist view of his own moral activity, every subsequent role he espouses must be understood as a mode of self-determination for which he bears final responsibility. For this reason, if he is prepared at all to enter into an association based on reciprocity and mutual recognition with other human beings, he can do so only in his capacity as a free moral agent. If he is an autonomous moral being, then in every subordinate goal he sets himself, and in every principle he adopts, he is also bringing into play that fundamental capacity for self-determination. He cannot repudiate or remain indifferent to the latter without, at the same time, withdrawing the claim he makes for the subordinate goals that are its expression.

This line of reasoning can quite obviously be extended so as to yield conclusions that cast light not just on the role in which I can present myself as a candidate for moral relationships with other human beings, but also on the terms of cooperation which I can offer to my prospective partners in a moral community. If they, too, are autonomous moral agents, and if they, too, can have obligations only by placing themselves under obligations, then what *could* I offer them except respect for this freedom of self-definition and self-engagement which they, like me, enjoy? Even if they were not to share my conception of moral personality; which, as I am assuming, is based on the doctrine of autonomy, and were to give priority to other attributes they possess, it seems clear that from my standpoint their establishment of these priorities would have to be regarded as itself an exercise of that same autonomy. In this context, it is important to emphasize once again a point that has already been made. This is that while self-conscious autonomy absorbs our other desires, wants, and aspirations by transforming them into so many forms of self-determining choice, it does not follow that these wants must be somehow derivable or deducible from the fact that we are autonomous beings. Quite obviously, many of them will pre-date the recognition of one's autonomy as a moral being; and in any case, they are absorbed into this autonomous condition not by some process of logical derivation, but by passing through a critical review as a result of which they are put forward, if at all, as claims with which others have to reckon as *my* choices, whatever their previous history and no matter how initially passive in relation to them I may have been.[33] They must, in other words, be *assumed.* The point that I am making here is simply that if we accept the doctrine of autonomy at all, we cannot avoid thinking of other human beings, for the purposes of possible moral relation-

[33] Sartre's views with respect to the logical relationship of "original" and "secondary" choices to one another are stated in *L'Être et le néant,* pp. 548–50. While he makes quite clear that this relationship is not one of deducibility but a looser one in which particular choices may contribute to a larger thematic unity from which they cannot be strictly derived, it would be too much to claim that he endorses the interpretation I have offered of total choice as a "resultant." Thus, Sartre argues that I can make errors about the nature of my own original choice and this inevitably suggests that it has a more "categorical" or "occurrent" character than I have suggested it does.

ships with them, as standing in this relationship to their own desires and wants.

This point has implications which make clearer how the aspiration to authenticity may facilitate the formation of moral relationships that can be truly binding. From what has already been said, it follows that the moral community that the existentialists project is one in which the only condition of membership is the very capacity for choice and self-commitment itself, and in which the members reciprocally recognize one another as "choosers." The force of this identification resides in the fact that it requires that each individual who is a member of such a community must regard himself, and be regarded by his fellows, as the sole and responsible arbiter of his own interests, and as controlling what may be called his "input" of claims into the public adjudicatory forum in which a common policy that resolves conflicts among claims must be formulated.[34] Thus the *"données"* of every moral problem are provided by the expressed preferences of human beings, each of whom speaks for himself and whose "vote" must be allowed to register as it stands, and not be interpreted out of existence or tacitly overridden by some theory of human nature that by-passes or disallows the explicitly declared preferences of the individual. Nothing is more alien to the general ethos of existentialism than the kind of moral paternalism that "knows better" than the individual moral agent what is good for the latter, or worse still, what the latter "really" wants. As often as not, this is done by appealing to some view of what is involved in moral personality as such; and when, as frequently happens, this view turns out to have substantive moral implications, these are established as antecedent premises on which subsequent joint deliberation must proceed, and which it is powerless to revise. By contrast, the existentialist insists that every element entering into the consideration of a moral problem must be "sponsored" i.e., must come in as the declared preference of one of the parties to such a deliberation; and his declaration is to be authoritative

[34] See S. de Beauvoir's statement, *Pour une morale de l'ambiguïté,* p. 198, that while "le bien d'un individu ou d'un groupe d'individus mérite d'être pris comme but absolu de notre action . . . nous ne sommes pas autorisés de décider à priori de ce bien."

for the other participants in the sense that none of them has the right to look behind or interpret this preference in any way that is not authorized by the person whose preference it is.

Perhaps the most important feature of the relationship between authenticity and obligation remains to be described; and in order to grasp its significance, one must understand how precarious and conditional such moral community as exists at any given time appears to the existentialists. As I have already indicated, there are writers on ethical theory who seem to assume the existence of a moral community as a presupposition of any distinctively moral activity on the part of individual human beings who belong to it. On this view, it does not make any sense to speak of the defining principles of such a community as reflecting any kind of choice on the part of its members; they constitute instead a datum of the moral life antecedent to, and presupposed by, the choices of individual moral agents. I have indicated too that existentialist writers, by contrast, are typically much more strongly impressed by the fraudulence of what passes for moral consensus, and by the fragility and the partiality of such genuine consensus as does exist. Because they see so clearly the insecurity and the ambiguity of our actual moral practices as judged by the standard of true mutuality, the existentialists conceive the relation of each individual to the moral community in the volitional mode and that community itself as a *realisandum* or as an "endless task" in the Kantian sense. This view in turn is inspired by the perception that our moral failures are as often due to our not recognizing certain classes of human beings as candidates for moral relationships at all, as they are to non-performance of duties within the sphere in which we do recognize the authority of moral principles. Precisely because the concept of autonomy is formal in the sense of abstracting from substantive rules of conduct, it makes possible a clearer focus upon the moral relationship between persons which is the precondition for a successful resolution of questions of conduct, as well as upon the problematic and vulnerable character of such moral community as exists.

If we now consider these views in the context of the theory of obligation and of the moral community sketched out in the preceding section, it is difficult not to conclude that the existentialists have made a valid and important point. It may well be the case that natural communities like the family can continue to exist and even thrive although their members simply fulfill the duties assigned to them by their roles within these communities, and no one explicitly formulates the nature of his role to himself in such a way that it incorporates a statement of the basic relationships between human beings on which that community rests. It seems impossible, however, that a moral community such as I have described should ever exist except as it is sustained by an awareness on the part of its members of the mode of relationship to others that it involves and by a conscious determination to persevere in it. For the moment we lose the sense of ourselves and of others as "choosers" or lose our belief in the importance of this mode of identifying one another, our capability for actions and decisions that are truly shared will be affected. In a moral community, the whole corpus of rules and policies must remain in principle permanently open for reconsideration and possible revision if that community is to be completely sovereign in the sense of being able to raise and to resolve in a manner binding on all whatever issues it may face. But in order to be sovereign in this sense, the members of a human group must recognize one another as endowed with the capacities of choice and self-commitment which make it possible for them to be participants in such collective choices.[35] To the extent that that recognition is effectively denied or is restricted by unilaterally imposed limits on the scope of choice, a moral community ceases to exist, and with it, relationships of obligation lapse. Those who might otherwise be subject to obligations will not have been permitted to act jointly with us to change our relations to one another in a way that would be binding; or perhaps not even they themselves will have fully grasped their capacity for so altering their own situation. In any case, in the absence of reciprocal recognition of one another as capable of this special kind of choice, a certain mode

[35] This notion of a collective or joint choice, which has been developed so extensively in the *Critique de la raison dialectique*, is not a recent addition to Sartre's ethical theory and can be found as early as *L'Existentialisme est un humanisme* where Sartre says that " (la) liberté se veut dans le concert." (p. 83.)

of human relationship becomes an unavailable option; and it is this mode of relationship that alone renders obligation intelligible.

Here then, we touch on the deep underlying motive for associating authenticity with obligation in the way the existentialists do. Because the various natural communities into which we are born only very imperfectly embody the ideal of human mutuality, we, as individuals, must continuously define for ourselves the moral community in which we effectively live. By so doing, we contribute in differing degrees to the expansion or contraction of such genuine mutuality as in fact exists; and if it is true, as I have argued, that mutuality is a condition of obligation, then we can properly speak of choosing to be obliged by choosing the mode of human relationship that makes obligation possible. Moreover, like all policies, the policy of living together with other human beings on the basis of a reciprocal recognition of one another's autonomy becomes effective *only* through corresponding choices made by individual human beings. When human beings single out their capacity for choice and self-commitment and place a value on it by seeking to extend and intensify their awareness of the choices that are open to them, and when they are able to describe these choices to themselves in such a way as to make evident the full burden of moral implication they carry, the making of such choices bearing on the constitution of a moral community will at the very least be facilitated. If, at the same time, they understand that only a similar recognition and prizing of the autonomy of other human beings can provide the framework within which the claims they may wish to make on others will have a place, they will surely perceive in the existentialists' positive evaluation of our capacity for autonomous moral choice, not just a facilitating but a necessary condition of the form of life they seek.

V

There has been one major exception to the existentialists' lack of interest in the social and institutional aspect of morality. At least since the end of World War II, the French existentialists have evinced a strong and continuing interest in Marxism, and have indicated—sometimes defiantly and sometimes rather wistfully—their awareness that its mode of dealing with moral questions represents a direct antithesis to the moral individualism of their own position.[36] This confrontation of existentialism and Marxism has led to a number of exchanges which have contributed in some measure to our understanding of the existentialist approach to questions of social morality; but these have been largely polemical exercises rather than attempts to build a general theory of human relationships on the foundation of the doctrine of autonomy. This last is what Sartre had promised to do "in a coming work" at the end of *L'Être et le néant,* but that work has never appeared.[37] In its place, Sartre published in 1960 the first volume of *Critique de la raison dialectique,* a major effort to reconcile the principal theses of existentialism with those of Marxism through a reinterpretation of the dialectical structure of human action or praxis.[38] In this book, Sartre goes so far as to speak of existentialism as an "enclave within Marxism"; but, while a final judgment on the relationship between the two as Sartre now understands them must await the completion of the *Critique,* a number of critics have already expressed doubts about the absorption of Sartre's earlier views by his more recently adopted Marxism and have suggested that on a number of points of crucial importance it is the latter that has had to accommodate itself to existentialism rather than the other way around.

By itself, the first volume of *Critique de la raison dialectique* is an enormous and—by reason of its formidably complex style and vocabulary alone—an extremely difficult book to understand. Many of the topics it takes up have little or nothing to do with ethical theory; and its central concern is rather with the phi-

[36] See, for example, Merleau-Ponty's *Humanisme et Terreur,* which marks the first major attempt by an existentialist to do justice to some of the insights of Marxism without accepting either its materialism or its determinism. Merleau-Ponty's political philosophy was to undergo considerable revision in his later *Les aventures de la dialectique* (Paris: Gallimard, 1955).

[37] *L'Être et le néant,* p. 722.

[38] A very useful summary outline of the argument of this book can be found in R. D. Laing and D. G. Cooper, *Reason and Violence: A Decade of Sartre's Philosophy—1950–1960* (New York: Humanities Press, 1964).

losophy of the social sciences. Its principal thesis is that our mode of understanding of social institutions and of social change is never wholly independent of our practical attitudes and commitments with respect to them, and that both take the form of certain conceptual syntheses or "totalizations" by which our social environment is organized with a view to action. In essence, this amounts to a new version of Hegelianism, qualified by a recognition of the underlying contingency of all human actions, individual or collective, and also by Sartre's express endorsement of a thoroughgoing ontological individualism according to which individual human beings are ultimately the only dialectical agents and any collective praxis must be understood as a complex function of an indefinitely large number of individual dialectics. In any case, a large place within Sartre's statement of this theory of society is assigned to the emergence of what he calls "groups" —human communities based on reciprocity—out of "serial" aggregates in which human beings cooperate with one another as they do in a queue, but without any recognition or acceptance of an effective identity binding them together. The paradigms which Sartre uses for his analysis of the emergence of groups are drawn from revolutionary situations in which a crowd suddenly acquires a conscious unity of purpose and acts as a single body. While much of what he has to say about such formations and the circumstances of scarcity and class antagonism which they presuppose, is very interesting, it would seem to fall more into the province of social psychology (insofar as the latter deals with the phenomena of self-identification among members of an emergent social group) than into that of ethics. Embedded in this theory of groups, however, there is a long discussion devoted to the "pledge" by which, a "group-in-fusion" is transformed into a permanent unit of social cooperation. In the course of this section, Sartre gives an account of human relationships based on self-created obligations which in its essentials runs parallel to the conception outlined earlier in this chapter.[39] While some of the special assumptions attached to this theory as well as the forbidding terminology in which it is couched make it unsuitable for use as a general statement of an existentialist theory

[39] *Critique de la raison dialectique,* pp. 381–460.

of obligation, its main points must be briefly noted here as a means of substantiating the general thesis of a compatibility between autonomy and obligation which I have been defending.

The most noteworthy feature of Sartre's theory of the pledge is its recognition that through a promise or its equivalent, human beings can change their situation vis-à-vis one another in such a way as to bring into existence reciprocal rights and obligations which then constitute effective limits on the exercise of each individual's autonomy. In language that often recalls—rather strangely—that of Hume's discussion of obligation, Sartre repeatedly calls the human group based on reciprocity an "invention" by which individual human beings produce a new form of relationship to one another by binding themselves (i.e. by restricting their own liberty of choice) on the condition that others do likewise.[40] This performance requires that each participant become what Sartre rather awkwardly calls a "third"—a kind of ideal, and in some sense at least, impartial agent who shares certain goals with others and identifies *their* actions in pursuit of these goals with his own. This new identity typically emerges in the course of some spontaneous joint action such as the taking of the Bastille. The pledge is essentially a formalization of the relationships so formed and is designed as a guarantee of the permanence of the newly-formed group against dissolution when the external dangers that were the occasion for its formation temporarily recede. Eventually, the permanent group takes on institutional form through the increasing differentiation of social functions and roles within the group and the consequent elaboration of codes of practice; and since the institutionalized group is always in danger of relapse into a purely external or "serial" mode of relationship among its members, the pledge has to be constantly renewed. Here it is important to note that Sartre recognizes that this renewal occurs not through explicit acts of swearing faith to one another but through any act of reciprocity such as aiding another who is in need. Indeed, as Sartre says, "it is always a

[40] On the other hand, Sartre asserts against Hume that a pledge or promise *can* effect an irreversible change in one's situation: "Le serment n'est ni une détermination subjective ni une simple détermination du discours, c'est une modification réelle du groupe par mon action regulatrice." (p. 441)

case—except in emergencies—of *renewing* the pledge."[41]

A number of passages are of particular interest because they express so clearly both Sartre's recognition of the possibility of a self-imposed limit on what an autonomous being may do, and his conception of the reciprocal understanding on which this self-limitation by each individual rests.[42] Thus we are told both that my belonging to the group is my free project and that this project by its nature makes a claim on each member of the group. It amounts, in fact, to an undertaking by me to satisfy the claims made on me in my capacity as a "third"; and this free undertaking is explicitly declared to involve a limitation of my liberty. In order that I may be able to count on other members of the group, each of them must be able to count on me; and they can be expected to respect limitations on what they may legitimately do, only if I honor their claim to a similar limitation on me. The pledge thus creates a "transcendence" of the group over its members which Sartre describes as an absolute right, and which he also speaks of as a "positing of man as an absolute power of man over man under conditions of reciprocity." In this way, through my own choice, obligation becomes a feature of my condition as it never was before; and it cannot simply be negated by my consciousness without thereby authorizing the use of violence by others to insure compliance. Finally, because the basis of human relationships within this newly created body is, for the first time, mutual recognition of self-imposed obligations toward one another, the pledge that brings the group into being is in fact, as Sartre says, "the beginning of humanity."

This beginning takes on an imperatival character by virtue of its being permanent in a way that makes it indefeasible for all future time; it thus refers the recognition of one human being by another back to the reciprocal affirmation of two common traits: we are one because we issued from the primeval slime at the same time and because each one enabled the other to do so with the concurrence of all the others. Thus we are if you please a unique species that made its appearance by a sudden mutation at a given point in time; but our specific nature unites us *qua* freedom. In other words, our common being is not an identical nature in each one of us, but rather a reciprocity that presupposes the

[41] *Ibid.,* p. 493. Emphasis added.
[42] *Ibid.,* pp. 439 ff.

setting of conditions on both sides; in approaching a "third" I do not recognize my own inert essence as it is manifested in another example. I recognize instead my indispensable accomplice in the act that will tear us loose from the soil, the brother whose existence is not distinct from mine and comes to me as my existence, but nevertheless depends on mine as mine does on his (with the concurrence of all the others) in the irreversibility of a free assent. . . . We are brothers in the sense that after the creative act of the pledge we are our own sons, our own joint invention. Moreover, just as in real families, this fraternity expresses itself in the group through a set of reciprocal and unique obligations which are laid down by the group on the basis of its situation and its goals (i.e., general obligations to render mutual assistance and obligations to perform particular actions or tasks in specific and rigorously defined situations.) But as we have just seen these obligations simply express the shared character of the underlying exigency and of the act of self-creation which has taken place and which constitutes the irreversible mortgage of our commitment with respect to future action.[43]

While these and other passages clearly establish a close correspondence between Sartre's conception of obligation and the theory of the moral community outlined in earlier portions of this chapter, other features of his position raise certain questions.

[43] "Ce commencement devenant pour chacun nature impérative (par son caractère de permanence indépassable *dans l'avenir*) renvoie donc la reconnaissance à l'affirmation réciproque de ces deux caractères *communs:* nous sommes *les mêmes* parce que nous sommes sortis du limon à la même date, l'un par l'autre à travers tous les autres; donc nous sommes, si l'on veut une espèce singulière, apparue par mutation brusque à tel moment; mais notre nature spécifique nous unit en tant qu'elle est liberté. Autrement dit notre *être commun* n'est pas en chacun *une nature identique;* c'est au contraire la réciprocité médiée des conditionnements: en m'approchant d'un tiers, je ne reconnais pas mon essence inerte en tant qu'elle est manifestée dans un autre exemple: je reconnais le complice nécessaire de l'acte qui *nous* arrache à la glèbe, le frère dont l'existence *n'est pas autre que la mienne,* vient à moi comme la mienne et pourtant dépend de la mienne comme la mienne dépend de la sienne (à travers tous) dans l'irréversibilité d'un libre consentement. . . . Nous sommes frères en tant qu'après l'acte créateur du serment nous sommes *nos propres fils,* notre invention commune. Et la fraternité, comme dans les familles réelles, se traduit dans le groupe par un ensemble d'obligations réciproques et singulières, c'est-à-dire définies par le groupe entier à partir des circonstances et de ses objectifs (obligations de s'entraider en général, ou dans le cas précis et rigoureusement déterminé d'une action ou d'un travail particulier) . Mais ces obligations—nous l'avons vu à l'instant—ne traduisent à leur tour que la communauté de l'exigence fondamentale et tout aussi bien de l'auto-création passée comme hypothèque irréversible de la temporalisation pratique." *(Ibid.,* p. 453.)

To take one example, there is in Sartre's account a very strong emphasis on the violence to which I expose myself from other members of the group by virtue of the pledge I have given as a member. There would seem to be some danger that this emphasis will obscure the very important distinction between the motive I have for keeping faith, and the valid basis for my obligation to do so. My motive may well be fear of the consequences of violating my pledge; but I would be under an obligation even if for some special reason I did not need to fear reprisals. In one place, however, Sartre goes so far as to say that the "indépassibilité" of the commitment assumed through the pledge may vary in degree from individual to individual, and that the prospect of violence in the event of infidelity serves to raise the level of this "indépassibilité," and thus to make it less probable that I will fail in my duty.[44] This is no doubt true in one sense, but it misses what is surely the distinctive force of the pledge which is to make non-performance and default *unjustifiable,* no matter what our tendency to keep or to break faith may be in the face of a certain level of prospective violence. That prospect may after all confront us whether or not we have pledged ourselves. What the pledge does is to disallow in advance any right we might claim either to do as we please or to resist such reprisals as our failure to comply may call forth from the group. On the other hand, as I have shown earlier, Sartre seems to recognize quite clearly that the core notion in obligation is that of a logical self-binding, and not that of a threat; and if at other times he argues that what effectively produces social cohesion is the prospect of violence, this may be explained by his evident feeling that too strong an emphasis on the internal logical structure of the pledge would tend to suggest that the latter is no more than a "reciprocal determination of discourse . . . a mere game of signs and meanings."[45] Nevertheless, these apparent inconsistencies do create some doubt as to whether Sartre would give the weight to the notion of logical self-binding within his conception of obligation which it seems to deserve, and as long as this doubt subsists, it cannot be said, with

[44] *Ibid.,* p. 459.
[45] *Ibid.,* p. 447.

complete confidence, that his views tally perfectly with those advanced earlier in this chapter.

A question arises also about the limited character of the groups within which, on Sartre's view, rights and duties come into being. The context of discussion makes amply clear that these groups stand in antagonistic relationships to other groups or social classes, and that the formation of a group typically takes the form of a response, through internalization, to a previous identification of it *as a group* by an antagonistic social class. It follows that the community thus formed and the obligations it comports are in no sense universal and include only those who, by their actions, demonstrate their affiliation. It may be that in his promised discussion of the way dialectical relationships among groups generate the movement of "History" Sartre will develop a theory along Marxist lines of the eventual emergence, through conflicts among restricted groups, of truly universal human community—an authentic "cité de l'homme." If so, it may well turn out that in such a society obligation will rest solely on the common human capacities of autonomy and rationality, and no longer on the special interests of restricted groups; but Sartre has also told us that we can know nothing of the freedom that will characterize that eventual society and presumably, therefore, nothing of the form that obligation will assume in it either.[46] Nevertheless, it does seem clear that in Sartre's view the momentum behind the movement toward such a state will be provided not by the internal logic of the idea of reciprocity but by the progressive resolution of the deepseated conflicts between material interests which, until they are overcome, render impossible the emergence of a common interest and the sense of a common human identity.

One may agree with Sartre that moral communities have material presuppositions, and still feel that he has underestimated the logical if not the causal power of the notions of reciprocity and justification. Even if it turns out that genuine social cooperation among different interest groups must await the emergence of new relationships of production and distribution of goods, the most

[46] *Questions de méthode* (Paris: 1960), p. 32. This study is bound in the same volume as *Critique de la raison dialectique*.

general features of such a new economic system itself must, one would think, be derived from, or at least pass the test of, some conception of the social arrangements that could justly be accepted by all elements in a society. This in turn presupposes a use of the notion of reciprocity beyond the limits of any restricted group. It is clear, too, that no restricted group can ever employ its moral vocabulary beyond the limits of its internal affairs for the purpose of justifying a *refusal* to seek larger and more comprehensive forms of social accommodation. It would, after all, be rather incongruous to claim a right to disregard systematically the interests of the very groups from whom a recognition of that right is then solicited. Insofar as such extra-mural use of the moral notions operative within a restricted group is contemplated at all, its legitimacy would be dependent on its taking the form of an appeal for a wider recognition and realization of the idea of reciprocity; and this is what Sartre with his rather fanatical emphasis on the limited character of groups has thus far failed to make sufficiently clear.

It is at just this point, of course, that the need will be most keenly felt for a truly and unconditionally universal form of obligation—one that goes beyond both the Sartrian conception of obligation as effective only inside restricted pledge-groups and the wider, "no right not to . . ." conception of obligation presented earlier in this chapter. This would have to be a type of obligation that would permit us to assert that it is our positive duty, in all historical circumstances and in all social classes, to do what we can to bring into existence a truly universal human community. Sometimes the demand for such a conception of obligation is deprecated on the ground that the only relevant weakness of the available theories of obligation is that they provide us with nothing to say to individual human beings or restricted moral communities (if there are such) that in actual fact neither seek nor propose a wider sphere of moral relationships. This, it may be claimed, is not a very serious deficiency, since the stance of such an individual or community, in the unlikely event of its being consistently maintained, could only be defined as a repudiation of the assumptions under which alone a wider moral community can even be sought. One may concede the force of this rebuttal and still feel that a conception of obligation as reciprocal self-binding cannot provide an adequate basis for certain moral attitudes to which, if we have them at all, we are likely to attach great importance. Specifically, we do feel that we have moral obligations of various kinds toward many human beings who are either temporarily or permanently incapable of true participation in a moral community because they cannot "bind themselves." Children, for example, are unable, before a certain age, to grasp the notion of justification and to make long-range commitments; and feeble-minded or deranged persons are permanently incapacitated in this respect. Then too, there are persons who have reached maturity in cultures quite different from our own in which the idea of basing moral relationships on voluntary reciprocal understandings is quite unfamiliar. Even at certain levels of our own society there are persons whose experience has been such that they are unable to attach much, if any, meaning to such ideas. Nevertheless, many people feel that moral restraints on what may permissibly be done are operative in these cases, in spite of the absence of any relationship based on mutual recognition of one another as autonomous moral beings. The question therefore arises of how such an extension of the notion of obligation beyond the range of effective moral community can be justified.

This is not a question that can be answered in a way that is likely to satisfy those who raise it. It is perhaps just possible that a deeper analysis of the principle of reciprocity and of the cognate notion of justification might show that even within restricted moral communities based on a common economic interest or shared racial characteristics there is nevertheless a tacit recognition given to the primacy of the human capacity for rational choice.[47] If so, it could be argued that moral relationships within such groups reflect a recognition that equal consideration

[47] Sartre may be implying something of this kind when he says that "le malaise secret du maître, c'est qu'il est perpétuellement contraint de prendre en considération la *réalité humaine* en ses esclaves (soit qu'il compte sur leur addresse ou sur leur compréhension synthétique des situations, soit qu'il prenne ses précautions contre la possibilité permanente d'une revolte ou d'une évasion) , tout en leur refusant le statut economique et politique qui definit *en ce temps* les êtres humains." *Ibid.*, pp. 190–91.

is due to their members by virtue of their possession of this attribute of human nature, and not by virtue of the other (e.g., racial) characteristics which may, nevertheless, for other reasons be subjoined to it as criteria of membership in this group. Obviously, such an analysis would present grave difficulties, but if any progress could be made in this direction, the basis would be laid for an even stronger charge of inconsistency against any group that refused like consideration to members of other groups in the event that circumstances were sufficiently favorable to permit them to extend that consideration without undue risk to themselves. Perhaps, too, other parallel lines of argument might be constructed to deal with the case of those who are incapable, whether temporarily or permanently, of sustaining moral relationships of the type proposed. After all, all of us are children before we are adults and any one of us may become mentally incapacitated, so we do have a stake in seeing to it that such persons are treated as having, within the limits of feasibility and prudence, the same rights and duties as they would have if they could speak for themselves, since in choosing for them we may well be choosing for ourselves. More than this it would probably be unfair to ask an ethical theory to establish. No ethical theory is likely to be able to show that loving concern for other human beings and perhaps for animate creation as such is a duty; and to this rule existentialism forms no exception.

CHAPTER IX

THE SIGNIFICANCE OF EXISTENTIALISM

In earlier chapters, I have on several occasions made a distinction between the substantive theses that are defended by the existentialists with respect to the nature of value and freedom, and the wider influence and significance that are often claimed for existentialism as a philosophical movement. I have also pointed out that my interpretation of existentialism as a movement of reaction against certain long-standing tendencies within the Western philosophical tradition raises serious questions about the appropriateness of the considerable popular response to existentialism. This response cannot, after all, have been inspired by a sense of liberation from the chains of a Platonic intellectualism that is in fact almost completely unfamiliar to the great mass of those who are drawn to existentialism in some of its more accessible forms. As I have noted, one might, in these circumstances, be tempted to conclude that the whole popular excitement over existentialism rests on an elaborate misunderstanding. On the other hand, if it could be shown that there is an affinity or parellelism between the developments within the history of moral philosophy which I have tried to outline and wider movements of Western life and culture, then it might become possible to interpret the reception accorded to existential philosophy—discounting certain purely eccentric manifestations—in such a way as to make it genuinely relevant to the actual content of existentialist doctrine. In this final chapter, I propose to argue that a parallelism of this kind does exist, and that in spite of its profound involvement with a somewhat arcane philosophical tradition, existentialism may appropriately be regarded as the philosophical expression of a movement within Western—and perhaps world—culture, the importance and scope of which can hardly be exaggerated.

This way of posing the question of the wider significance of existentialism assumes that philosophy in general, and ethical theory in particular, develop in substantial independence from other movements in the societies that cultivate them; and that a special explanation is therefore in order when major interest in some philosophical doctrine is shown by the general educated public. Those who, like the Marxists, reject this assumption and treat philosophical doctrines as coded expressions of the situation and prospects of some society or social class at a certain stage in its historical development will naturally approach the whole question I am raising here in a quite different way. Marxists have in fact characterized existentialism, in both its philosophical and popular forms, as a philosophy whose clientele is the Western entrepreneurial bourgeoisie. What is said to be the desperate sense of isolation of that group from the forward movement of history allegedly finds its counterpart in the extreme moral individualism of the existentialists. While many interpreters of existentialism have been content to attribute its special ethos to particular crises in the life of countries like Germany after World War I and France during and after World War II, and have thus failed to provide any intelligible account of the strong elements of continuity with earlier phases of Western moral philosophy that existentialism reveals, there have been Marxists like G. Lukacs who recognize these historical affinities and are prepared to convict virtually the whole post-Kantian tradition of proto-Fascism.[1] The grotesque distortions of history to which this line of interpretation has led cannot be dealt with here. Instead, by giving a brief account of the extra-philosophical movements with which the gradual emergence of voluntaristic ethical theory does run parallel, I hope to show that any characterization of that evolution in purely political or economic terms misses its deepest significance.

---

[1] The high-water mark of Marxist denigration in this field was set by Lukacs' *Die Zerstörung der Vernunft* (Berlin: Aufbau-Verlag, 1954).

I

While there are great and obvious difficulties in the way of any attempt to chart the evolution of the sense of selfhood within a society or a culture, it is impossible not to feel that a profound and accelerating change has been taking place over a period of several centuries in the way human beings conceive their powers and responsibilities as moral agents. For a very long time— indeed, for the vast majority of us, until quite recently—the cir- cumstances of life of almost all human beings have been so ne- cessitous and so restricting as to make it virtually impossible for them to think of themselves as exercising effective control over any significant aspect of their lives. Under conditions of enforced passivity, or rather, of activity exclusively within the limits of cer- tain pre-established social roles, it was inevitable that such ideas as were formed of moral personality should have had a strongly "naturalistic" cast. When one's mode of life and social role are not susceptible of any significant modification, a clear-cut distinc- tion between one's nature as a human being and one's "station and duties" will not be easy to make. As a result, what one "ought" to do will quite naturally come to be thought of as some- thing very like self-evident truth, capable of being "read off" from the social world we inhabit. It seems plausible, moreover, to suggest that intellectualism and its cognate ethical theories build upon (and owe a large measure of their plausibility to) such a mode of life in which the possibilities of significant choice are so radically curtailed as to find only a subordinate place in the pic- ture human beings form of themselves as moral beings.[2]

Now it is this state of affairs in which human beings are born into a world of wholly determinate social roles and relationships that has been gradually changing. At first, during earlier centu- ries of the modern era, and indeed up to the nineteenth century,

---

[2] This view seems to have the support of S. de Beauvoir, when she says that "moins les circonstances économiques et sociales permettent à un individu d'agir sur le monde, plus ce monde lui apparait comme donné." (*Pour une morale de l'ambiguité*, p. 68.)

an enlargement of the possibilities of life was realized for only a tiny and privileged fraction of the total population. More recently, larger and larger segments of the population of Western countries and significant minorities within the non-Western world have been drawn into this movement. What is of special interest in that evolution from the standpoint of this study is not so much the immense and fateful transformation of the material instrumentalities of human life, but rather the progressive internalization and, as it might be called, "voluntarization" of much that was previously accepted and espoused without question and indeed without any sense that an individual commitment might be involved. As the objective possibilities of freely fashioning one's own life have increased, ideas of self-determination and of the necessity for a personal ratification by each individual of the mode of life proposed to him by his society have come to occupy a larger and larger place in the conception we form of ourselves.[3] To a considerable extent, of course, this sense of a personal participation in the creation of the self attaches to relatively superficial details of personal style and manner, but it has also penetrated to the deeper levels of selfhood and to basic ideals of life and modes of relationship with other human beings. At all levels, this new and essentially critical form of self-consciousness reduces the claims of custom and authority to set the course of an individual life to so many *données,* all equally subject to the judgment and decision of the individual moral consciousness.

It would not, I think, be an exaggeration to say that for the first time in human history large numbers of human beings have come to think of themselves as autonomous moral agents, capable of raising and resolving for themselves all questions about what they are to do. Here, then, is a real analogue to the drama of transition from a pre- or quasi-moral condition to a full assumption of responsibility for one's own life that is celebrated by the existentialists. No doubt we were moral beings all along in the sense

[3] For an excellent interpretation of the theme of autonomy in nineteenth century history, see F. Schnabel, *Deutsche Geschichte im neunzehnten Jahrhundert,* (Freiburg: Herder and Co., 1929). Vol. 1. Many interesting comments on the "culture of the will" can be found in the critical essays of Lionel Trilling. See *The Liberal Imagination* (New York: Doubleday, 1950), and *The Opposing Self* (New York: Viking Press, 1955).

of having a capacity for choice, and of exercising it within the narrow limits set by the technological and institutional frameworks of earlier societies; but it is also true that in a special sense we *make* ourselves moral beings by adopting a certain perspective on our lives and on those of others. Because the existentialists concentrate their attention not so much on the finer internal substructures of a fully moralized human life as on the contrast between being a fully self-conscious moral agent and the condition of life in which free moral personality is either not recognized or is suppressed, they speak with special directness to the highly focused and explicit kind of moral consciousness that has emerged in its distinctive form in the course of modern Western history and is still new enough not to be disposed to take itself for granted. In spite of passing fads and excesses of one kind or another, the recognition given to existentialism as well as to its forerunners in the history of ethical theory may accordingly be regarded as reflecting an authentic affinity between its main theses and the movement toward personal autonomy that is perhaps the distinguishing feature of modern Western culture.

Nothing testifies more convincingly to the existence of this affinity than do the distinctive preoccupations of much of the imaginative literature of twentieth-century Europe. I have in mind not so much the "literature of existentialism" (i.e., the novels and plays that are either written by existentialist philosophers themselves, or directly inspired by their writings), but instead, certain works that have evidently taken form in virtually complete independence of any direct philosophical influence and therefore constitute evidence of a particularly valuable kind bearing on the moral atmosphere of the time.[4] The common theme of these works, as of much of modern literature, is the situation of human beings who have lost contact with (or repudiated) the social institutions and the related systems of belief that claim to provide authoritative moral guidance to the individual, and who accordingly live in what must be—from the standpoint of their previous experience—a peculiarly truncated moral world. Their situation is that now frequently described as "alienated." This somewhat

[4] I have in mind here writers as different as André Malraux and R. M. Rilke, Samuel Beckett and Paul Valéry.

too glibly employed term is unobjectionable if it is simply meant to characterize a state in which an individual is thrown back on his own moral resources as a result of being no longer willing or able to accept the claims to unconditional validity of some externally imposed code. In any case, among the works of imaginative literature that seek to render this situation, there are those that can only be called testaments of despair, and others that seek with very different degrees of success to project an affirmative ideal of what human life can be under this new dispensation. Perhaps only in the work of Franz Kafka are the stark lineaments of this truly modern situation rendered without artificial despair or enthusiasm, and above all without any tincture of ideological partisanship.[5] The extraordinary power and directness with which Kafka's fables speak to the modern imagination make it very difficult to believe that they do not express something in our sense of life that goes much deeper than any literary fad.

I do not wish to be misunderstood as suggesting that this special affinity that existentialism has with the modern spirit is so close as to preclude the possibility that the latter might find expression in any other conception of the moral life. There is, after all (as I have noted), a variant concept of autonomy that associates it with the existence of objective norms, and attributes to each human being the capacity and the right to interpret and apply these norms for himself. Moreover, as a matter of historical fact, the movement toward a liberalization of the conditions of social life has typically based itself on such intellectualistic conceptions of autonomy rather than on a radical voluntarism of the existentialist type. Nevertheless, while conceding all this, one may still wonder whether such ostensibly intellectualistic defenses of liberalism are not more deeply tinged with voluntarism than their leading proponents have often grasped. Not only does the assignment of a right to each human being to interpret moral laws for himself suggest a measure of scepticism with respect to the patency of these laws; but it is also not clear how in practice a

[5] I have developed this view of Kafka's work at greater length in my article, "Kafka and the Primacy of the Ethical," *Hudson Review*, Vol. 13 (1960), pp. 60–73.

right to interpret would be distinguished from a right to choose one's principles of action. Once people come to think of themselves as having to "decide" questions of interpretation at all levels of the moral life, the intellectualistic compulsion to duplicate each such decision in the form of a corresponding determination of an objective moral principle and thus to project it into some antecedent realm of truth seems likely to lose much of its power. If that is so, the final destination of all ideologies of self-determination and moral freedom may be expected to approximate to a position very like that which the existentialists now represent.

II

Throughout the period during which these changes have been taking place, there has been an accompanying current of speculation about the effects that might be expected to follow upon a widespread acceptance of a voluntaristic and individualistic conception of morality. Since the middle of the last century, this speculation has reached flood proportions and it has ranged from expressions of exalted enthusiasm over the prospect before us to warnings of the dangerous implications of moral freedom. In the latter category, writers from Dostoevsky onward have laid great emphasis on what they take to be the demoniacal character of an unqualified moral freedom, and have argued that the only logical issue for such a freedom must be a violent act of destruction directed against the values of the established social order and ultimately against the self, i.e., suicide. The assumption shared by writers who take this view is that the freedom they condemn is of such a nature as to be incapable of finding expression through the acceptance or creation of any stable moral relationships to other human beings, and therefore must assume the form of a violent repudiation of previously accepted values for which there is no longer felt to be any adequate foundation. Such views as these appear to be rather widely accepted, and have certainly influenced the reception accorded to existentialism in many quar-

241

ters. They are also exploited by certain versions of religious "existentialism" which expose their adherents to the icy drafts of non-being just long enough for them to become thoroughly chilled, and correspondingly amenable to being led back into what is, in spite of certain renovations suited to the contemporary taste, still recognizably a religio-moral edifice in the old style.[6]

There are, I think, good reasons for believing that this "Dostoevskian" view of the implications of moral autonomy is mistaken. At the same time, however, it is important to understand that it owes such plausibility as it possesses to an experience of disorientation and shock that often does accompany a shift from one general conception of morality to another like that of existentialism. This disarray reflects a belief that no distinction is any longer possible between purely individual preferences and generally valid moral principles. The source of this belief may be found in a feeling that while existentialism may not prejudice *what* we can say in a normative way, it often seems to leave us without a means of saying it. It rules out any use of the factual model for interpreting moral truth, and yet provides no new means by which we can express an order of values that is not finally arbitrary. The result is that moral judgments as a class are pushed into a limbo in which no general rational principles operate at all. The impulse to claim general authority for certain principles still survives, but it is saddled with an ethical vocabulary that cannot give a meaning to this conception. I am forced to see that my favored moral judgments and their opposites are profoundly alike in being nonlogical acts of preference, but I am unable to point to anything that substantiates my sense of the unique status enjoyed by my principle, beyond the very fact that it is mine, and that can hardly serve as a basis for any kind of su-

[6] Sartre has explicitly declared that "l'apparition, dans l'entre-deux-guerres, d'un existentialisme allemand correspond certainement—au moins chez Jaspers—à une sournoise volonté de ressusciter le transcendant." (*Critique de la raison dialectique,* p. 21) . Sartre declines to discuss the case of Heidegger in this connection on the ground that it is too complex. In Heidegger's writings since the war, however, with their suggestions that man must listen for the "call of being," there are unmistakable signs of such a return to a more traditional conception of being as a source of a message that has relevance to human concerns. See Heidegger, *Über den Humanismus* (Frankfort: V. Klostermann, 1949) , pp. 28–29.

prapersonal authority.[7] To the extent that I do not merely identify with my own preferences, but try to accept a moral principle
only when the grounds for its acceptance are such as to be equally
compelling for everyone, I am searching for a standard that is not
itself internal to one of the two conflicting views. At this final
level of the moral life, however, there is none to be found; and
the realization that there is no possibility of an extrinsic justification for the moral life can lead to doubts as to whether, under
these new auspices, that life is possible at all.

Nevertheless, however painful we may find this dislocation of
the moral life that is produced by the apparent absence of any
model for the expression of an ordering of values that is not
purely individual, it will very likely be temporary and may yield
in time to a saner appreciation of the possibilities that are still
left open by a morality of freedom. I have already tried to show
that there are such possibilities, and that among them is a type of
human relationship characterized by effectively binding obligations. Instead of investigating these possibilities that are left open
by an acceptance of a morality of freedom the Dostoevskian critic
proceeds to read the psychological reactions noted above and the
destructive forms of conduct in which they sometimes find expression back into the very doctrine of moral autonomy itself of
which they are then declared to be the necessary logical issue.
This is a plainly inadmissible procedure. What those who employ
it forget is that if the world does not have a "meaning" in the required sense of generating absolute moral directives, then neither
does this fact about the world—that it does not provide absolute
norms—have the power to do so.[8] No policy of action is justified

[7] This seems to me to be what Sartre is saying when he speaks of the
discovery that "toutes les activités humaines sont équivalentes" (*L'Être et le
néant*, p. 721).

[8] One could wish that Albert Camus had grasped this point more clearly. In
his *Le Mythe de Sisyphe* (Paris: Gallimard, 1942), he appears to argue that
the very pointlessness of human effort is to be espoused as the one value that
survives the wreck of all the rest. This is in effect to substitute a penchant for
action for action's sake for all the ordinary reasons we have for acting in one
way rather than another, and from such a view it is just a step to an
identification of true autonomy with the life-style of the hero and the
"adventurer" and the ethos of the *acte gratuit*, which Sartre has rightly
declared to be something very different from authenticity. See my review of
Camus' book, *Philosophical Review*, Vol. 66 (1957), pp. 104–07.

by the fact that its opposite—in this case, the traditional moral norms that the nihilist violates—is not somehow endorsed by the universe. It is, of course, possible that a perception of the fraudulence of an endorsement of this type which we had previously taken at face value may have the paradoxical effect of making a violation of the norm so endorsed seem attractive. There is no reason, however, to think that this type of reaction would be very widespread; and where it occurs it would seem more likely to be motivated by the oppressive rigidity of the moral discipline that has been cast off than by anything inherent in the experience of moral autonomy as such.

We should not, however, jump to the conclusion that, because there is no valid basis for the prophecies of calamity we have been reviewing, we should look forward to a general acceptance of an autonomist ethic with unreserved enthusiasm. There are, in fact, certain drawbacks connected with the use of the concept of autonomy: first, as an instrument for describing the moral reality of the world we actually live in; second, as representing an ideal which we should seek to realize ever more fully in our own lives and in those of others. To these I now turn.

III

The difficulties connected with the use of the concept of autonomy as an instrument of description has already been touched on in the course of an earlier discussion of the divergent interpretations of moral freedom put forward by Sartre and Merleau-Ponty.[9] The point was made that there are real and important differences among human beings with respect to their degree of internalization and explicit assumption of the policies implicit in their modes of conduct. While all human beings may very well possess the capacity to transform automatic and customary behavior into fully intentional "action," there is no reason to think that it is equally easy for all of them to do so; and it is manifest that they, in fact, bring areas of greatly varying extent within their lives under explicit decisional control. If under these

[9] See ch. 7, pp. 158 ff.

244

circumstances we nevertheless proceed to give an account of our own moral experience and that of other persons in which we make use of a set of concepts that at least suggest that an exhaustive "voluntarization" of our experience has already taken place, a very peculiar picture of the actual moral world will result. Specifically, all distinctions of degree and quality with respect to the responsibility individuals bear for their actions will be erased when the latter are portrayed as endowed with a full awareness of the whole range of options that confronts them.

Nowhere does the danger inherent in this procedure emerge more clearly than in Sartre's critical essays, especially in his "existential psychoanalyses" of Baudelaire and Jean Genêt, but also with certain differences in his treatment of anti-Semitism.[10] In these often very brilliant and perceptive studies, Sartre applies his general doctrine that the function of a properly conceived psychoanalysis is to disengage from our actions the total choice of ourselves which we in fact have made and for which we alone are responsible. This conception of psychoanalysis is contrasted with the Freudian position, which, according to Sartre, seeks the sense of our actions in an "unconscious" which is disjoined from the ego and its choices and for the content of which we—our conscious selves—bear no responsibility.[11] To the degree that this proposed revision of psychoanalytic theory corrects a tendency to transform the unconscious into an inaccessible and mysterious entity, it can have a very beneficial effect; but questions begin to arise when Sartre proceeds to impute the total life-policy he infers on the basis of a scattering of biographical data to the subject of the investigation as *his* choice of himself. The difficulty here stems not so much from the fact that the events of a man's life may admit of several interpretations and that Sartre often does not seem to recognize the inherent ambiguity of the evidence

[10] Sartre, *Baudelaire* (Paris: Gallimard, 1947) ; *Réflexions sur la question juive* (Paris: P. Morihien, 1946); and *Saint Genêt: comédien et martyre* (Paris: Gallimard, 1952) .

[11] A quite different and, I think, more accurate interpretation of Freud's doctrines in their bearing on morality can be found in P. Rieff, *Freud: The Mind of the Moralist* (New York: Viking Press, 1959) . In certain respects the "ethic of honesty" which Rieff attributes to Freud is not so very different from Sartre's own position, although the affinity is much closer in the case of Merleau-Ponty.

with which he has to deal, but rather from Sartre's failure to make any allowance for the inevitable discrepancies between his own perspective on the system of choices that *is* an individual human being, and the often much more limited perspective of that individual himself. Even if we do not challenge the accuracy of any of the assumptions of fact that underly Sartre's interpretation of a given individual's life, and concede a real plausibility to his version of the latter's total choice of himself, it still remains to be determined whether that individual ever entertained a comparable vision of himself and his life, and if so, with what degree of clarity and explicitness and completeness. This is to say that in some sense an individual must be able to recognize himself in the account the existential psychoanalyst gives of his life. While we may be prepared to impute to a person some intentions and some choices that he is unwilling to recognize as his own by appealing to notions like Sartre's "bad faith," there must be real limits in the form of empirical controls of some kind on the use that can be made of such arguments if they are not to turn into devices for establishing any hypothesis about another person's intentions which it may please us to advance. In Sartre's analyses, there is often a kind of non-stop escalation from a not very large evidential base to highly abstract formulations of the total choice through which these data are to receive a meaning. Little or no attention is paid to any evidence bearing on the relationship between the subject's perspective on his own life—the sense the recorded events had for him—and the analyst's perspective on that life. If these differ in ways that cannot be accounted for by *ad hoc* hypotheses of bad faith, and if (as seems likely), the subject's picture of his own moral history is a much more blurred and ambiguous one in which alternatives and consequences are not laid out with anything like the clarity characteristic of the analyst's presentation, then to substitute the explicitness and completeness of the latter for the opacity and particularity of the former will inevitably introduce serious distortions into our understanding of the life under consideration.

The criticism I am suggesting can be expressed in the following way. It has already been shown that Sartre, like most existentialists, adheres to the doctrine of ontological individualism according to which all actions are the actions of some individual human being, and the rationale of all actions must be in some sense an internal structure of that individual's life. One major implication of this doctrine is that all the accounts and explanations that historians and social scientists give of apparently collective actions must decompose the latter into an indefinitely large number of individual acts with their convergent (or divergent) rationales.[12] Except perhaps in the case of groups bound together by explicitly acknowledged quasi-legal relationships, the practical difficulty of performing such an analysis would be formidable and very likely insuperable; but quite apart from such difficulties, an even more serious issue arises at the level of theory. If, as is so often the case, the individuals participating in such collective movements have very imperfectly and partially internalized the rationale of the action imputed to them, may not any advantage gained by substituting individualistic for holistic concepts in the explanation of such actions be balanced by a corresponding distortion, through overexplicitness, of the actions of the individual participants? In any case, a great deal of our linguistic apparatus for the description and explanation of action seems to be designed so as to permit us to talk about collective actions without the kind of imputation of conscious intention on the part of individual persons on which the existentialist appears to insist. This holistic idiom in which much of our discourse about history and society is carried on has on occasion played into the hands of those who believe that there is a genuinely supraindividual kind of agency, but that fact by itself does not seem to be a sufficient justification for refusing to recognize the ambiguous and indeterminate character of the relationship of individuals to collective actions which makes an intermediate mode of describing such actions a practical necessity.

The second major criticism of existentialism which I wish to suggest is one which, like the first, concerns a possible failure to appreciate the limits that in practice must be observed in seeking to achieve an ideal—that of self-conscious moral freedom—which

[12] For a critical discussion of the claims of "methodological individualism," see E. Gellner, "Explanations in History," *Proceedings of the Aristotelian Society* (1956), Supplementary Vol. 30, pp. 157–76.

in itself is perfectly valid. Specifically, it needs to be understood that by assigning an unqualified priority to the special kind of freedom and self-awareness that the existentialist prizes so highly, we may be led to sacrifice other elements of moral personality. Is it not likely that a conception of the self that is centered on its capacity for explicit volitional self-determination and that proclaims the desirability of an intensification and extension to all areas of life of a highly developed sense of the alternative possibilities of action and of the necessity for choice will tend to interfere with a certain spontaneity and naturalness in our relations to others and to ourselves? To be sure, Sartre has declared that choice may equally well occur not just after conscious deliberation but also when we act passionately and on the spur of the moment. In this way, he may seem to have forestalled an interpretation of his views as encouraging a hypertrophy of the volitional life. Nevertheless, it is hard to resist the conclusion that the effect of a conscious and principled espousal of the ideal of authenticity might be just that; and if so, there are good grounds for fearing that the strenuous culture of the moral will thus initiated might not be an unambiguously desirable goal.

The fact is that there are a good many important aspects of human life to which the notions of choice and decision apply only in a rather strained sense.[13] It is by no means clear, for example, that one can *choose* to love or to trust another human being. It is certainly possible to choose not to perform the actions that are the natural expression of such attitudes; and it is even possible to perform or to try to perform those actions even in the absence of the real feelings with which the latter are normally associated. It seems very likely however that any attempt to substitute a kind of volitional fiat for these feeling-states or, worse still, to transform the latter into volitional acts would produce at best a very unstable and imperfect facsimile of the "real thing." This point, in turn, may be developed in such a way as to suggest a

[13] In formulating this criticism of existentialism, I have benefited from a study of the work of Erik Erikson, especially his *Childhood and Society* (2d. ed.; New York: W. W. Norton and Co., Inc., 1963), and *Insight and Responsibility* (New York: W. W. Norton and Co., Inc., 1964).

wider dependence of our systems of choices on the affective dispositions by which they are accompanied. While no set of facts about what we like and dislike can by itself settle any question about what we will do or ought to do, it does seem to be true that an effort of self-definition that is not based on a certain measure of self-knowledge and a recognition of one's own proclivities and interests is unlikely to develop much momentum. There is a sense in which all of us may be said to *learn* what our long-run preferences really are and what kinds of lives we are effectively willing and able to lead over the long pull. This is the kind of knowledge of ourselves that other persons with longer and wider experience of the world can often help us to acquire. While we are often and no doubt rightly unwilling to accept such counsel, it would be folly to deny that there are any such "facts" about ourselves that need to be taken into account. Sometimes the existentialists seem to have come close to making such a denial, as for example when they insist that all such predisposing affective states themselves express some deeper choice that we ourselves have made. As I have already suggested, there is no obstacle of principle to a broadening of the existentialist concept of a "situation" to include psychological factors, both those that are common to all or most human beings and those that may be idiosyncratic, in such a way as to do justice to the affective dimensions of selfhood while still reserving a central place for the act of critical appraisal and choice. It is clear that in the absence of such a recognition of the special importance of these affective states, a purely volitional ethic that isolates action and choice from the underlying powers and interests of the psychological self might prove a brittle and impermanent guide to life.

This sense that volitional activity emerges from and is sustained by the very aspects of human personality that it is called upon to criticize and perhaps to redirect, has so often been associated with a failure to do anything like justice to the special function of the moral will, and the special kind of independence in which that function is performed that even a reference to it may be misunderstood as an abandonment of the whole notion of autonomy. Such is not my intent here; and the positive thesis for which I am arguing is one that is perfectly consistent with the central doctrines outlined in earlier chapters. This conception of the place of the moral will within human personality as a whole may be conveyed by means of a somewhat hackneyed simile to which I would append just one further detail. If we compare human personality to an iceberg, then the relatively small exposed portion could be regarded as corresponding to that portion of our lives that is subject to the scrutiny of the moral will. The much larger submerged portion of the iceberg would represent the habitual and quasi-automatic—although by no means necessarily "unconscious"—routines of human life insofar as these are not made the theme of moral interrogation. The innovation I propose is simply that this iceberg should be thought of as one that can be turned over in any direction so that there is no portion of it that cannot be exposed. In terms of this image, then, the point I have been trying to make about the dependence and the independence of moral choice would simply be that the iceberg cannot be completely exposed at any one time and that a particular portion of it can be exposed only if other portions are submerged. Literally, this amounts to saying that while none of the multiple relationships we continuously sustain to the whole of our human environment is immune to becoming the object of critical attention and revisionary choice, it is not possible for all such relationships to be subject to such a review simultaneously or continuously without grave consequences for the integrity of the very moral life they compose. In fact it is tempting to go somewhat further and to suggest that successful critical revision of certain elements in our moral experience can occur only to the extent that others remain undisturbed. To the extent that some existentialist writers may have tended to suggest that the strength that accrues to human beings from the undisturbed operation of such settled dispositions is to be replaced by a conscious and total and continuous act of explicit self-creation, they have not only very greatly exaggerated the powers of critical self-objectification that human beings possess but have also run the danger of mutilating human nature as a whole in the interest of *one*—albeit a central one—of its faculties.

IV

Serious as these reservations and criticisms which I have just been formulating certainly are, they clearly call for a more careful effort to set the theses of existentialism in the context of other valid perspectives on the human fact, and not for a simple abandonment of the former. There is, however, another line of criticism which needs to be taken into account if the long-run interest of what the existentialists have to say is to be justly assessed. The criticism I have in mind would take the form of an initial recognition that during a period of transition from one "form of life" to another such as I have attempted to describe, a philosophy such as existentialism might legitimately claim a certain pertinence and interest. It would then go on to question whether that interest could survive the disappearance of the mode of life and of social relationships that gave real point to the existentialist's denials, by providing him with something to reject. When everyone has come to think of himself as an autonomous moral being and the choice-character of all moral principles has been universally acknowledged, will not the reiteration of the corresponding existentialist theses come to seem truistic and even vacuous in the absence of any living sense of morality's possibly being anything other than what it is universally understood to be? Just as communism is sometimes described as an ideology that has a point and a function only during a difficult period of transition from preindustrial to industrial society, may not existentialism and all the other versions of post-Renaissance Western individualism be by-products of a transition from one sense of moral selfhood to another and may they not come to seem extravagant and even in certain respects unintelligible in a society that has completed this transition?

In spite of the surface reasonableness and plausibility of this argument, it is, I think, mistaken, and that for reasons on which I have not touched before but which go a long way toward explaining the contemporary appeal of existentialism. The fact is, that especially in some of its more popular formulations, existentialism is at least as much a protest against certain trends within the urban and industrial society of the present day as it is a repudiation of the closed, morally determinate society of the past. As so many commentators on the current cultural scene have made clear, there is a very real question about the place that the ideal of personal autonomy can claim in the emerging society of the future. It may be that the very technological and scientific progress that has so immensely expanded the possibilities of human life will impose forms of social organization that limit the exercise of personal freedom quite as drastically as did the penurious and technologically primitive society of the past. Even today it is as difficult for a great many people in our society to think of themselves as autonomous participants in a joint and voluntary shaping of their lives as it ever was for their fellows of another day. There are even more pessimistic observers who see the whole stretch of post-Renaissance Western history with its ideal of personal autonomy as a kind of false dawn which, they believe, is now yielding to a quite different kind of society in which individual freedom will not be a value at all. However that may be, there can be no denying the existence of forces within our societies and perhaps within ourselves as well that make for depersonalization and moral passivity, whether we view these as survivals from a dark past or as harbingers of an even darker future. While these persist, they will in greater or lesser measure hinder the emergence of a society in which, through reciprocal recognition and acceptance, human beings can jointly and freely participate in the direction of their own affairs. And as long as that goal is not achieved, one may hope that existentialism—under whatever name—with its insistent emphasis on the centrality within human nature of the capacity for constructing alternatives and for choosing among them, will elicit an intelligent and serious response.

INDEX

Action: in theological voluntarism, 32; existentialist concept of, 60, 100; and value 116–21; and possibility, 118, 124–25; and determinism, 147–52; and autonomy, 154–62 *passim;* and choice, 163–68; two components of, 173; as criterion of convictions, 176, 182–83

Akrasia: Aristotle on, 7*n*

Alternatives: 118–19; 146–52 *passim*

Anxiety: existential, 134–35; Sartre on, 155*n*, 161*n;* and freedom, 241–43

Aquinas, Thomas: as intellectualist, 9–11, 19; and Ockham, 22

Aristotle: ethical theory of, 5–8; on ontology, 81–82; on natural kinds, 87; on choice, 145; on man as social being, 207

Augustine, Saint, 9*n*

Authenticity: existentialist theory of, 200–8; and obligation, 217–24; Heidegger on, 216*n;* criticized, 247–50

Autonomy: as central theme of existentialism, xiv–xvi, 145, 153–62; in Ockham, 26; in theological voluntarism, 32; in idealism, 36–37; Kant's theory of, 38–42, 44–47; Nietzsche's view of, 53; not internal power of soul, 80; intellectualistic interpretation of, 140, 240–41; Sartre's theory of, 153*n*, 156*n*, 157–60; Heidegger's theory of, 153*n;* analyzed, 156–62; and consistency, 185–86; normative implications of, 200–8; and obligation, 217–24; in modern world, 238–41; criticisms of, 241–52

Bad faith: Sartre's view of, 112*n*, 195–96, 246; Simone de Beauvoir on, 168*n*

Baudelaire, Charles, 245

Baumgarten, Alexander, 38

Beauvoir, Simone de: ethical writings, xv*n;* on bad faith, 168*n;* on moral development, 204*n;* on autonomy, 207–8, 237*n;* on good of others, 221*n*

Being: existentialist concept of, 79–88 *passim*, 96; Aristotle's treatment of, 81; Heidegger and Sartre on, 84*n;* as logical operator, 91–92; experience of, 92*n;* and value, 133; Heidegger on founding one's being, 172–73

Being-in-itself: and phenomenological reduction, 68–70; contrasted with world, 74–75

Being-in-the-world: 66–67, 73, 98–99

Bentham, Jeremy, 13–14

Brentano, Franz, 65

Brunner, Emil, 31–32

Calvin, John, 26–27

Camus, Albert, 243*n*

Choice: Aristotle's account of, 8, 163; voluntaristic use of, 14–15; in Kierkegaard, 29–30; in Kant, 41–42; in Nietzsche, 52; not mental event, 60, 163–69 *passim;* and value, 133; and value judgments, 141–42; Heidegger and Sartre on, 145; and prediction, 150–53; of world, 151*n;*

and consciousness, 159*n;* existentialist theory of, 162–72; and moral principles, 174–87; and social codes, 198; as involving temporal stretch, 218*n;* limits of, 248

Concepts: of human being in existentialism, 82–104, *passim*

Conceptual analysis: and existentialism, 83–86; Merleau-Ponty on, 94

Conflicts of principle: 178–80

Consciousness: Husserl's theory of, 61–63; existentialist theory of, 66–72; metaphorical descriptions of, 91; perceptual, 96; nonthetic, 158–60; and choice, 159*n*

Cudworth, Ralph, 11–12

Dasein: Heidegger's concept of, 71, 80*n*, 87*n*, 89*n*, 91*n*, 95*n*, 97*n*, 98–102, 119, 149*n*, 150*n*, 171*n*, 200*n*

Death: Heidegger's interpretation of, 173–74; Sartre's view of, 173*n*

Descartes, René: as voluntarist, 26*n*, existentialist reaction against, 59–60; and Husserl, 62–63; conception of God, 182

Determinism: existentialist critique of, 145–53

Dilthey, Wilhelm, 100*n*

Dispositional properties: and value properties, 122–23; and autonomy, 159–62 *passim*

Dostoyevsky, Fyodor, 241–44 *passim*

Duns Scotus, 72*n*

Education: and morality, 203*n*

Emotivism: and existentialism, 65

Essence: real, 6–7, 42, 59; and being, 84–85, 93; and concepts, 102*n*

Essentialism: in existentialism, 87–88; in ethics, 204–5

Ethical theory: of existentialism, xi–xvi, 72–77, 107–114; 190–92, 235–52 *passim;* in English-speaking world, xiii–xiv, 189–90

Existence: Kierkegaard's conception of, 29–30; as *Verstehen,* 100–1

Existentialism: contemporary attitudes toward, xi–xii; as ethical theory, xi–xvi, 72–77, 107–114, 190–

92, 235–52 *passim;* in history of philosophy, 3–4; and voluntarism, 16, 71–72; popular interest in, 16–17, 235–36; religious forms of, 32–33, 242*n;* and Protestantism, 36*n;* and Nietzsche, 54–55; not subjectivistic, 59–60; and phenomenology, 66–73; French, 46, 75*n;* 225; onotological terminology of, 79–80, 88–94; and science, 89, 146; and language, 93, 101–3; as voluntaristic, 107; and "open question" argument, 126–32; on value judgment as act, 140–43; as anti-metaphysical, 146–47; on autonomy, 153–62; on choice, 162–74; on moral principles, 174–87; and utilitarianism, 178*n;* on human conflict, 193–95; and Marxism, 225, 236; and literature, 239–40; criticisms of, 241–52

Facticity: and being-in-the-world, 99–100; in Heidegger and Sartre, 169–70

Fichte, J. G., 35

Freedom: in Kant, 39, 145; dependence of truth on, 73; in moral judgments, 140; and autonomy, 145, 155, 161–62; and prediction, 148–51

Genêt, Jean, 245

God: Aquinas' conception of, 9–11; will of, 19–20; in voluntarism, 20–21; Ockham's account of, 22–26; Protestant views of, 26, 31–32; Kierkegaard's view of, 28–30; Sartre's critique of, 115, 133

Good: naturalistic analysis of, 20; and right in G. E. Moore, 127–29; interpretation of, 142–43

Hedonism, 20

Hegel, G. W. F.: treatment of autonomy, 37, 44–46; on master and slave, 194; on finite conation, 206

Heidegger, Martin: as ethicist, xiii, 75*n*, 109*n*, 111*n*, 200*n;* later writings, xv*n;* and Nietzsche, 37*n*, 71*n;* and Husserl, 57–58, 60–61, 66*n*, 71, 87*n;* on truth, 69*n*, 107*n*, 119; and

designer : Gerard A. Valerio
typesetter : Kingsport Press, Inc.
typefaces : Baskerville
printer : Kingsport Press, Inc.
paper : Warren 1854 Medium—Finish, 480
binder : Kingsport Press, Inc.
cover material : G.B.S. S-535 Book Cloth

DATE DUE

10/18			
APR 2 5 1978			